T0159964

THE LITTLE BOOK OF

CHANEL

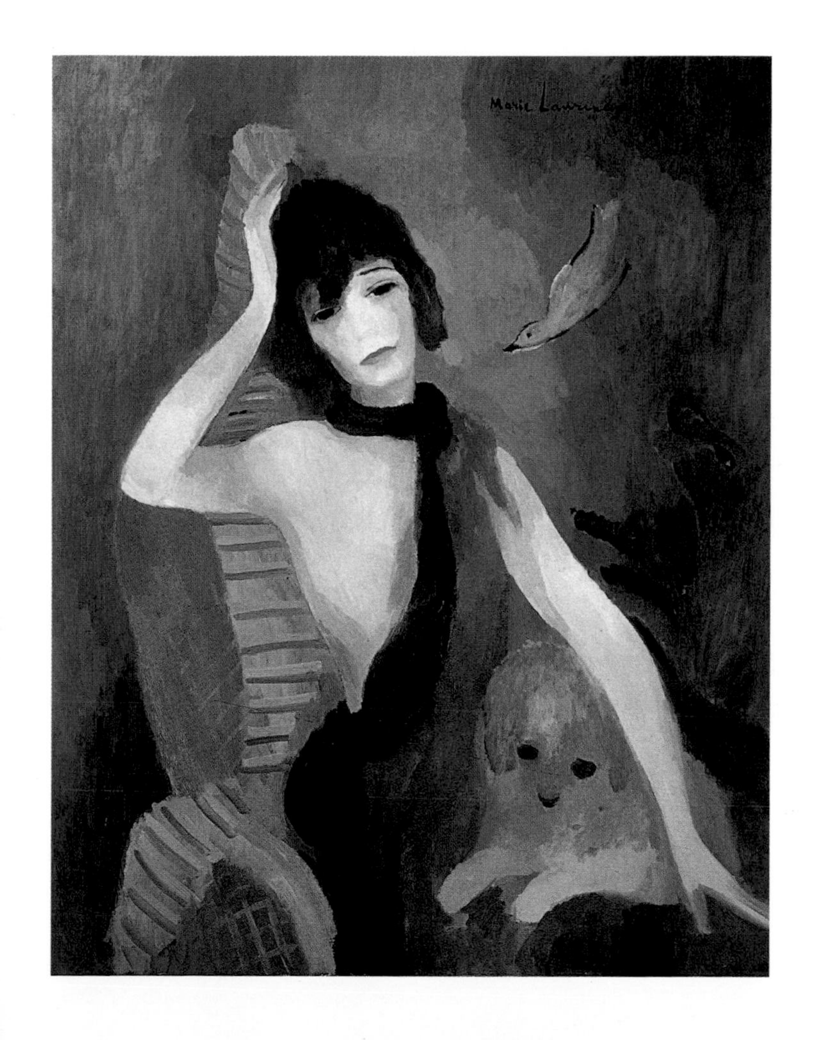

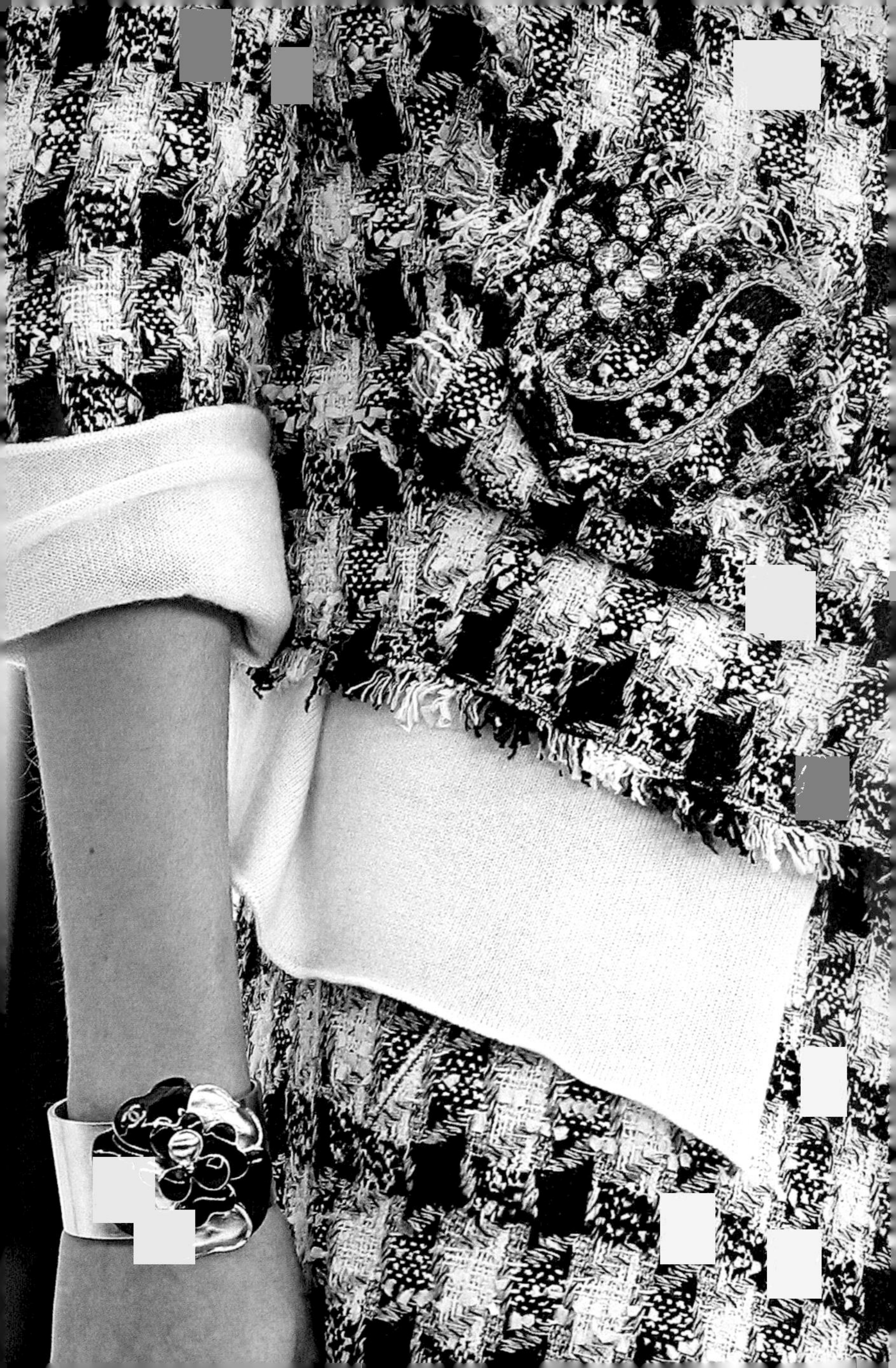

THE LITTLE BOOK OF

CHANEL

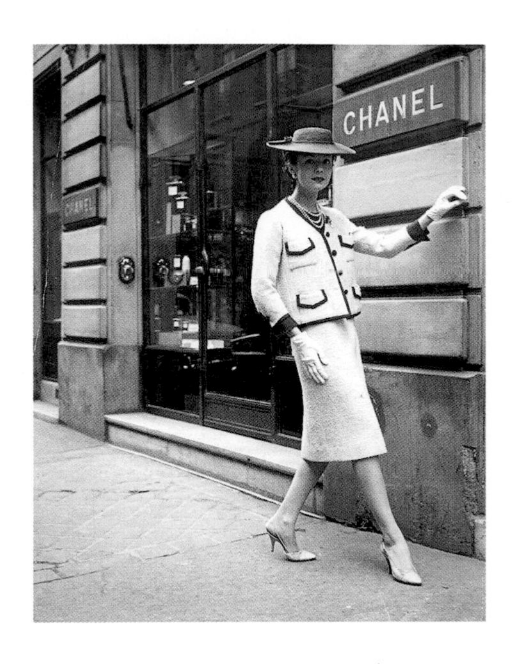

EMMA BAXTER-WRIGHT

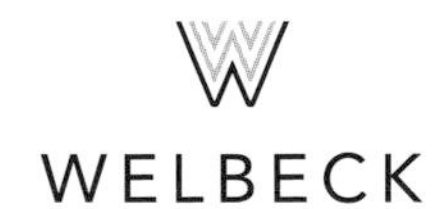

WELBECK

Having studied fashion at St Martin's School of Art and history of art at Bristol University, Emma Baxter-Wright has taught fashion journalism at the University of the Arts London and UCA.

She has contributed to many publications, including the *New York Observer*, *Cosmopolitan* and *Marie Claire*, and is the author of two photographic books on the English fashion photographer Brian Duffy and *The Little Book of Schiaparelli*. Emma lives in London, England.

For Otis, who chose a lifestyle not an education, because it's with what cannot be taught that one succeeds.

First published in 2012 and 2017 by Carlton Books Limited

This edition published in 2020 by Welbeck
An imprint of the Welbeck Publishing Group
Based in London and Sydney.
www.welbeckpublishing.com

30 29 28 27 26 25 24

A CIP catalogue record for this book is available from the British Library.

ISBN 978 1 78097 902 1

Printed in Dubai

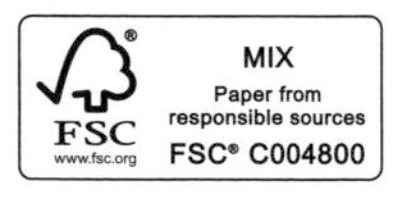

Contents

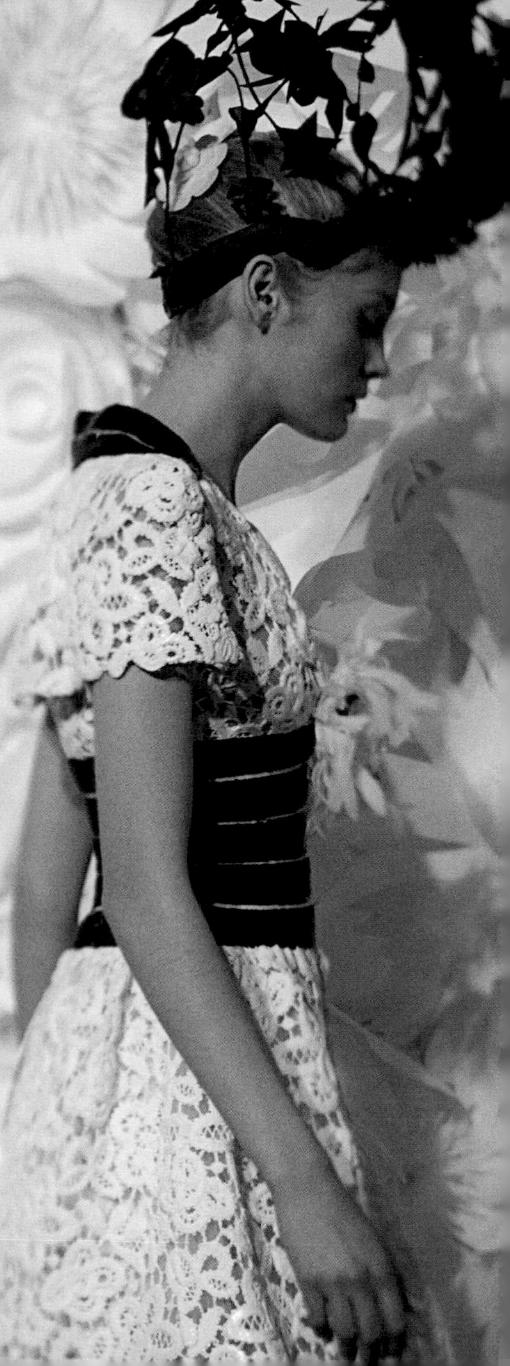

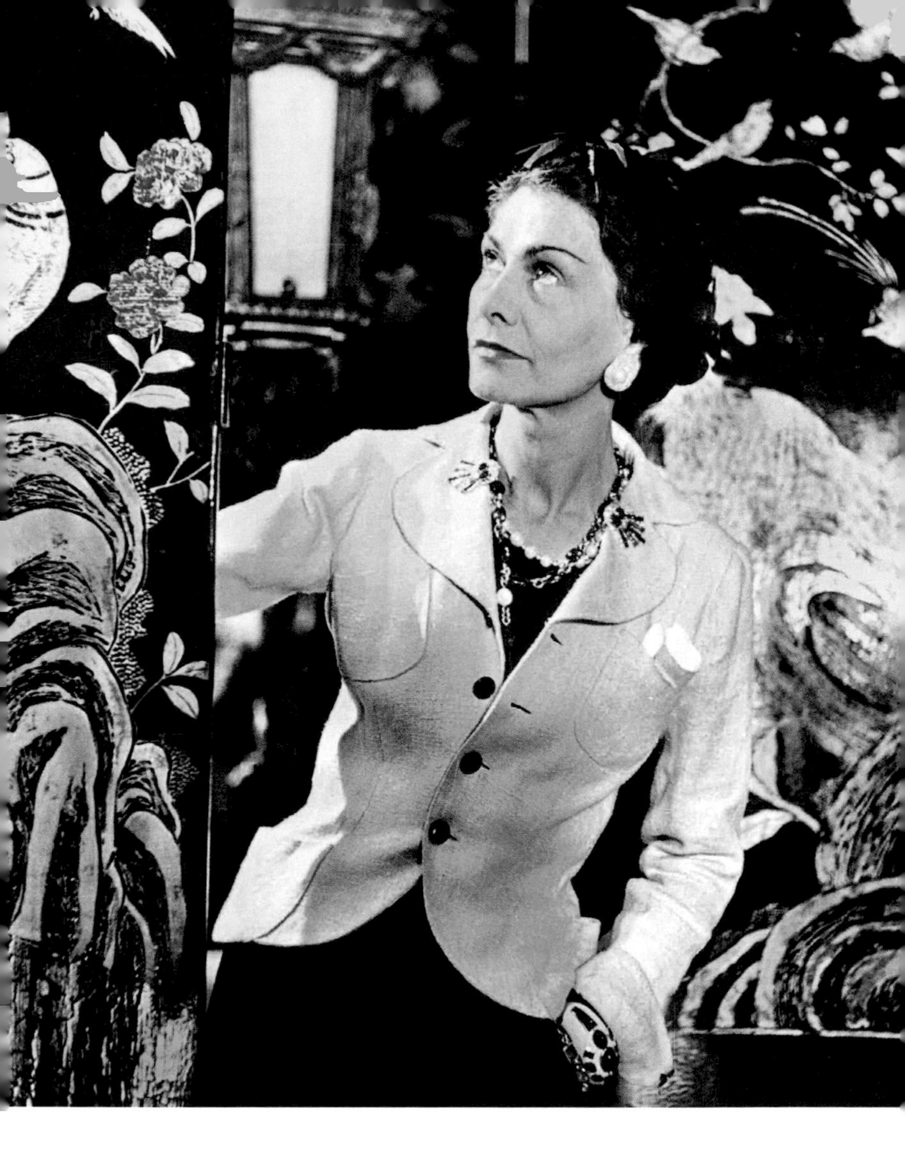

Above Chanel photographed in her suite at the Ritz Hotel in Paris, surrounded by her famous antique Coromandel screens, circa 1937.

Introduction

"May my legend gain ground – I wish it a long and happy life."

Coco Chanel, on her reputation

More than anyone Gabrielle "Coco" Chanel understood the value of her own self-created mythology and she played the part brilliantly. This exceptional and exasperating woman, who told a litany of lies to perpetuate the ongoing mystery and confusion that surrounded her life, was the first to recognize the couturier as a modern-day celebrity. If the job of the couturier is to continually re-invent fashion, then Chanel made a skilful alliance between her professional work as a designer and her personal life story, brutally deconstructing the past, rearranging the truth and then presenting a controlled image of herself as the role model for what became a global brand. At a time when fashion was dominated by male designers, she single-handedly rejected society's version of femininity in favour of her own fabulous style, based on a functional modern aesthetic. As one world was ending and another was about to begin, Chanel seized the opportune moment and with visionary insight gave women what they wanted, just before they recognized the need. She took the basis of a man's wardrobe to create feminine power, providing a democratic dress code that ultimately delivered freedom, equality and understated classicism. Her status was enhanced by her complicated personal life, which always had an impact on her professional work, but as her rags-to-riches story unfolded, it was she who became the influential force as a designer, lover and collaborator, flitting seamlessly between high society and the avant-garde art set.

A self-imposed exile of over a decade derailed her trajectory, and that may have been the end of the fairytale, but for Chanel the vital creativity never waned. Reinvention was part of her psyche, and when Chanel returned to work at the age of 71 she successfully consolidated her contribution to fashionable modernity and rebuilt her public image, to the point that even now, many years after her death, she remains the immovable figurehead behind the House of Chanel.

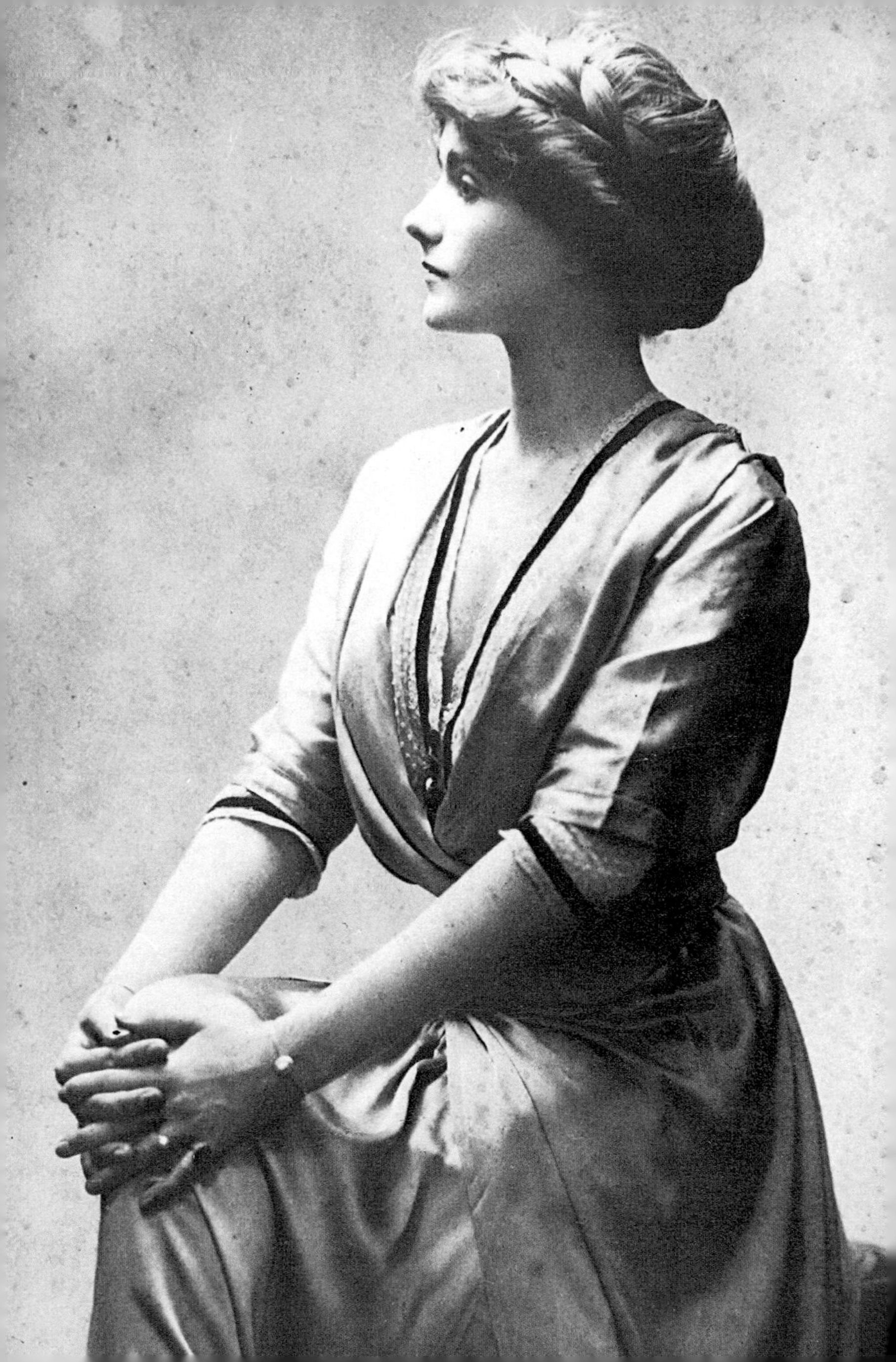

The Early Years

The details of Chanel's early life have always been shrouded in mystery and half truths, deliberately kept that way by a woman who preferred to forget, conceal and frequently provide misinformation about her miserable origins. It is often overlooked that the woman who ultimately had such a profound effect on changing the face of twentieth-century fashion, a pioneering champion of freedom and modernity, was actually born in the preceding century.

Delivered in the poorhouse on the 19 August 1883 in the small market town of Saumur, on the river Loire, Gabrielle Bonheur Chanel was the second illegitimate child of a young peasant girl called Jeanne Devolles and her wayward boyfriend Albert Chanel. Although the couple married soon after the birth, their relationship was always troubled, and when Jeanne died prematurely, Albert, who was unwilling or incapable of looking after his five children, sent the boys to work on a farm and the three girls to a convent orphanage run by nuns.

Life within the high abbey walls at Aubazine was certainly harsh for a young 12-year-old girl and, though not necessarily cruel, almost certainly without love. Gabrielle was made to wear black and it was here that she spent many hours in silent solitude, learning how to sew and potentially developing her appreciation of austere simplicity.

The girls spent their holidays with their paternal grandparents in the small garrison town of Moulins and by the age of 18 Chanel was working as a clerk in a small shop that specialized in lingerie, linen and hosiery. Early ambitions of a career on the stage were kickstarted when she began singing at various café-concerts around the town. Small, dark and distinctly different from the other girls who performed alongside

Opposite An early photograph of Chanel, aged 26, at the start of her career and before she cut her long, thick, textured hair into the trademark short bob.

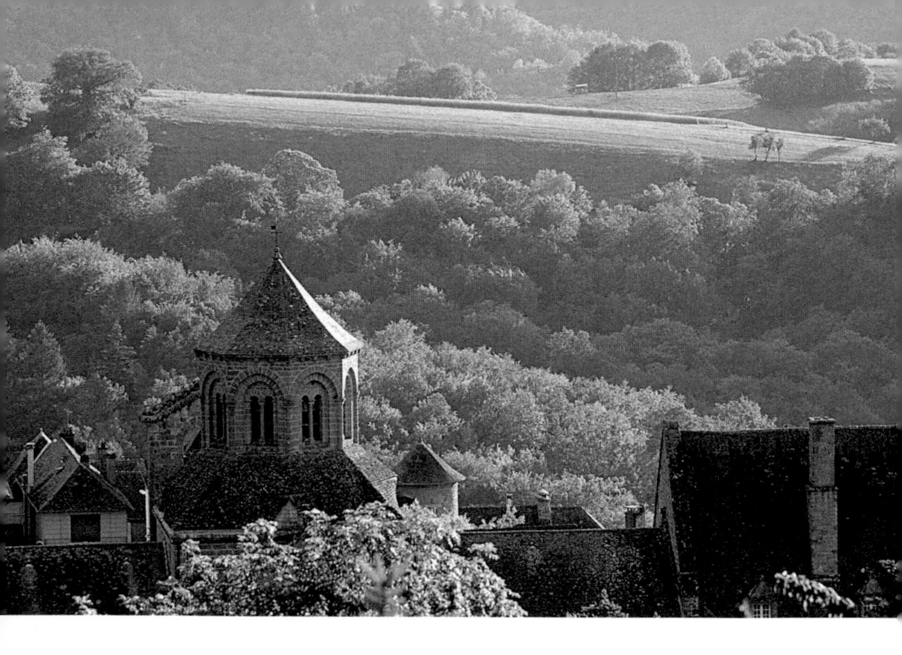

her, it is thought her vaudeville repertoire consisted of only two songs: "Ko-Ko-Ri-Ko" and a vacuous ditty about a lady from Paris who had lost her puppy dog, "Qui Qu'a Vu Coco?". Her popularity grew, and soon she became known by the little word that appeared in both songs: "La petite Coco". The nickname stuck, eventually becoming synonymous with a global brand that encapsulated the ultimate in Parisienne style.

Gabrielle "Coco" Chanel was starting to gain a succession of wealthy, educated, sometimes even titled, admirers, and saw an obvious way, through her association with these men, to shake off the social stigma of poverty and enter into a higher social tier. Étienne Balsan was one such admirer; rich, attractive and without the snobbery often associated with his class, he spent his time pursuing personal pleasures and breeding racehorses. At the age of 25 Coco agreed to live with him at his estate Royallieu on the outskirts of Paris. Balsan certainly had other mistresses living with him, and Coco was known as his *irrégulière*, but through her unorthodox choice of dress she chose to differentiate herself from the other women. While most courtesans of the day still wore lavish Belle Époque-style dresses with elaborate trims and fussy frills, all of which hampered movement, Coco dressed with the utmost simplicity.

Photographs of her at this time show a young girl wearing clothes more suited to a little boy: cropped trousers, with flat boy's boots, a plain white shirt with a Peter Pan collar and a man's tie loosely knotted into a bow. With hindsight these pictures reveal a fundamental strategy, that of re-appropriating the clean uncluttered lines of classic menswear for women. Never content with a life of idle beauty, Coco kept herself busy, learning to ride and making and trimming hats for herself and her friends with some considerable success. It is hard to unravel just how happy she was, but a determination that she should never be a "kept woman" potentially fuelled the idea that she could turn her hat-making pastime into something more serious. She wanted to go to Paris and make a career for herself as a *modiste* – a milliner – and boldly suggested to Balsan that he set her up with a small shop. Although he refused her proposal, he did agree to finance a business for her from his Parisian apartment, at 160 Boulevard Malesherbes.

The dashing English millionaire Arthur "Boy" Capel was, according to Coco, the one true love of her life, and on this it is agreed she was telling the truth. Capel was a friend of Étienne Balsan's who started to appear more frequently at the chateau in the spring of 1909. He was

Opposite Exterior view of the Abbey and convent at Aubazine, where Chanel and her two sisters were placed in the orphanage and taken care of by nuns when their mother died.

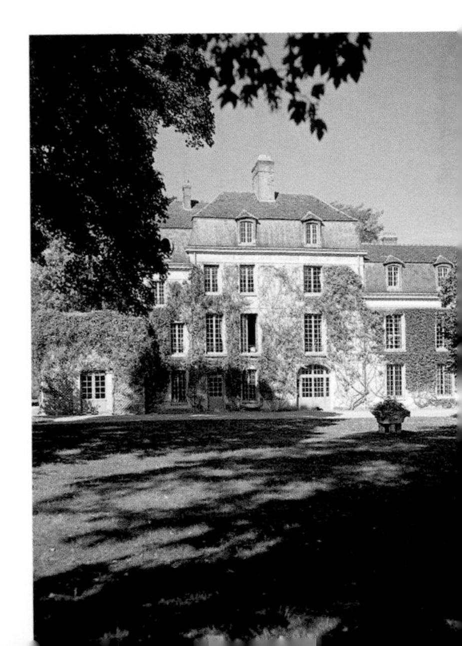

Right Château de Royallieu, the grand estate outside Paris owned by Étienne Balsan, and where Chanel learnt to ride.

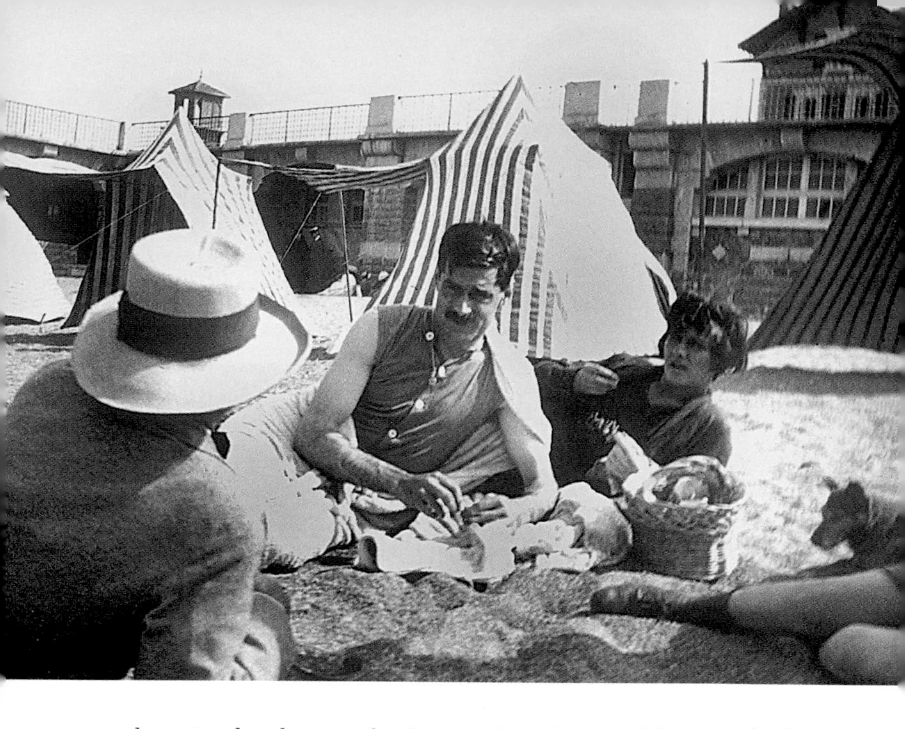

a charming, handsome polo-player, with an irrepressible desire for fast living and adventure. Having earned his fortune through the coalmines in northern England, he had an entrepreneurial spirit and took the idea of Coco's hat-making much more seriously than Balsan, who laughed it off as a passing fancy. For a time the trio muddled along uncomfortably, but Coco had fallen completely in love with Capel and when she ran away to live with him in Paris, the two men were left negotiating who exactly would pay what, to continue financing Coco. Finally they came to a gentlemen's agreement to share costs: Capel would cover the business expenses, while Balsan provided the premises.

Above Chanel with her lover, the Englishman Arthur "Boy" Capel, and their friend the sugar magnate Constant Say, on the beach in Saint-Jean-de-Luz in 1917.

Opposite This 1913 caricature by the satirist illustrator Sem for *Le Figaro*, shows a dancing Chanel caught in the arms of a polo-playing Boy Capel, who is depicted as a centaur.

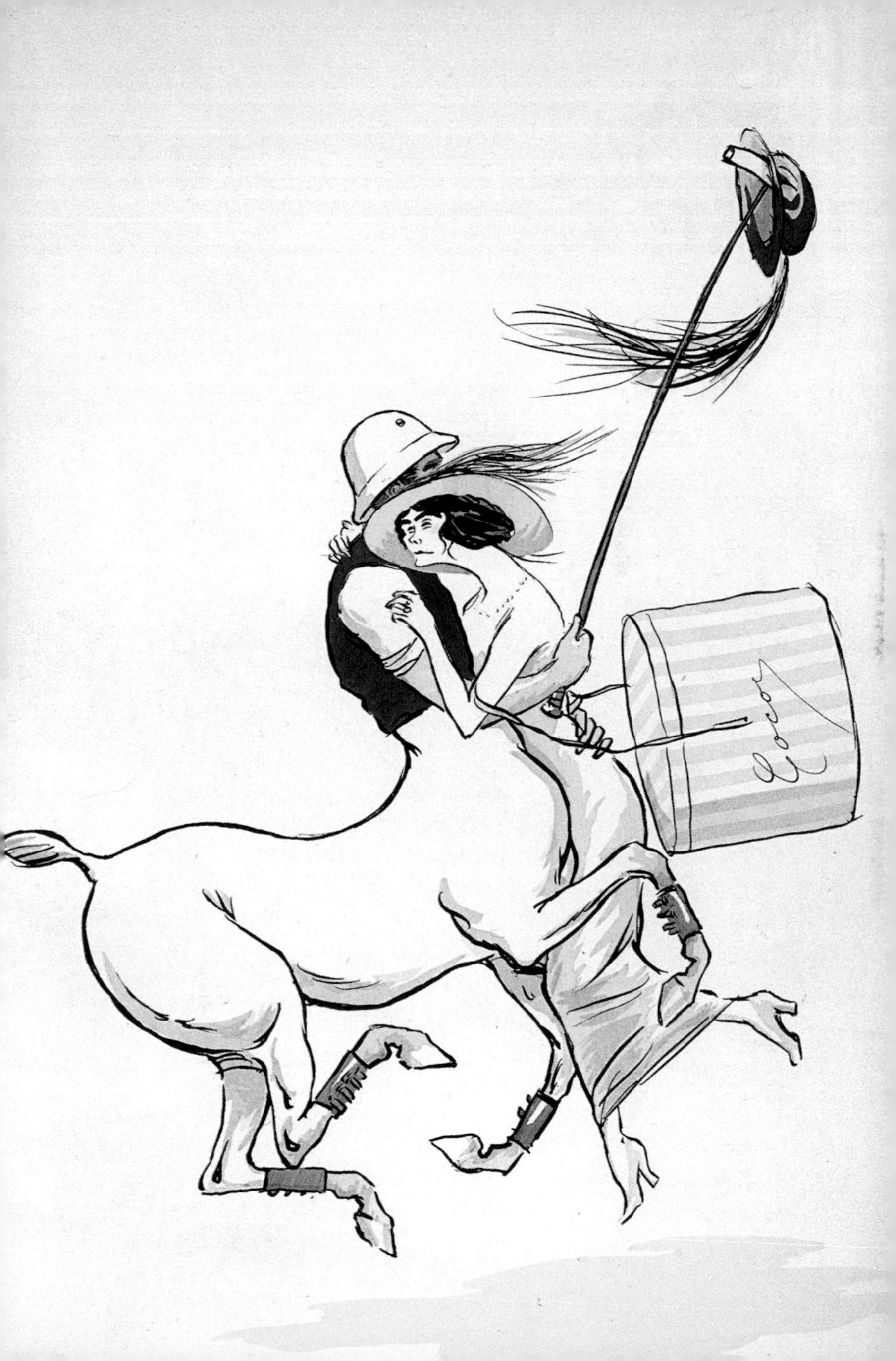
Coco

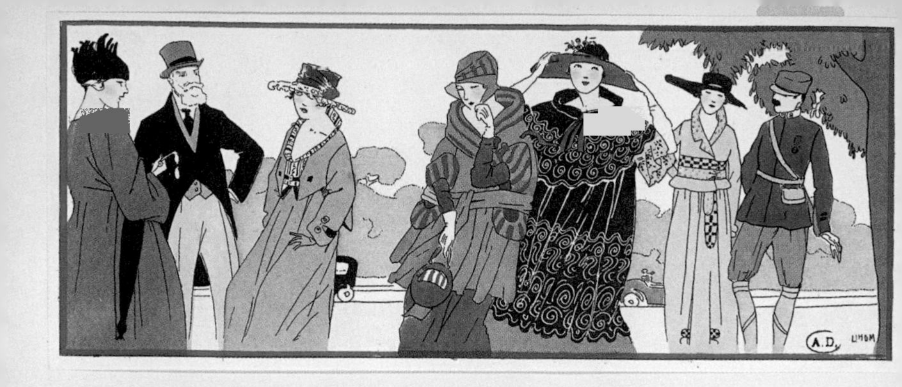

Mademoiselle Chanel was on her way. Years later she recalled to Salvador Dalí, "I was able to open a high-fashion shop because two gentlemen were outbidding each other for my hot little body." Friends and family came to buy, as did Étienne's former mistresses, all of whom were charmed by Coco's chic simple hats, which were often just bought from Galeries Lafayette and cleverly embellished. Word spread, success came almost immediately, and having outgrown the space in the apartment, Capel agreed to secure commercial premises for Coco in the centre of the established couture district. On 1 January 1910, what was to become the foundation of an empire opened its doors at 21 Rue Cambon. The sign above the door simply read "Chanel Modes".

Above Fashion illustration from the magazine *L'Élégance Parisienne,* April 1917, which shows "The Latest Fashion Creations", including hats by Chanel.

Opposite Early examples of Chanel's jersey suits. The cardigan jacket and new fuller, shorter skirt provided a suit that was far less restrictive than the extravagant fashion of her rivals.

Deauville, Biarritz, Paris

Chanel started her business selling the hats she was already making: the lease for her premises at 21 Rue Cambon stated that she had no right to make dresses as there was already a dressmaker in the same building. The hats, however, received rave reviews in the influential magazine *Les Modes* and were sought after by the popular theatre actresses and singers of the day.

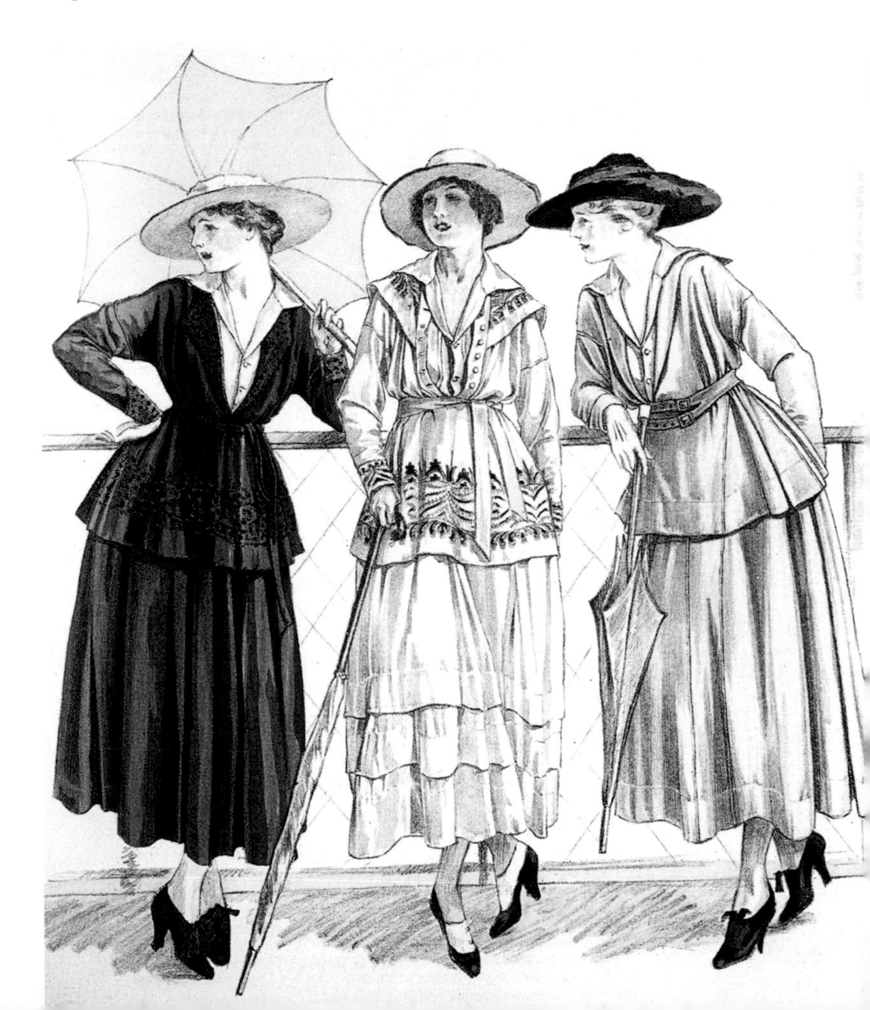

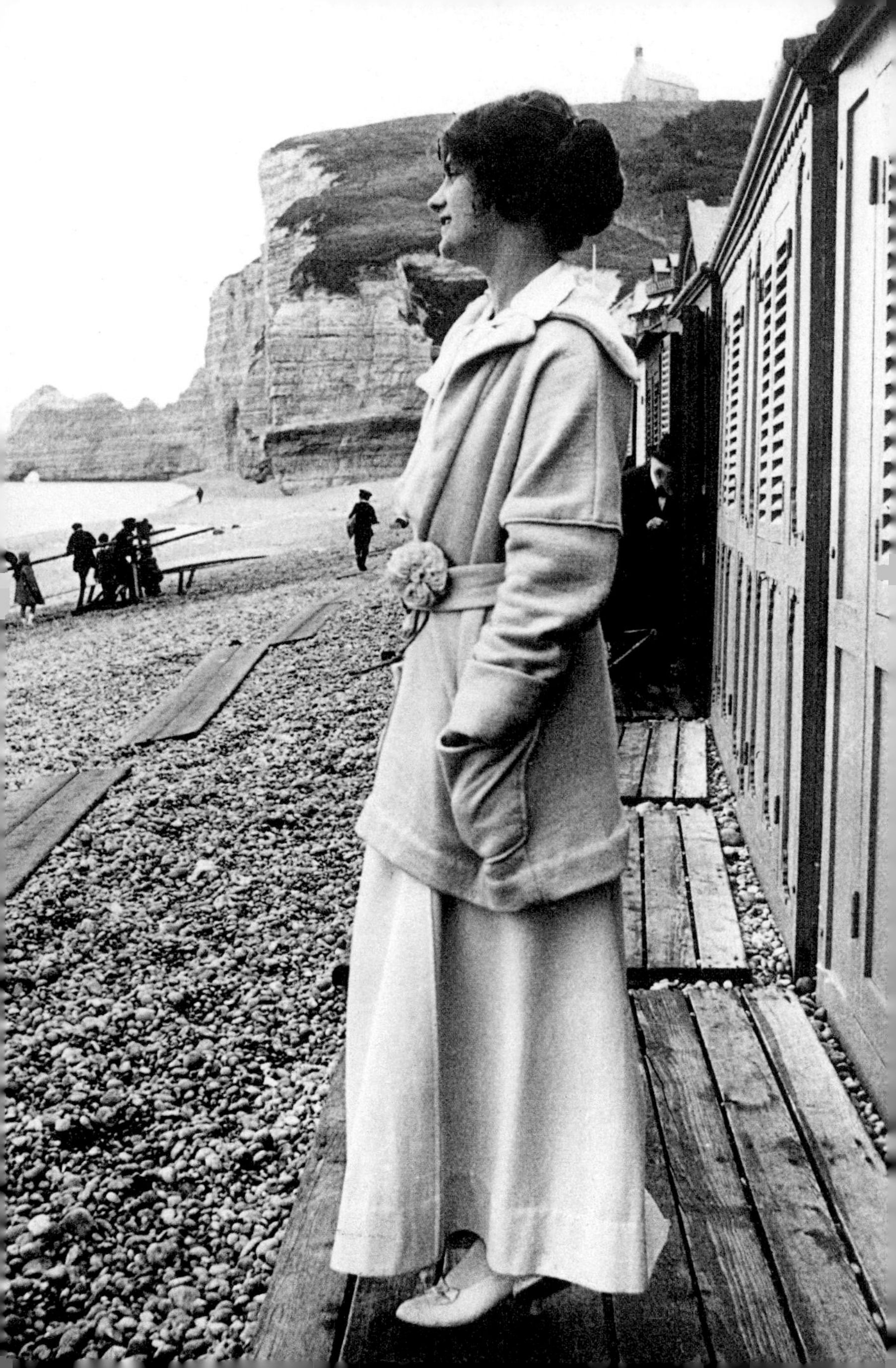

Coco was a reactionary. She detested the headache-inducing hats of the fussy Belle-Époque era, heavy with plumage and gauze, so instead offered hats that relied on understated minimalism. Often they were large, but without ornate garnish; sometimes she used a single feather or grosgrain ribbon as decoration. The fashionable dress of the day was dominated by a desire for romanticism, elaborate ruffles and frilly details. The totally restrictive S-shaped corset, popular at the beginning of the century, had been challenged by the success of Paul Poiret's high-waisted empire line, but fashion was still aimed at dull society women who led inactive lives. Clothes from Jeanne Paquin, Jacques Doucet and Poiret were all heavy with colour and surface decoration, grandly sumptuous and theatrical.

Opposite Chanel loved sunbathing and swimming at the seaside. Here, she is photographed in one of her own jersey cardigans at a beach in France in 1917.

Below The familiar Chanel logo adorns the awnings of her first shop outside Paris, which opened in the fashionable seaside resort of Deauville in 1913.

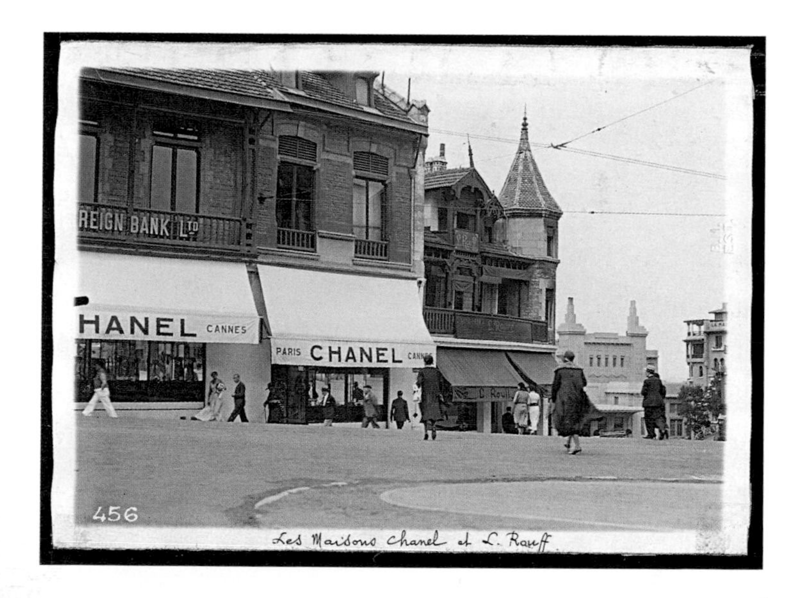

Coco, who was slender and sporty, had other ideas, and her own desire to be independent provided the basis of her fledgling collection of clothes for her first boutique, which opened in Deauville in 1913. The fashionable resort on the north coast of France appealed to Coco: its component parts of dazzling sunshine, healthy sea air, wealthy men and thoroughbred horses provided her with another chance for reinvention. Financed by Boy Capel, the shop was located in the chicest part of town and had a striped awning bearing the words "Gabrielle Chanel".

Coco's first pieces were created in response to her own need to live freely and oppose women's repression. Functional clothes were inspired by the Normandy fishermen, sailor's shirts with open necks, loose linen

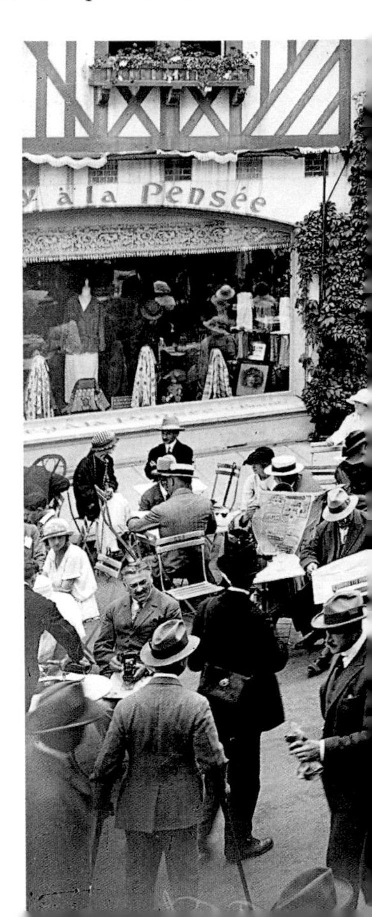

Right The chic coastal town of Deauville in Normandy became popular with wealthy Parisians for weekend and summer excursions during the 1920s.

Overleaf left Chanel opened her first couture house, opposite the casino in Biarritz, in July 1915, to provide a fashionable wardrobe for the cosmopolitan clientele who flocked to the Atlantic coast resort.

Overleaf right Chanel started using Rodier jersey in 1917 because it had the properties of cashmere without the expense. It draped beautifully and was perfectly suited to winter sportswear such as this stylish skater outfit from 1929.

pants, long skirts and turtleneck sweaters, all designed for comfort and ease. Encouraged by the scorching weather, Coco even made a very demure swimsuit for women to bathe in, using the soft jersey fabric she had discovered in one of Boy's sweaters. When war broke out Boy, who was called to arms, encouraged Coco to stay put and keep the shop open in Deauville. His business instincts proved to be right, as business boomed under the patronage of wealthy women who sought refuge at the seaside.

A year later, Boy swept Coco off for a weekend away in Biarritz where they stayed at the Hotel du Palais. Seemingly unaffected by war, the Basque town provided the perfect location for Coco to repeat the

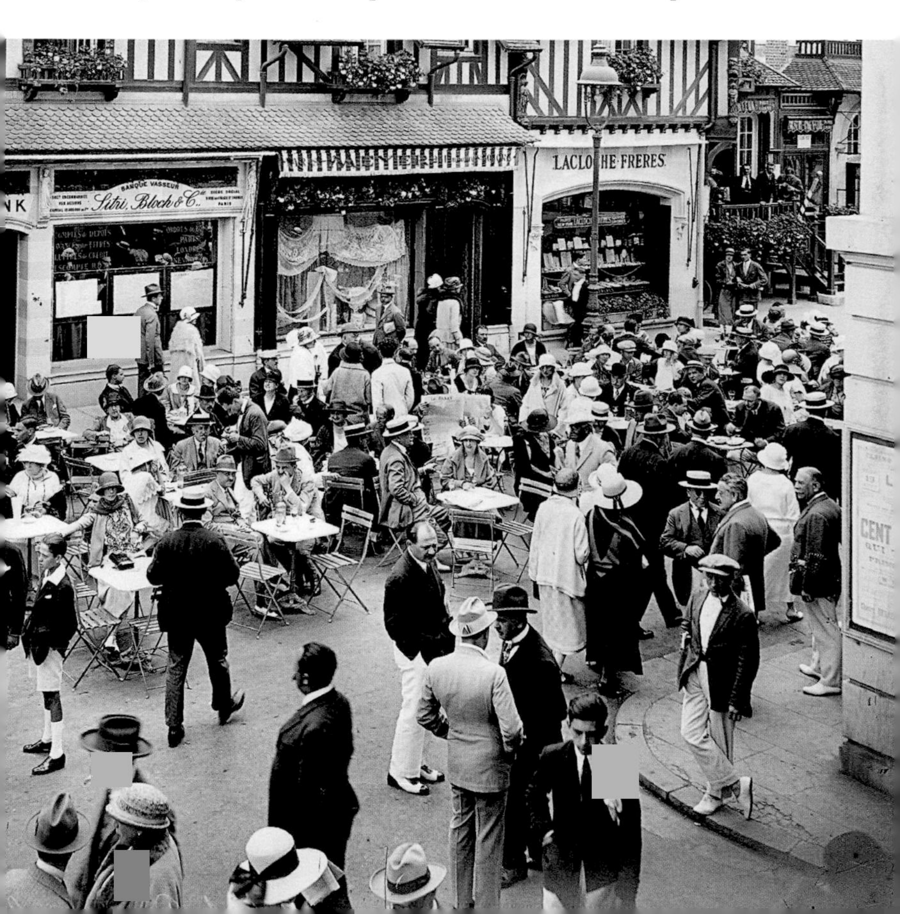

success of Deauville. Here, in July 1915, she opened her first couture house in a villa facing the casino, catering for a cosmopolitan clientele who were crying out for luxury as a distraction from the brutality that surrounded them. The war had upended fashion as it existed, but Coco was inventive, improvising with available fabrics such as Rodier's knitted jersey, and producing clothes that provided a modern aesthetic as well as practicality. She understood the changing world, and while her clothes were never cheap (dresses were priced at 3,000 francs each) she had refined a new functionality that combined fluidity with pared-down elegance. Orders flowed in from Madrid, Bilbao and even the Spanish court. By the end of the war Coco was doing so well financially that she was able to reimburse Boy for his initial funding, and could finally declare her total independence. In Paris she expanded her business, moving across the road to a six-storey building at 31 Rue Cambon, which to this day remains the centre of operations for the House of Chanel.

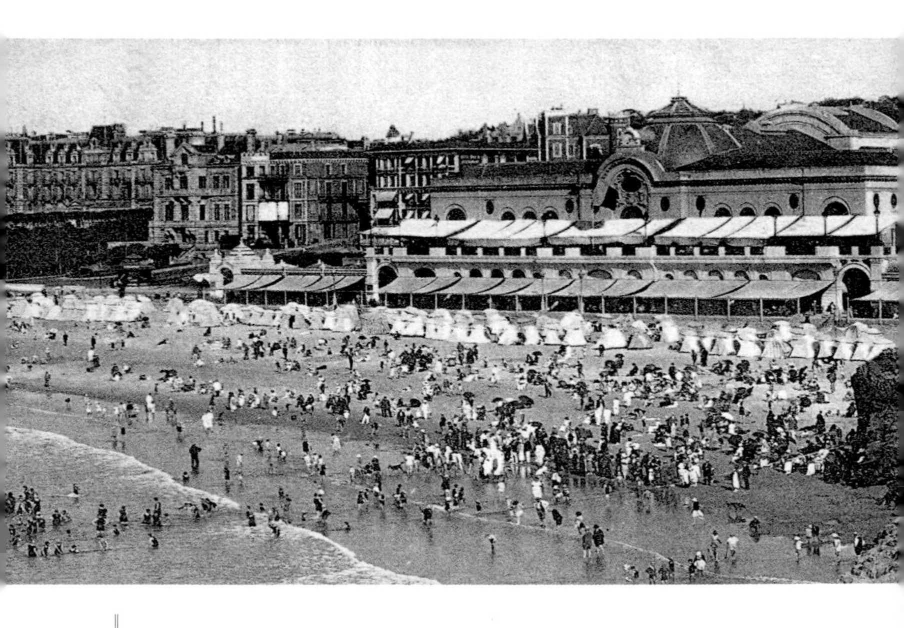

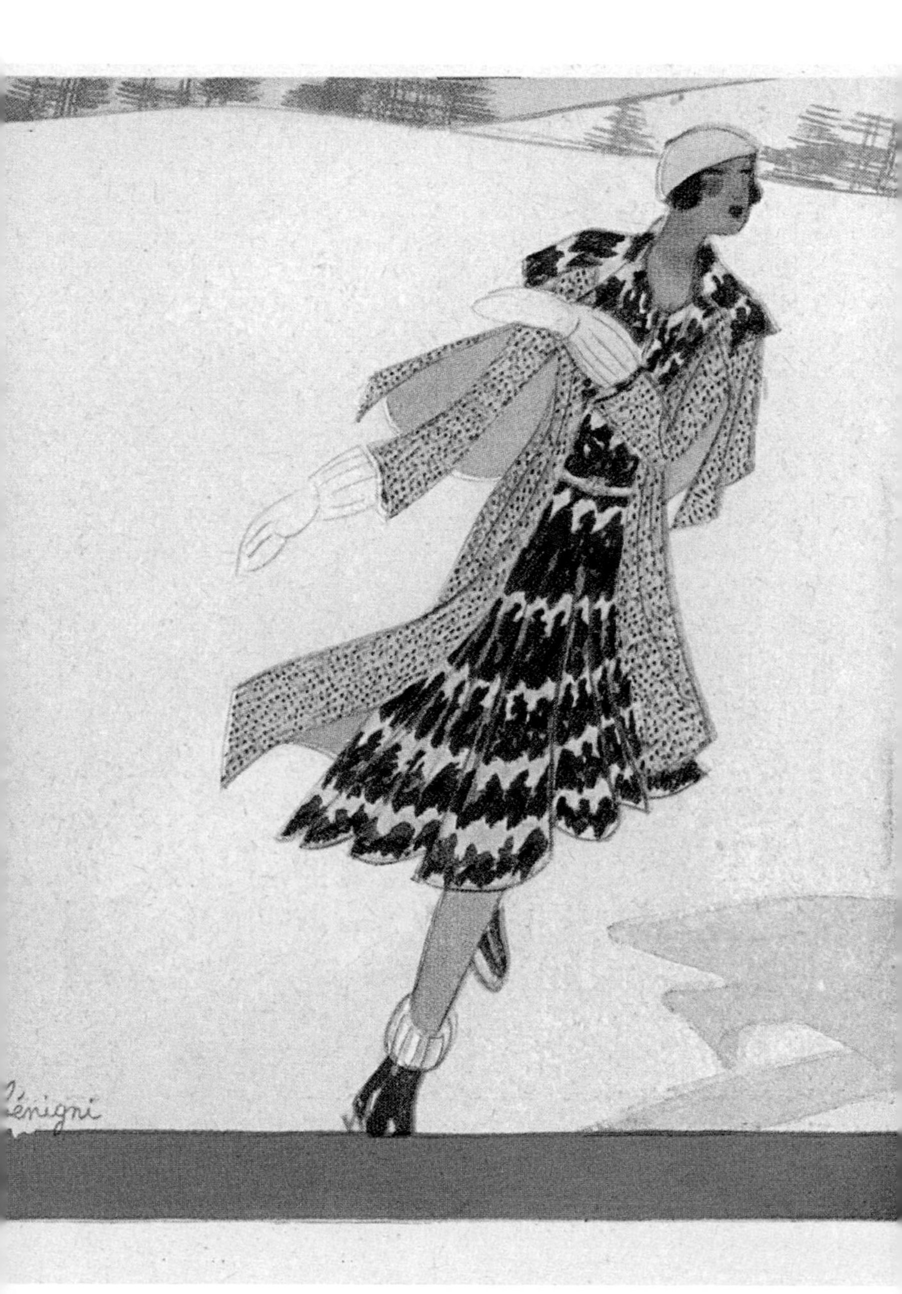

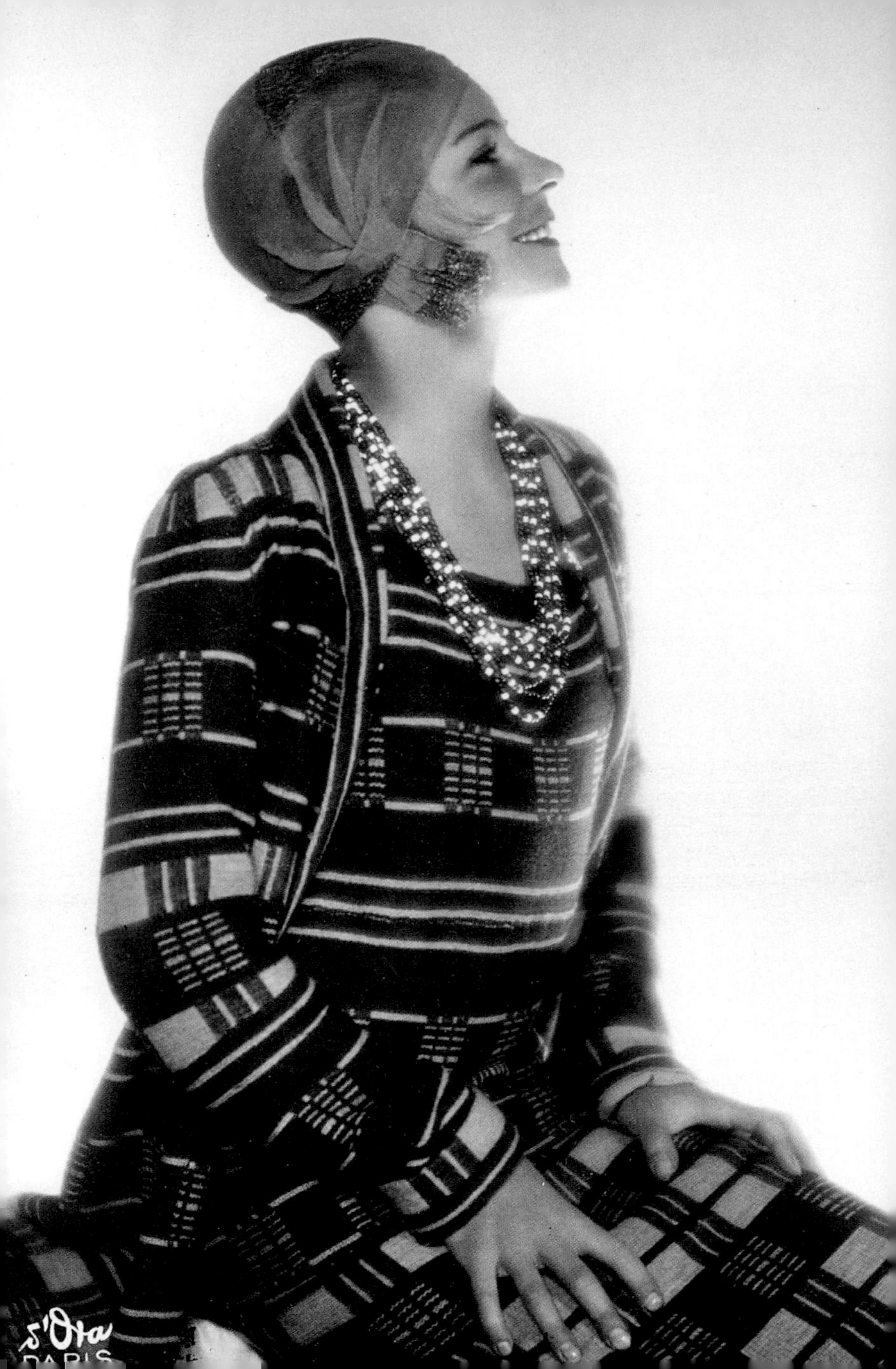
d'Ora

Though inextricably linked, like the intertwining Cs of Chanel's logo, Capel and Coco had a complex love affair, bound together but pulling in different directions. Coco knew that Boy had many other liaisons and due to her social status was unlikely ever to propose, but it was a devastating blow when in 1918 he married a beautiful young aristocrat called Lady Diana Wyndham – and there was worse to come. In December 1919, Boy was fatally wounded when the speeding convertible he was driving from Paris to Monte Carlo burst a tyre and overturned. Years later Coco told her friend Paul Morand in a conversation that was published as a memoir: "In losing Capel, I lost everything. He left a void in me that the years have not filled." The reality was that a grief-stricken Coco withdrew to lick her wounds for a time. When she returned with a hardened heart, the process of renewal continued as her domination of Paris gathered pace.

Opposite This outfit is a typical example of Chanel's early modern sportswear, made in a soft jersey fabric, which ensured both comfort and freedom. The unstructured cardigan jacket became a staple piece throughout this period. Photograph by fashion and portrait photographer Dora Kallmus, known as "Madame D'Ora", in 1929.

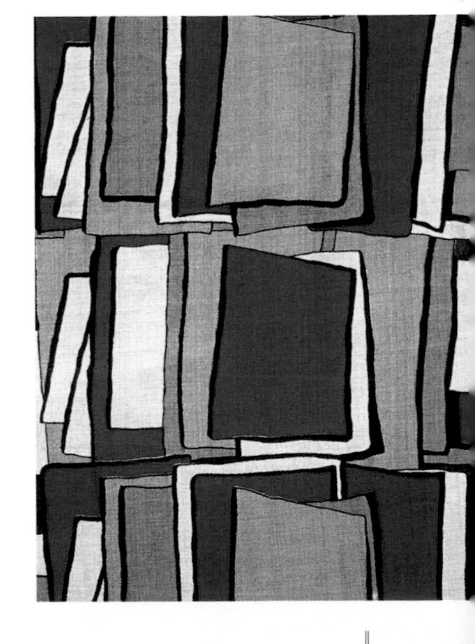

Right Chanel designed with a limited colour palette that included black, white, beige, red and blue, as shown in this detail of a modern geometric print, circa 1929. Made from wool and silk, the fabric was used for a dress.

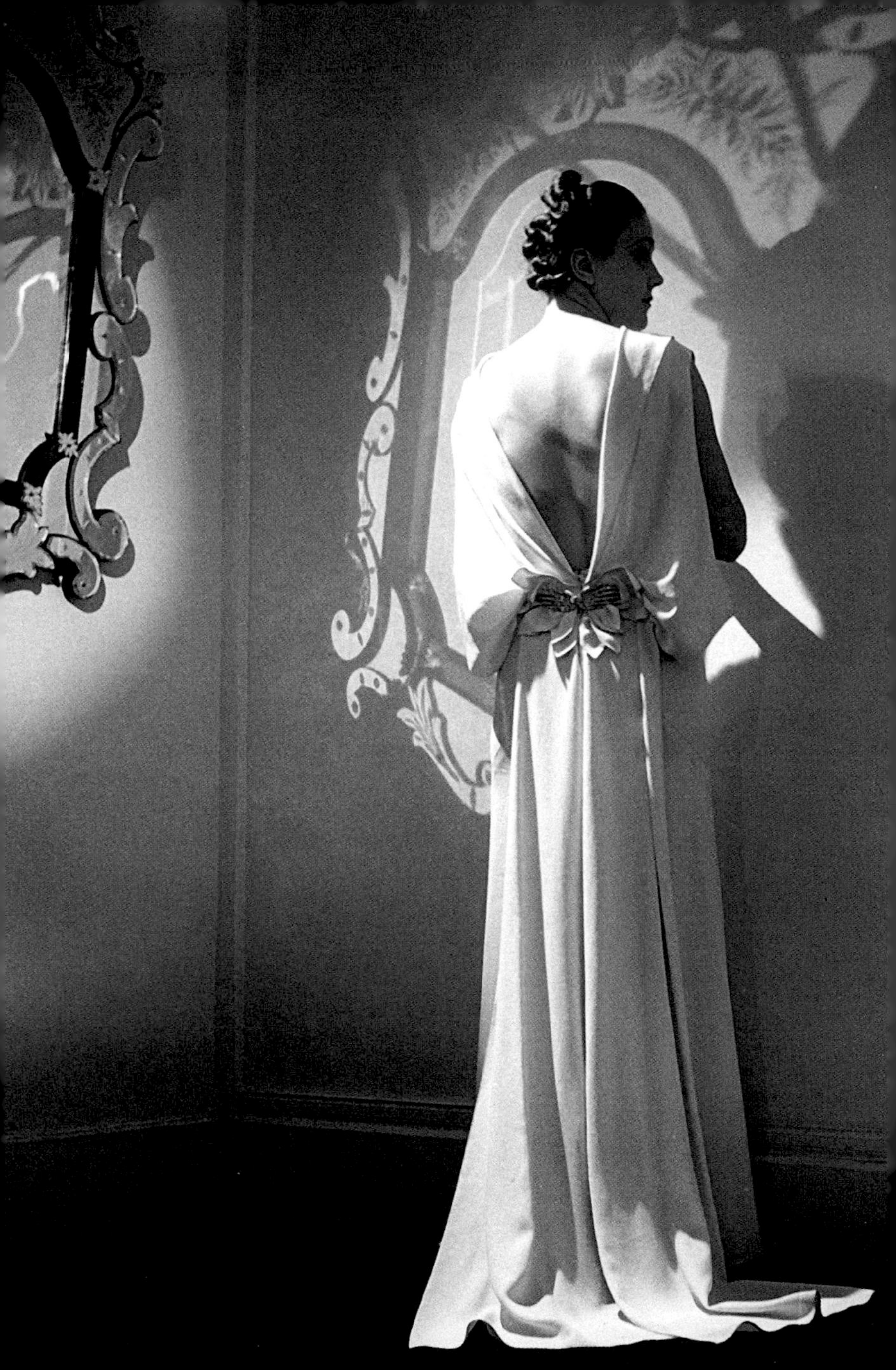

The House of Chanel

"Fashion is not an art, it is a job."

Coco Chanel

Coco Chanel was unlike any other designer in that she did not design on paper or make sketches. Her talent lay in her instinctive knowledge of how to dress the uncorseted female form. At the start of her career she lacked technical expertise and, having carefully chosen the fabrics, would explain verbally to her staff what she wanted. This was often a harrowing process for everyone: Coco barked orders at her assistants, and models were made to stand for hours while she endlessly pinned and repositioned the fabric until she was satisfied.

Coco understood that postwar life required simplicity and that society had changed dramatically. She was responsible for a major shift in women's fashion that relied on clean lines and mass production. Taking advantage of her social connections, she enlisted the help of the Balsan brothers to secure silk from Lyon, while Boy helped her acquire tweeds from Scotland. When fabric was difficult to source, she simply found a way to successfully utilize what was available: cotton jersey, flannel and broadcloth. Fur was impossible to find and consequently so highly in demand that clients usually didn't ask too many questions as to the origin of the skins. Coco used whatever she could get hold of, such as squirrel and white angora rabbit, for bands of fur around hemlines and cuffs.

Opposite Eveningwear in the 1930s was extravagant and luxurious. This white satin gown with a dramatic deep V back features a decorative bow, something Chanel started to incorporate on the front and back of her dresses during this period.

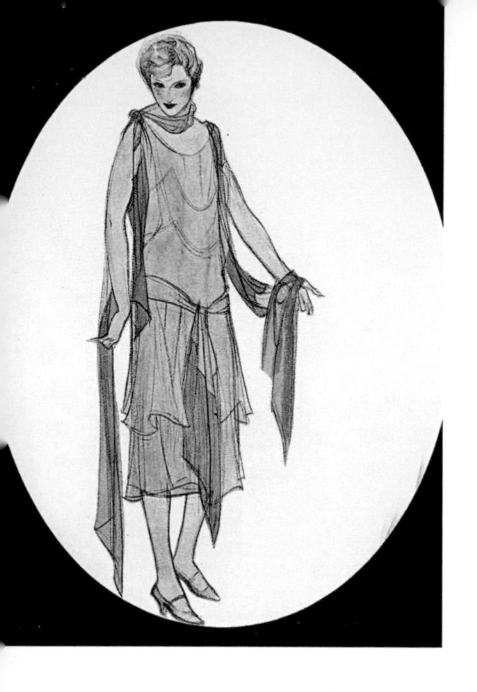

Left Hemlines fluctuated during the 1920s. Here, illustrated by John La Gatta for an American fashion magazine in 1925, chiffon scarves are tied round the hips and at the shoulder line to create a fashionable pointed handkerchief effect.

Everything Coco did in her personal life had an impact on the brand, as her design philosophy was based thoroughly on herself and what she liked to wear. She exemplified the *garçonne* look with her chic bobbed hair and lithe physique; she wore slim sweaters and drop-waist skirts with a pulled-down cloche hat, creating a look that became known in New York and London as "the flapper". Coco was sporty and she loved riding horses and outdoor life at the beach, which kept her slim, tanned and, by all accounts, much younger looking than her actual years. In 1920 *Vogue* magazine wrote: "Everything she does makes news – the first quilted coat, the narrow crepe de chine dress inside a cage of tulle, and the suntan which she cultivates."

During the 1920s the economy boomed for the privileged, and Chanel opened more premises to provide her wealthy clients with expensive items she had cleverly remodelled from "poor clothes". In the heart of Paris she consolidated her empire in Rue Cambon as she took over her third shop, at number 29, later adding numbers 25, 27 and 23, as well as opening another boutique in the chic Riviera town of Cannes.

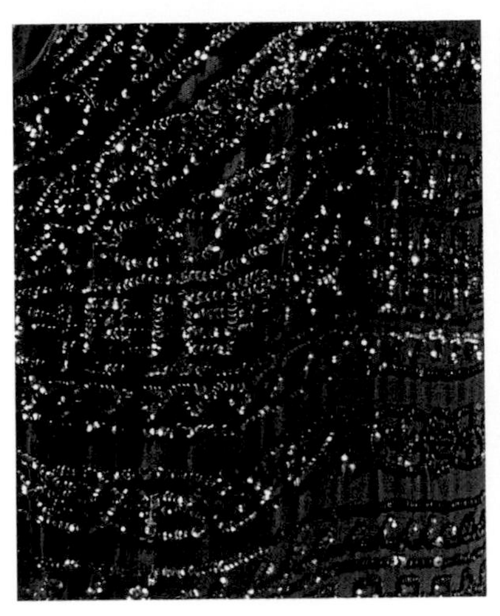

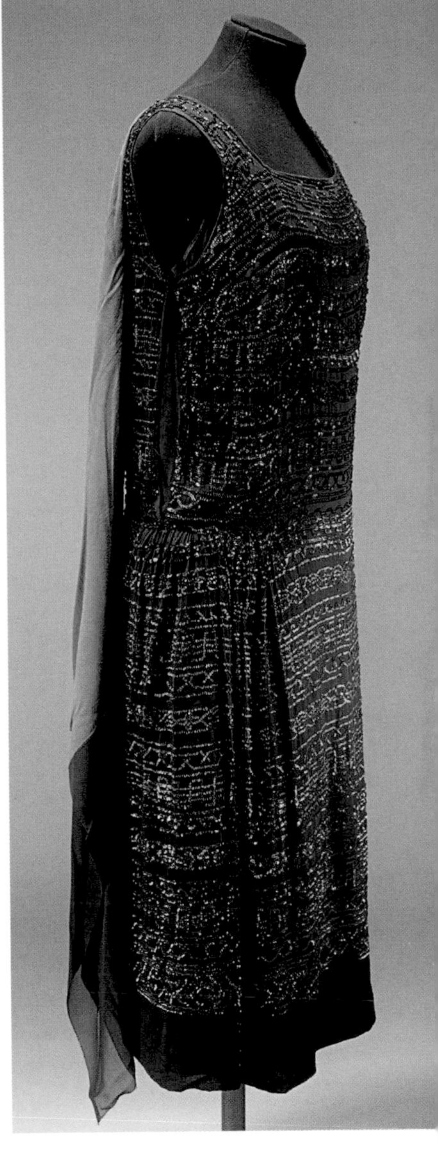

Right and detail above A black silk crepe dress embellished all over with sequins and embroidery in midnight blue and light blue. The chiffon scarf attached at the back hangs slightly longer, to create the fashionable fluid hemline.

The Slav Period

Throughout her life Coco was unashamedly influenced by the men she associated with. Sergei Diaghilev, Igor Stravinsky and her new lover, the Grand Duke Dmitri Pavlovich (a handsome but penniless playboy), were all Russian émigrés who had escaped the Revolution and come to Paris, bringing with them a somewhat fictionalized version of Russian life that the French people fell in love with. Coco had complicated relationships with all three men, but was influenced by their artistic and cultural heritage, immediately sensing that romantic Russia could have great commercial appeal. Inspired, she went on to produce a collection of traditional peasant clothing that she called her "Slav period". The war had disrupted textile production and fashion houses became increasingly starved of luxury fabrics, so Coco found a way to embellish plain black crepe de chine with stunning embroidery, resulting in beautiful cloth that could rival the finest couture fabrics. The fashion world was surprised by her use of intricate embroidery but, as ever, it was the structural simplicity and wearability of these pieces that made them so popular. Sticking to a dark colour palette and then strategically embellishing with vivid colours, she made rustic-looking shift dresses, tunics and waistcoats, and reinterpreted a traditional belted blouse with a square décolletage called the "roubachka" style. The collection appeared in *Vogue* magazine in 1922 under the headline "The Peasant Look".

Opposite Taking inspiration from simple peasant shapes, Chanel created a plain black wool shift dress and used intricate gold embroidery to decorate it with simple Russian folk art, circa 1924.

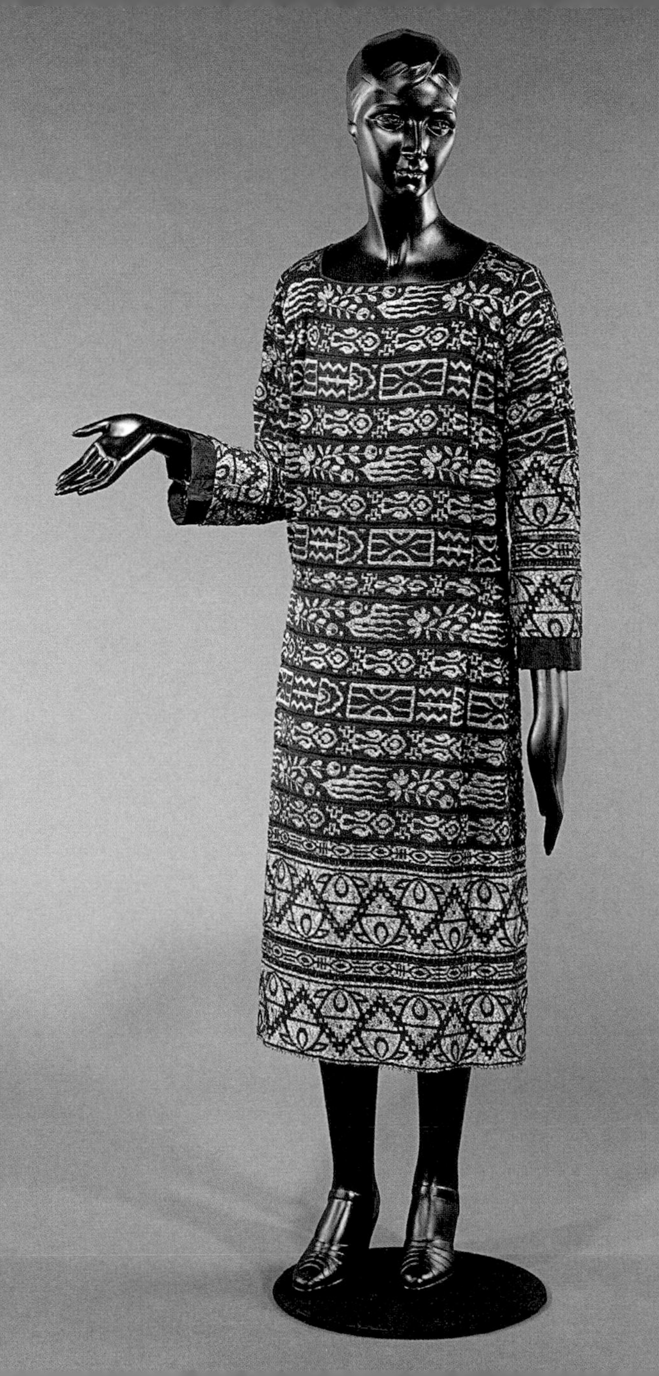

Coco commissioned the sister of Dmitri, the Grand Duchess Maria Pavlovna, to produce the exquisite embroidery for her. Using the skills of the expatriate Russian community as her workforce, Maria went on to run a successful business she named Kitmir, employing about 50 women. The Kitmir atelier (who also supplied embroidery to other couturiers) initially produced everything by hand, which was both time and labour intensive. Coco demanded speed and perfection and she dismissed the idea that the folkloric embroidery had to be hand-stitched, instead providing three sewing machines for the workshop that produced comparable results more efficiently. Always a commercial innovator, Coco felt the decorative effect of the Balkan motifs lost none of their aesthetic impact simply because they were made by machine. For her the finished visual effect was more important than traditional authenticity, as was later exemplified by her extravagant use of costume jewellery.

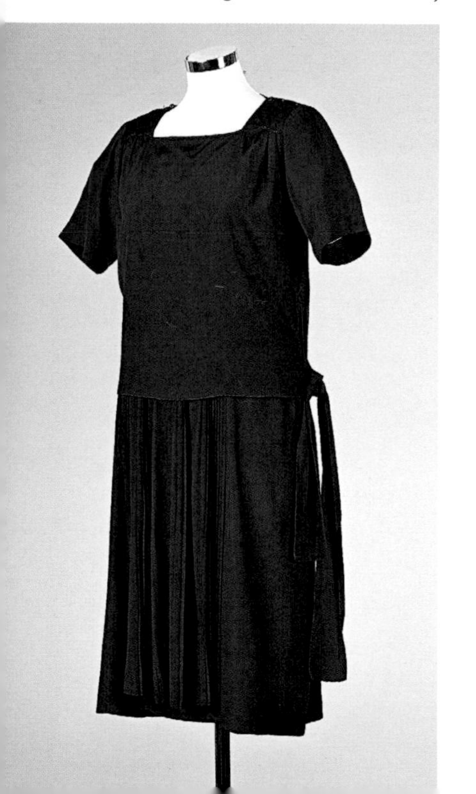

Left The square neckline of this little black dress made from silk crepe, circa 1926–27, is typical of Chanel's "Slav period". The loose apron-like bodice, which is fastened with press-studs at the shoulders, floats over the finely pleated skirt and has long ties that fasten at the back.

Opposite This 1922 sleeveless shift dress is made from silk georgette, which flares from the hips and features the uneven hemline so popular at the time. It is decorated all over with clear glass bugle beads and metallic gold and black thread embroidery.

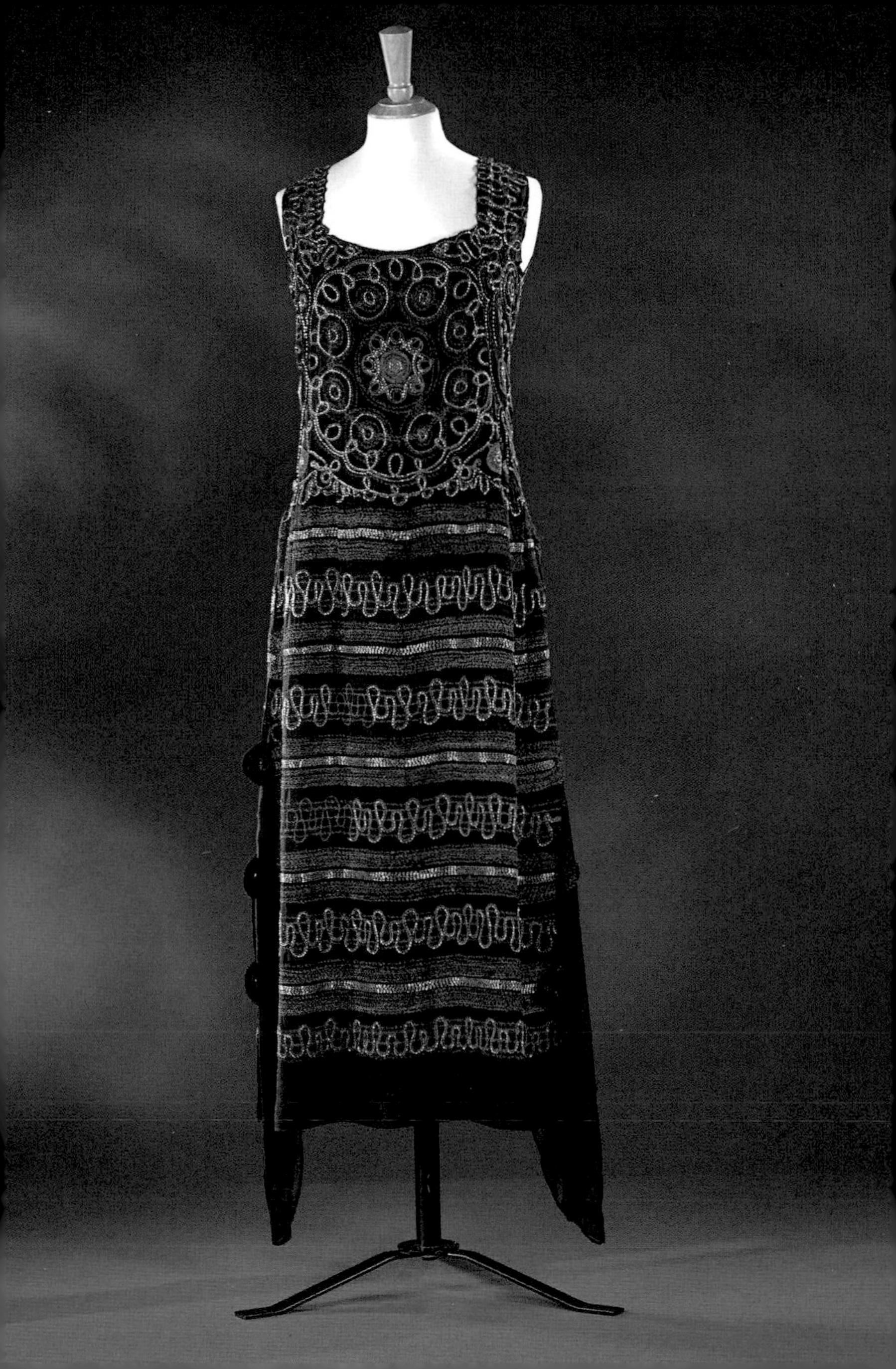

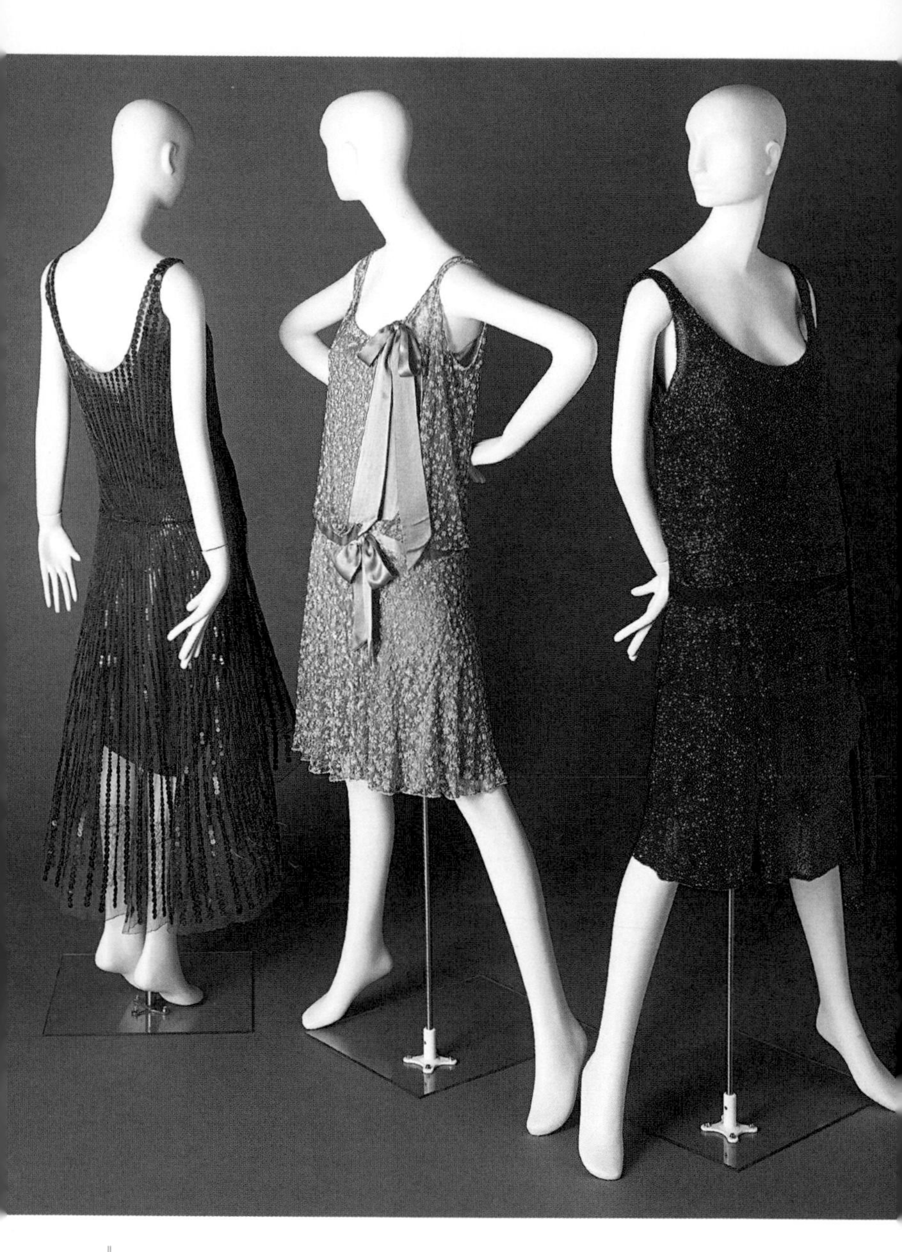

Flapper Dresses

The roaring, reckless Twenties went on to become known as the Jazz Age, a time when those who could afford it were hell-bent on hedonism. Cocktails, cabaret and non-stop dancing were the popular pursuits, and Chanel's tubular shift dresses, elaborately decorated with intricate beading, sequins and gold thread embroidery, were "must-have" items. Made from chiffon and tulle, these evening flapper dresses were sleeveless, fluid and flattering for the new boyish body that society women were starving themselves to achieve. Many were expertly cut in one piece to avoid ugly side seams. Hemlines were still fluctuating: there were asymmetric hems and the pointed handkerchief hem, which prettily covered all options, but Coco's instincts were to keep her dress lengths rising. Apart from the visual modernism of the slightly shorter skirt it had a functional purpose too – it was easier to dance in a dress that liberated the leg.

Opposite In the 1920s, Chanel's tubular Flapper dresses led the way. Drop-waisted with skimpy skirts, they were often heavily decorated, such as this blue silk tulle evening dress (left), which is decorated with metal sequins, and the 1925 lace dress (centre) covered in crystal beads with silk ribbon bows at the neckline and hips, 1925. The drop-waist shift dress (right), from 1925, with gathered tiers and a side sash, is made from crystal beads on silk chiffon in bright red, which was one of Chanel's favourite colours for eveningwear.

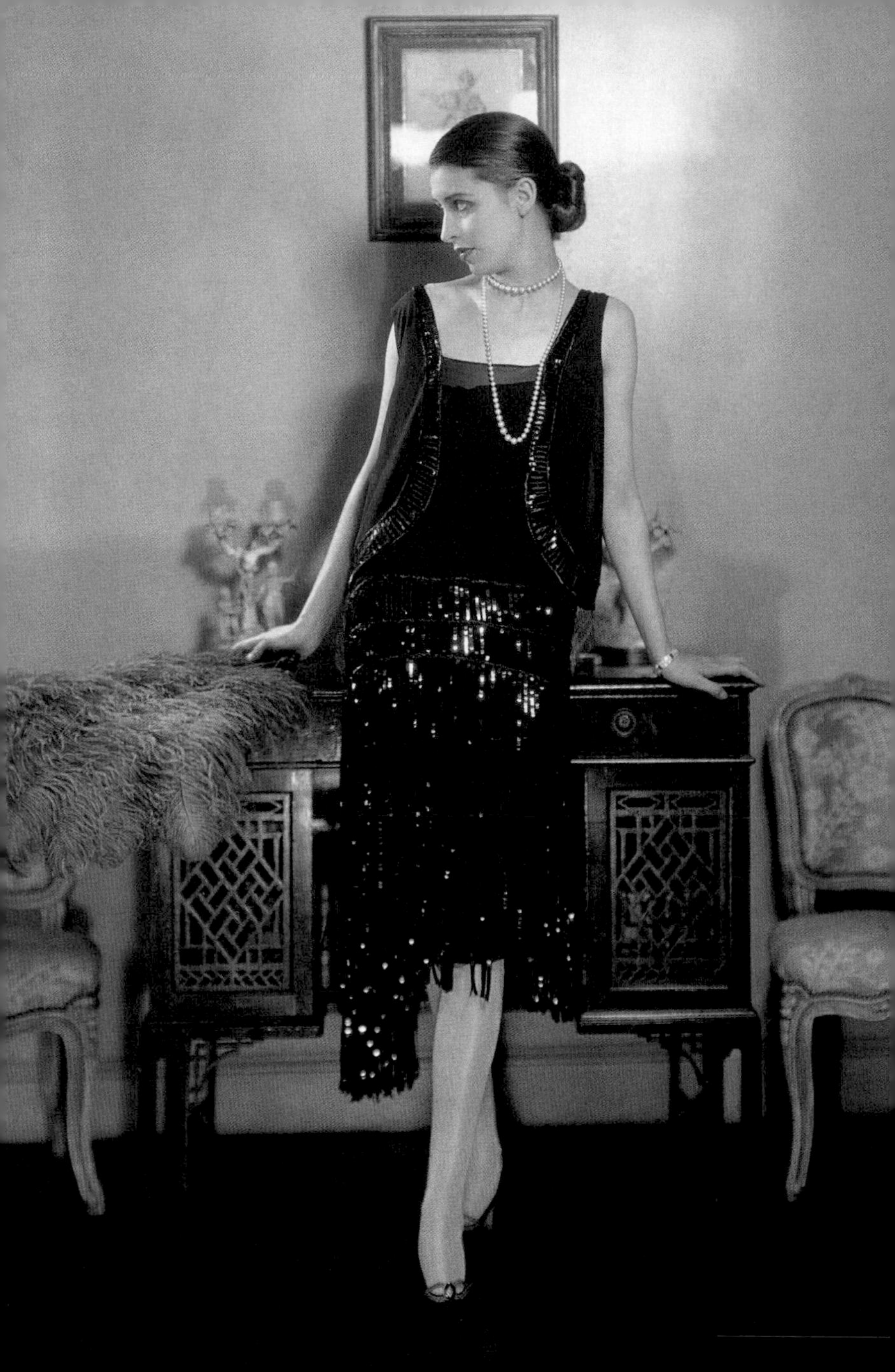

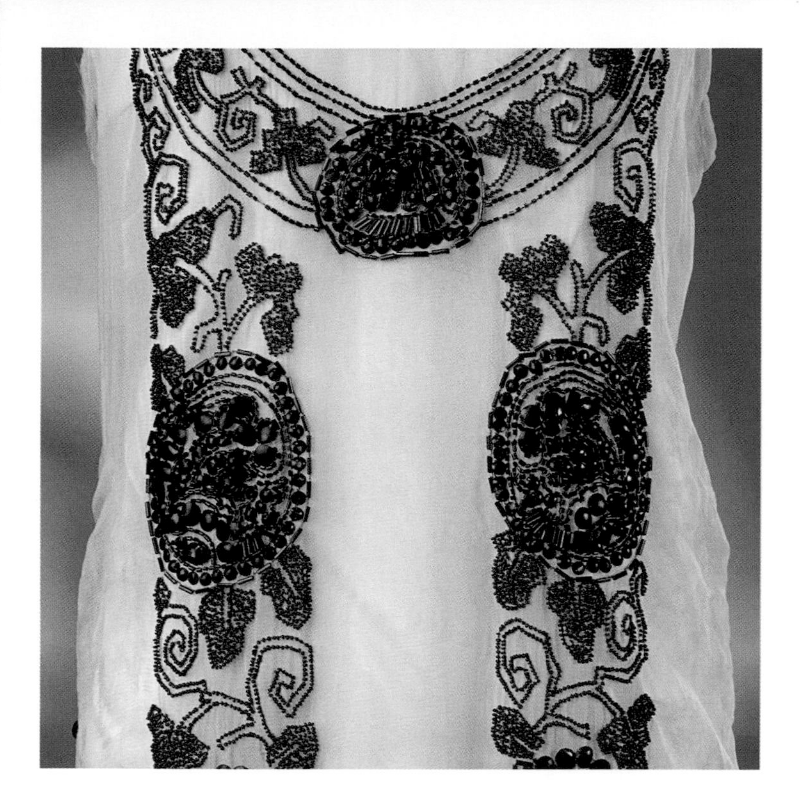

Opposite In the early 1920s, Chanel's "Slavic" period became a great success after the earlier triumph of her jersey collection. Her association with Russian, Duke Dmitri Pavlovich, inspired her to pay homage to the Russian culture. She employed Dmitri's sister, the Grand Duchess Maria, and other exiled royals to execute the fantastic hand-embroidery and decorative beadwork, which embellished her finished garments. The evening line showcased "waterfall" gowns sparkling with crystal and black jet beads, such as this black bolero and fringed paillette-embroidered dress worn by model Marion Morehouse, in the Paris apartment of Condé Nast, 1926.

Above Exquisite jet handbeading on an ivory Chanel column dress from 1919. Art Deco played a prominent role in the fashion trends of the 1920s with geometric shapes based along natural lines.

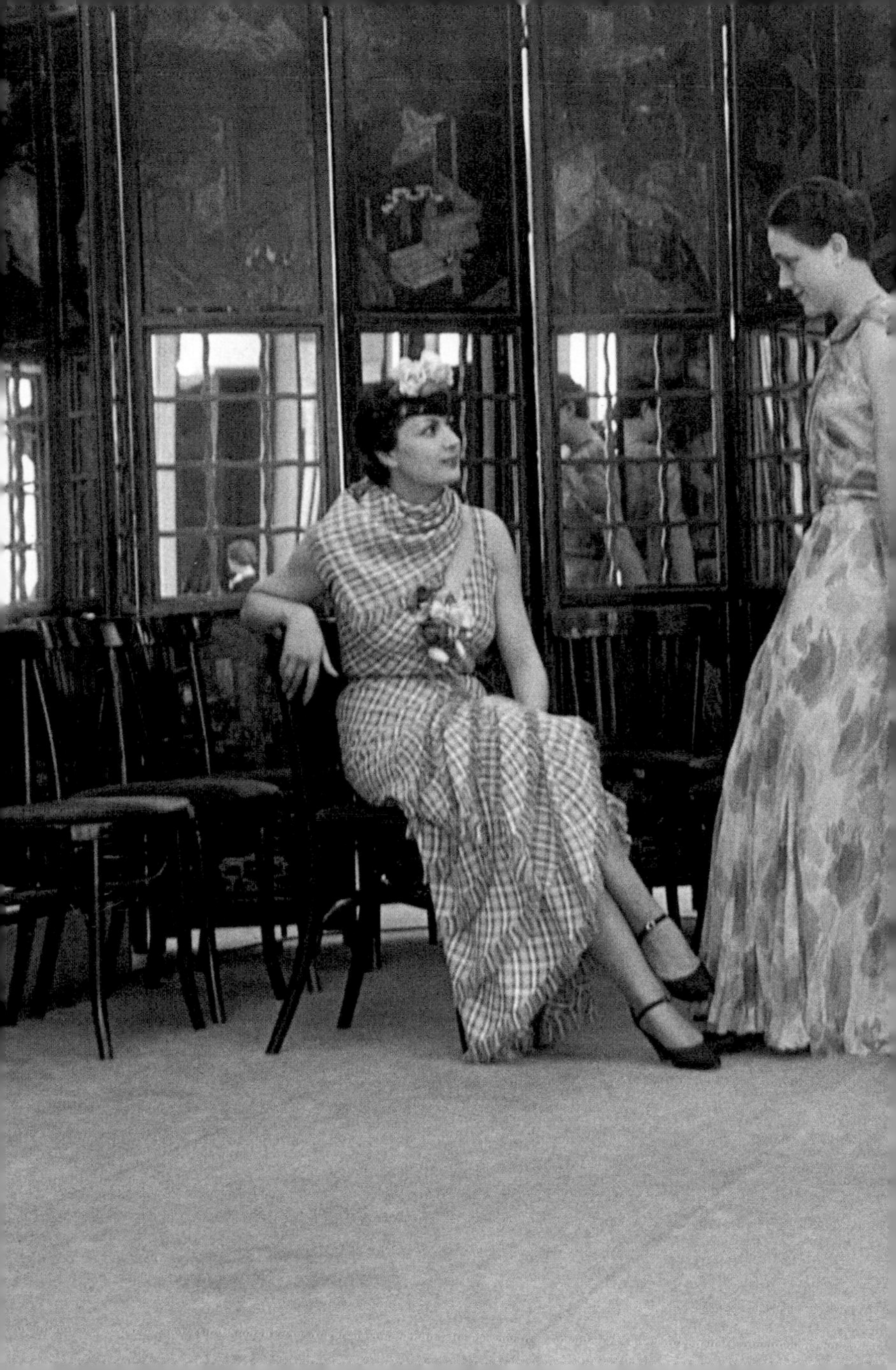

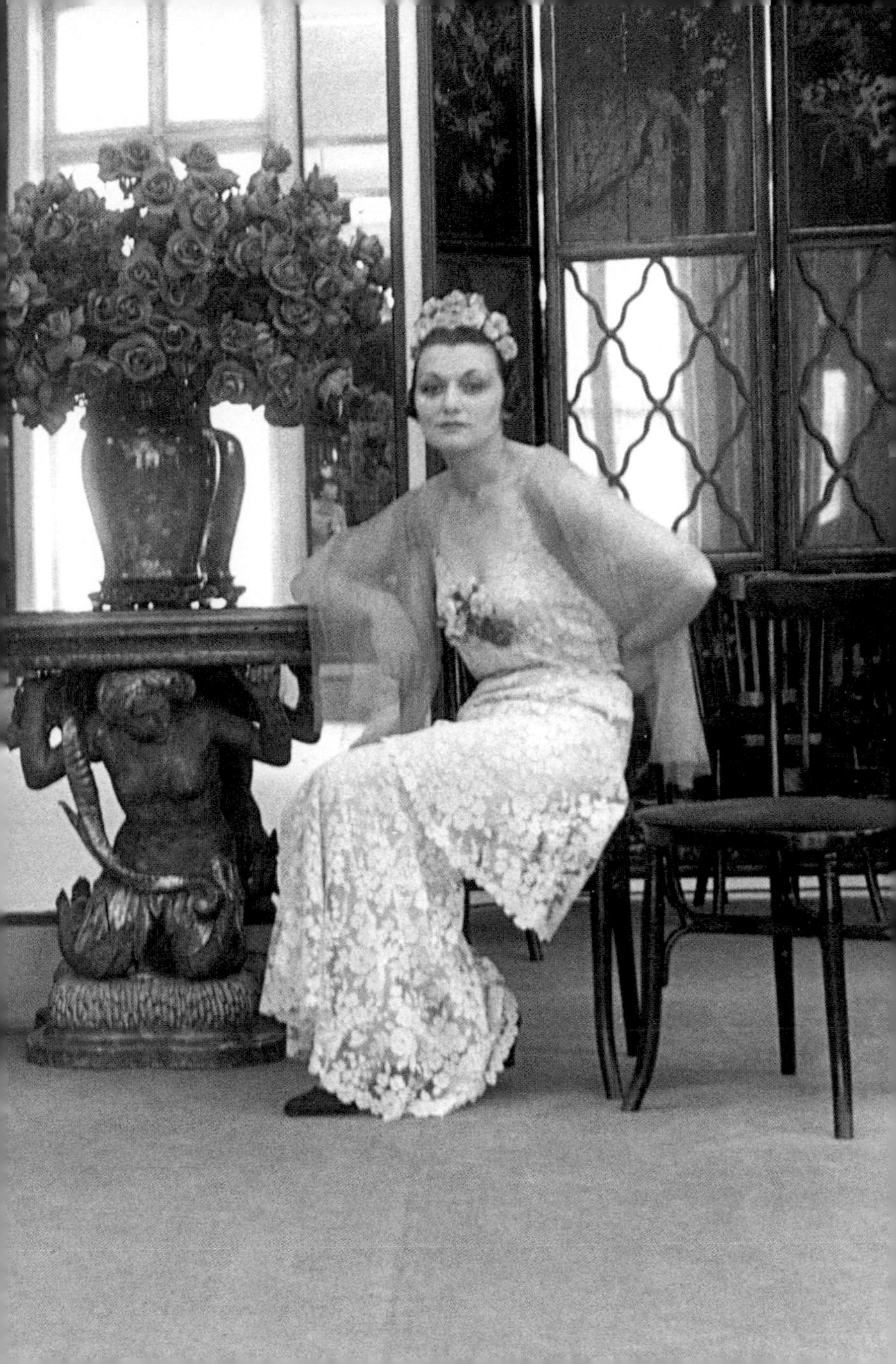

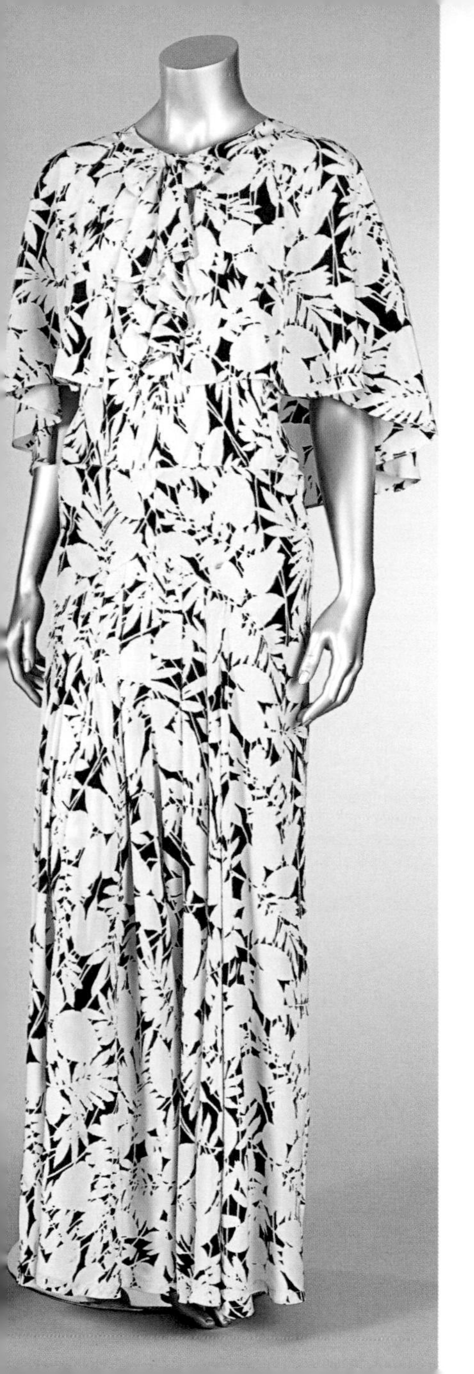

Previous pages By the mid-1930s there was a definite return of the waist to its normal position, and eveningwear, which tended to be body moulding, was longer again. Taffeta, velvet, silk and lace were the preferred fabrics and Chanel often complemented her romantic evening dresses with ribbon and flower decorations and also white carnation headdresses, as seen here on the right.

Left This crepe-de-chine evening gown from the early 1930s is printed with a stark floral design of white leaves and foliage against a dark background. Pleated panels, cut on the bias to allow fluid movement, are incorporated into the front and back of the skirt, and the flounced sleeves are cut from petal-shaped panels.

Opposite Chanel made it her signature to use the same fabric for a dress or a blouse that she used to line the jacket or coat. This green muslin coat with its loose, unstructured opening is lined with silk, using the same "falling leaf" print for the matching dress, circa 1927.

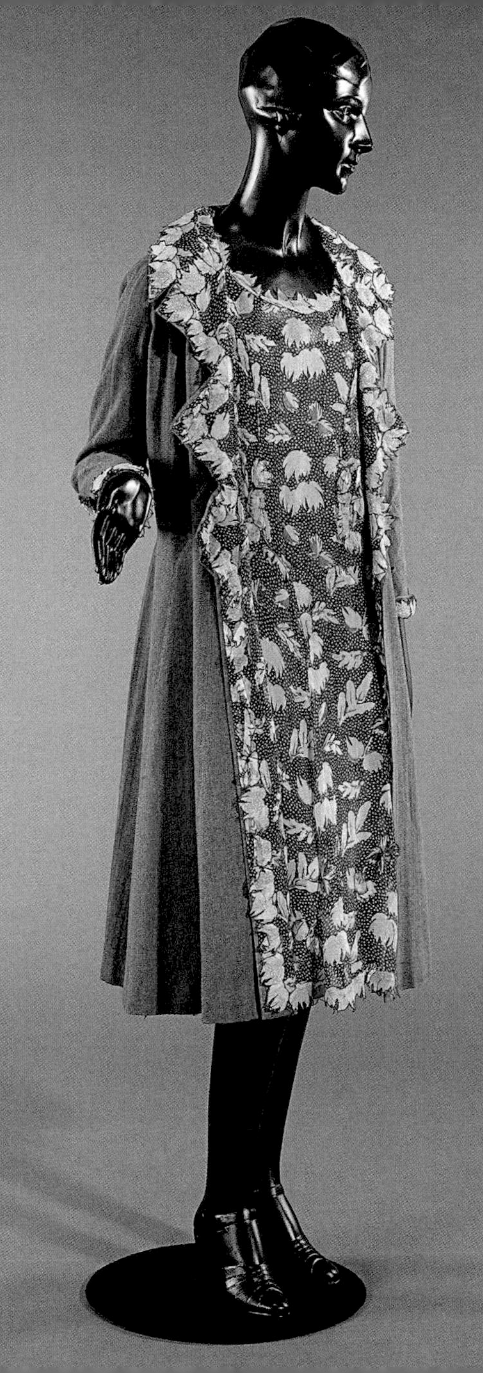

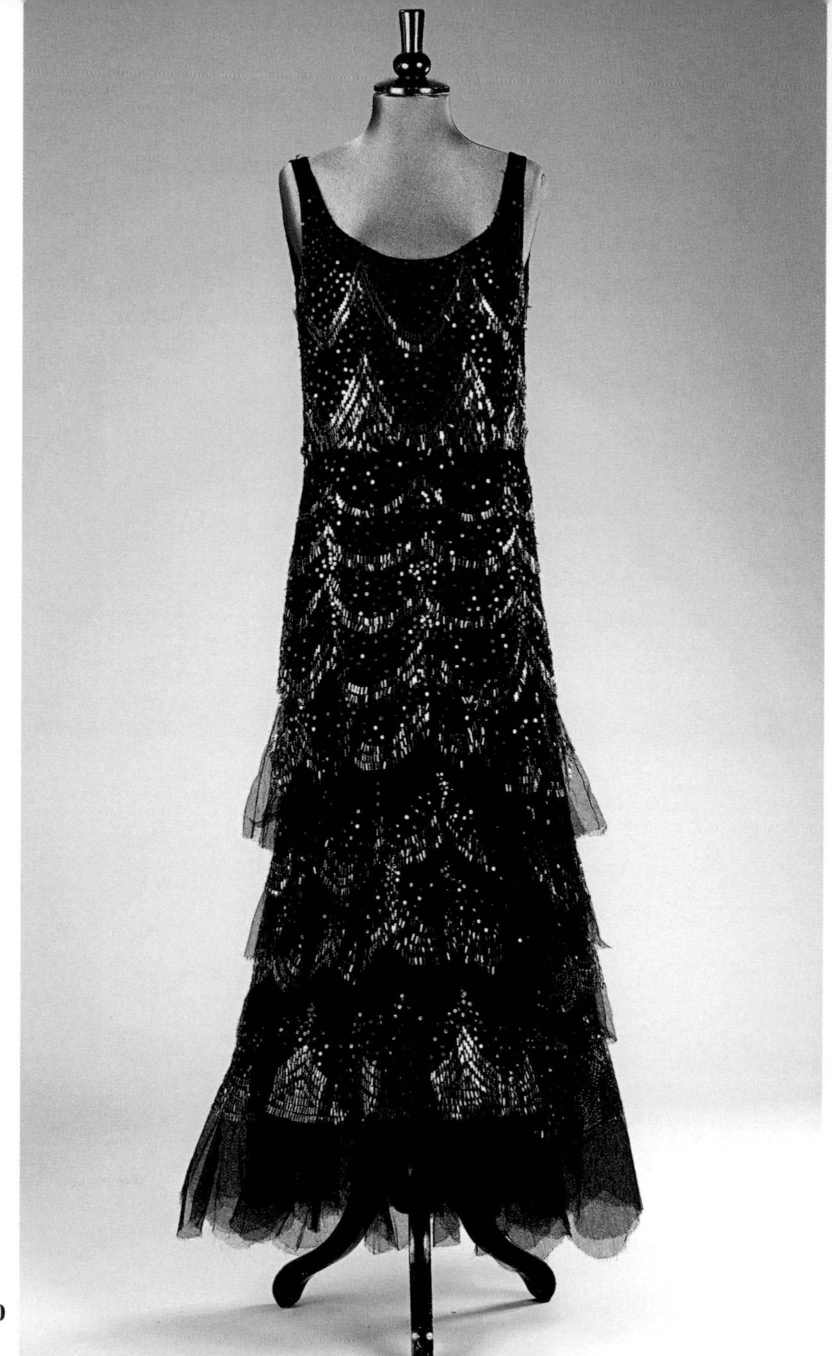

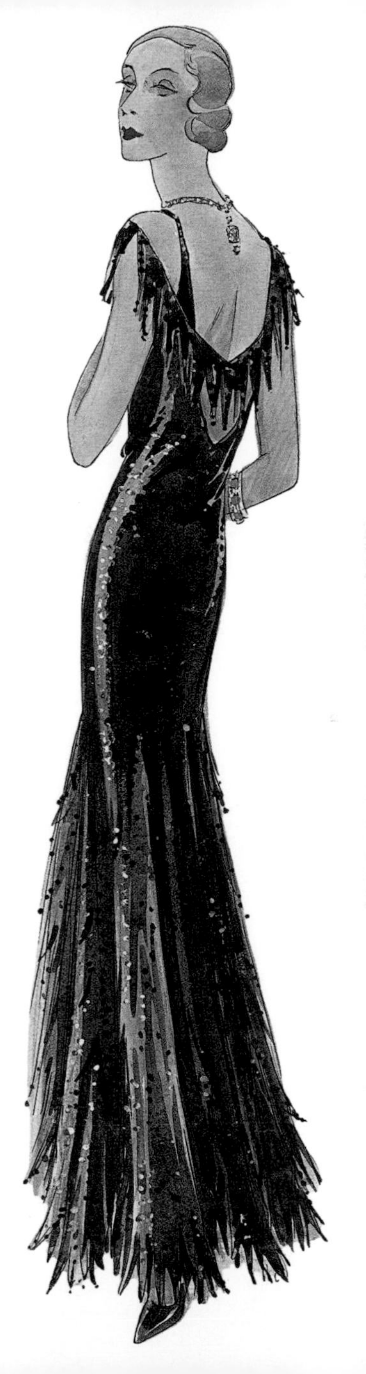

Opposite For this black silk tulle evening dress from the early 1930s, Chanel has used intricate beading work and swags of gold sequins to decorate it. It is gently flared from below the hips in four tiers to allow ease of movement.

Right A fashion illustration featured in *Vogue* magazine shows Madame Paul Dubonnet wearing a black sequinned evening gown by Chanel, circa 1934.

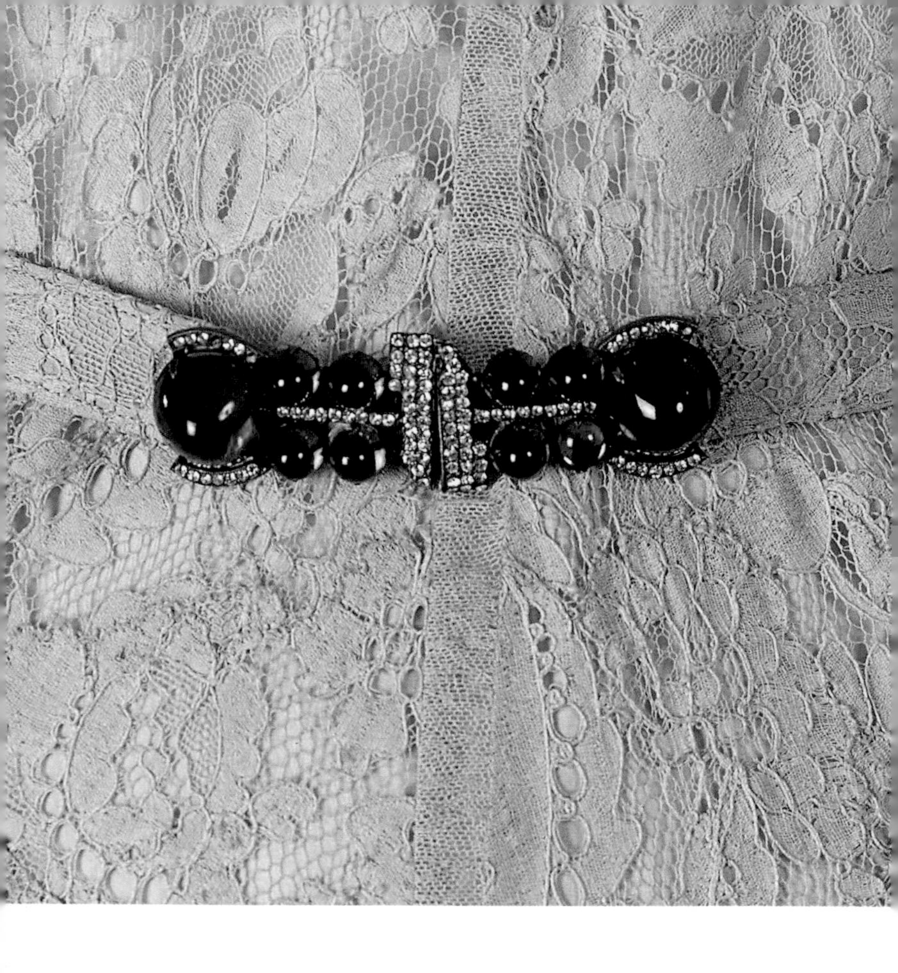

Opposite and detail above Unlike other industrial processes, which Chanel felt could not compete with hand-crafted skills, machine lace kept its key characteristics of elegance, lightness and luxury, and was cheaper to produce. This figure-hugging lace evening dress with three-quarter length sleeves split from the inner elbow and gently gored skirt, is made from intricate panels cut into the body of the dress and dates from 1935. The skinny waist belt (above) was designed as part of the dress. The metallic snap fastening is covered with white lead glass and translucent blue glass beads.

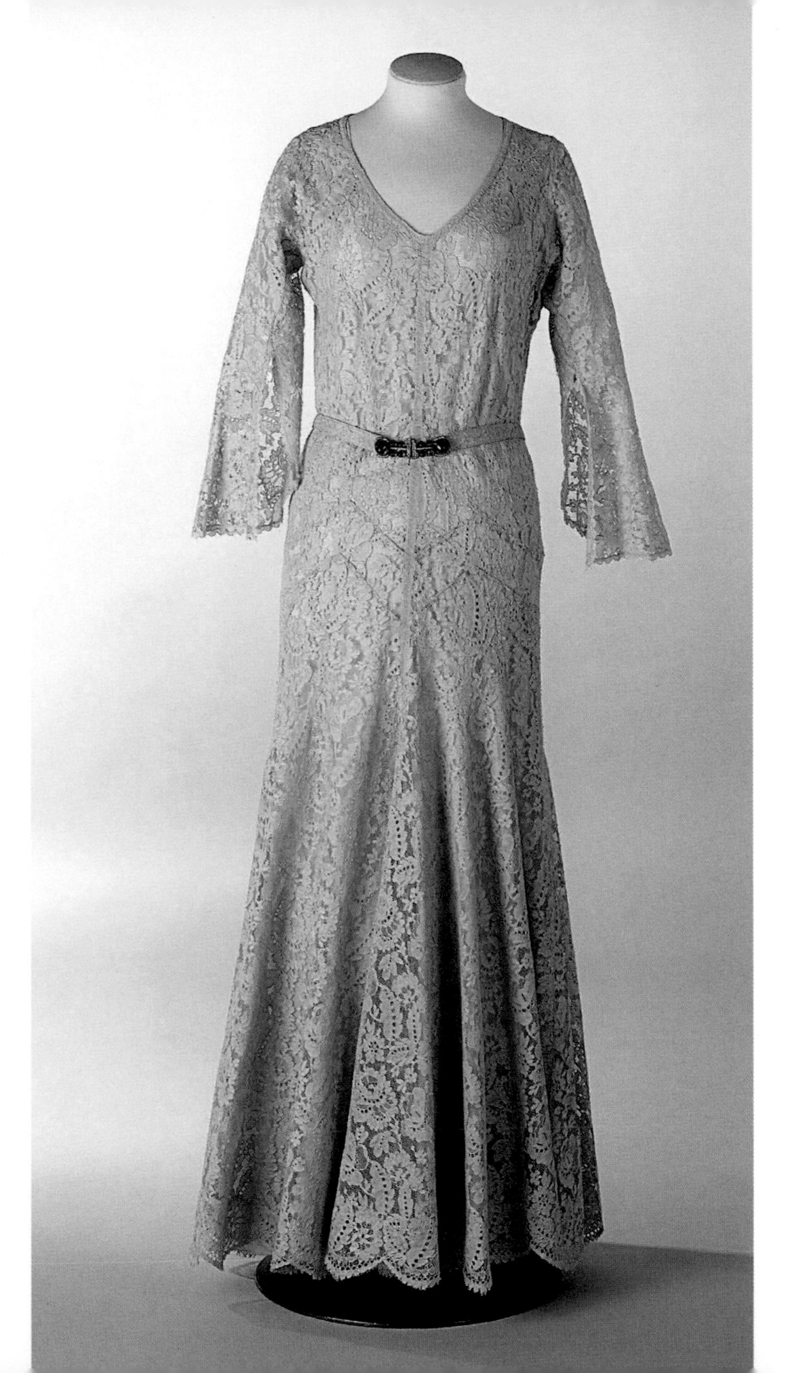

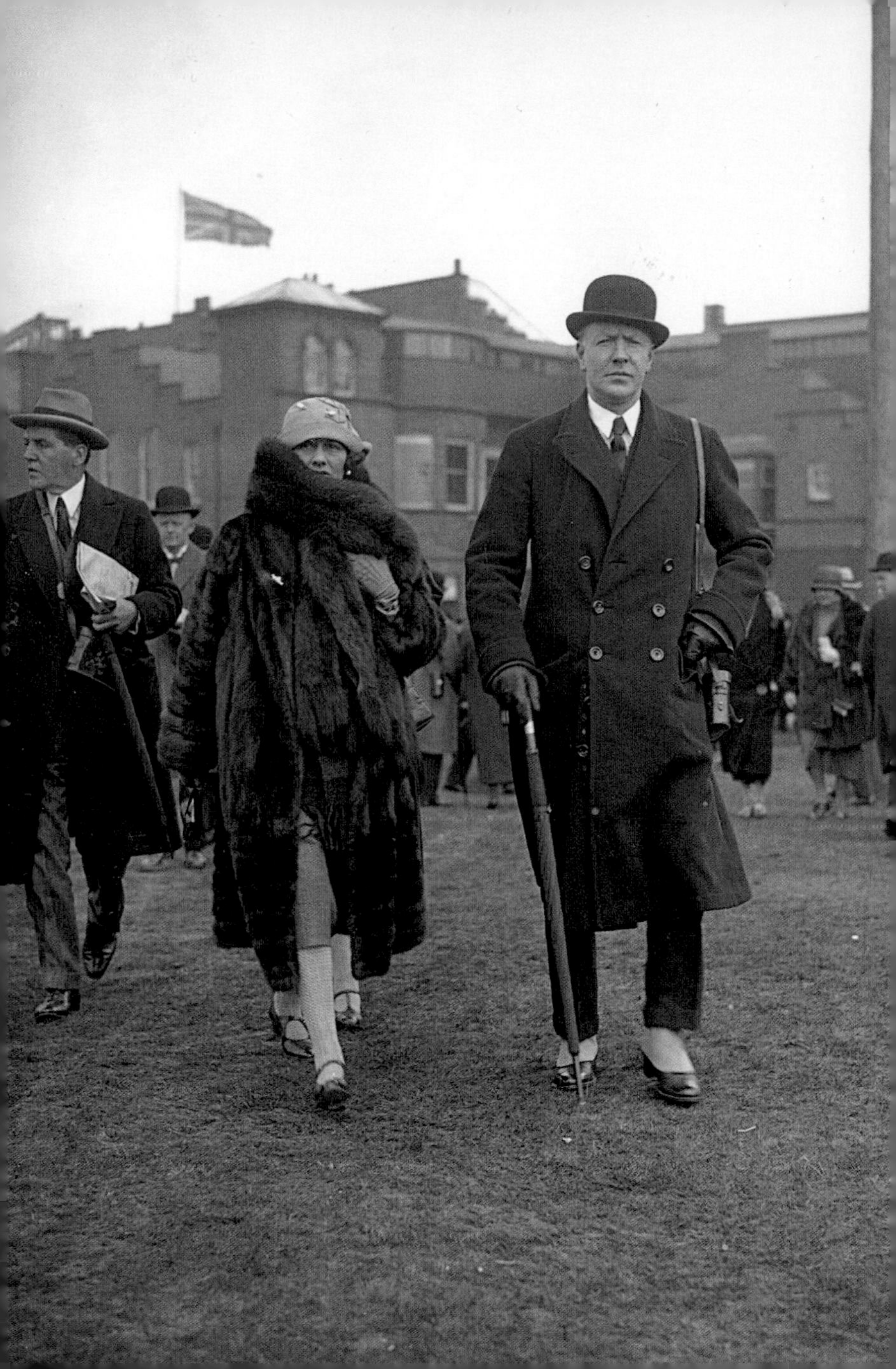

The English Influence

By the mid-1920s Art Deco dominated interior design and architecture, and the tubular lines of this movement were mirrored in the narrow silhouette of women's fashion. Coco had always hated ostentatious theatricality and as the decade progressed she honed her style, simplified her designs and used less and less surface decoration in her work. Her ten-year love affair with the Duke of Westminster (known at the time as the richest man in England) resulted in collections that were heavily influenced by sporting fixtures of the English aristocracy. During her time with him, Coco went fishing, shooting and sailing, and was often photographed wearing an assortment of his tweed hunting jackets, shirts and waistcoats. The cardigan, which became a wardrobe staple for fashionable women everywhere, is said to have derived from the English cricket field. In Coco's hands it became an item that was multifunctional; made from fine-knit jersey, it was easy to wear over a slim straight skirt but also purposefully useful as she ensured the pockets were actually big enough to use. Fishing trips to Scotland with the Duke introduced Coco to traditional Fair Isle patterns and Scottish tweeds, both of which were quickly appropriated into her upcoming collections.

Opposite Chanel with her lover, Hugh Richard Arthur Grosvenor, the Duke of Westminster, at the Grand National racetrack in Liverpool, March 1925. Chanel wears a cloche hat and heavy hand-knitted beige stockings.

Right The Prime Minister of Britain, Winston Churchill (right), with his son Randolph and Chanel at a boar hunt, the Mimizan Hunt, in northern France, 1928.

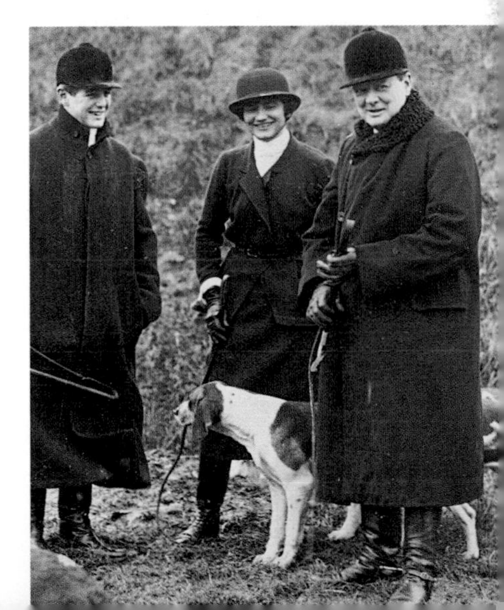

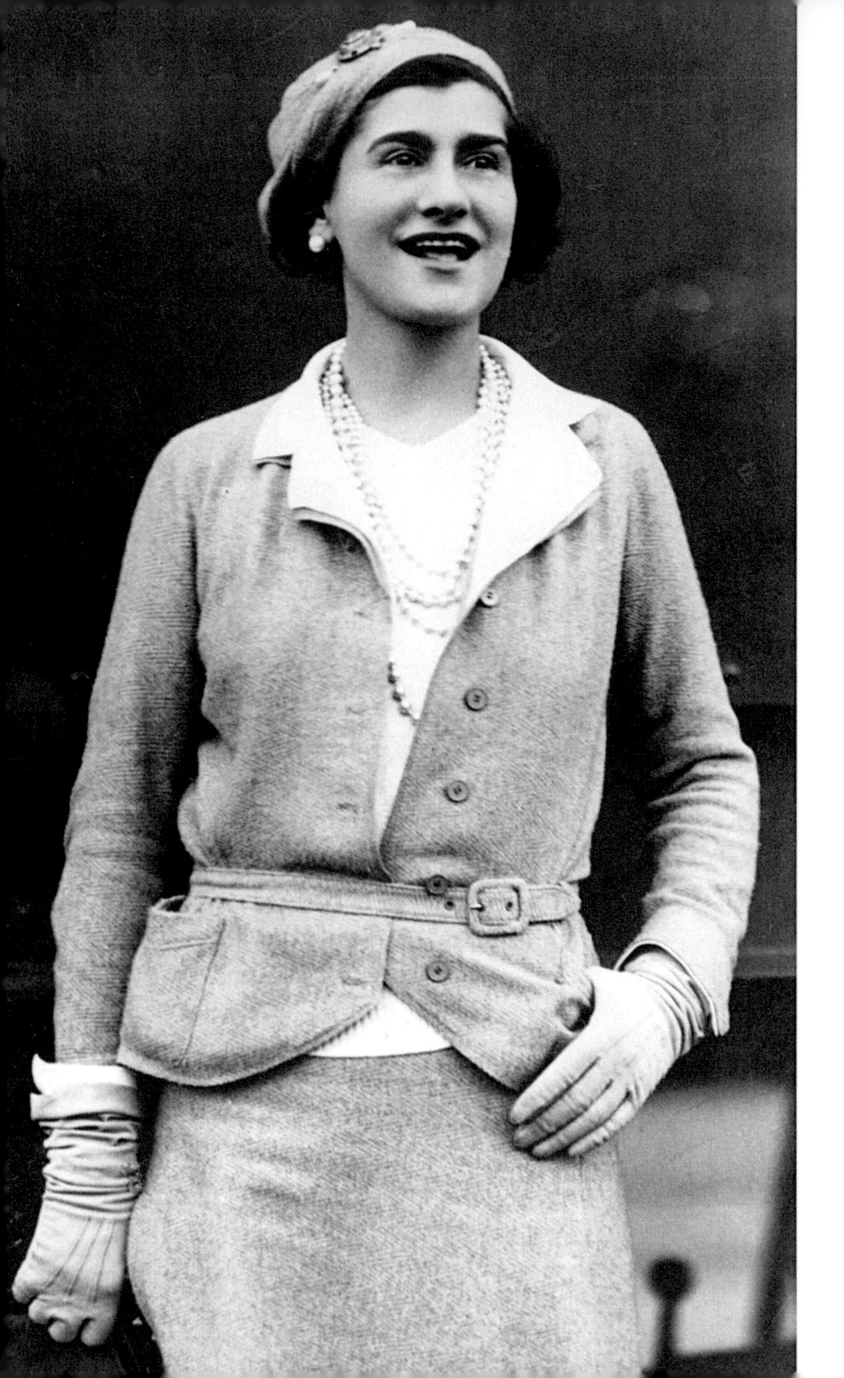

CHANEL

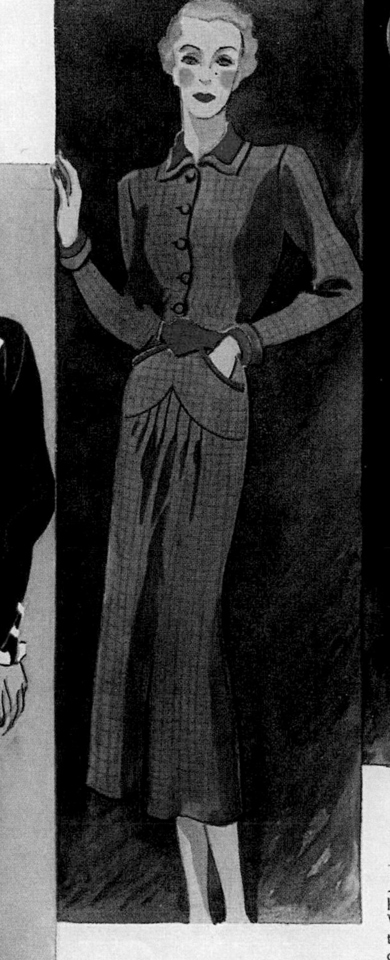

Buttoned bodices, with basques cut full, or flat, are Chanel's contribution to the winter fashion picture. Watch her little collars, fitted close to the throat and frequently faced, or doubled with another colour.

The black woollen dress on the left with white collar and cuffs, is fastened with clips at the shoulders and wrists. A red leather collar and belt of the same, bring novelty to the light navy check-woven woollen dress, while an interlaced leather belt adorns the raspberry wool marocain frock.

The first example of a Chanel suit that could be called an early template for the classic item we recognize today came in the mid-1920s, proof if it were needed that real style is timeless. Early incarnations of the suit were made of a soft wool jersey called kasha and textured tweeds. Coco usually included a three-piece ensemble for each new season, which consisted of a skirt that contained a slight flare to facilitate movement, a jacket, sometimes trimmed with matching fur collar and cuffs, and a silk satin blouse. Her attention to detail was meticulous: the jacket would be lined using the same fabric as the blouse, hours were spent perfecting the fit of the sleeve, which provided total ease of movement, and the inside was stitched as beautifully as the outside. From these formative versions the Chanel suit went on to become an instantly recognizable standard of understated elegance.

Previous left Here, in 1936, Chanel looks comfortably stylish in one of her early suits, casually belted at the waist and with workable pockets. She rarely appeared without her trademark accessory of several ropes of pearls.

Previous right This 1937 print advertisement for Chanel of three outfits shows meticulous grooming and attention to detail in collars, cuffs and belts. The silhouette is fitted, with broad shoulders and a definite return to the waist. Skirts are slimline with just a small flair for movement; these afternoon day dress show the hem dropped almost to the ankle.

Opposite A 1930s woman's magazine advertisement for Chanel showing outfits from her new spring/summer collection. The fitted coat-frock in white cotton pique and the pink organdie suit, which has all-over white embroidery, are both decorated with oversized bows at the neck, a favourite Chanel detail at the time. The slim-fitting silk jersey dress in black-and-white "*pieds-de-poule*" (a fake weave) uses crisp white cotton piqué for the reveres, hat and gloves.

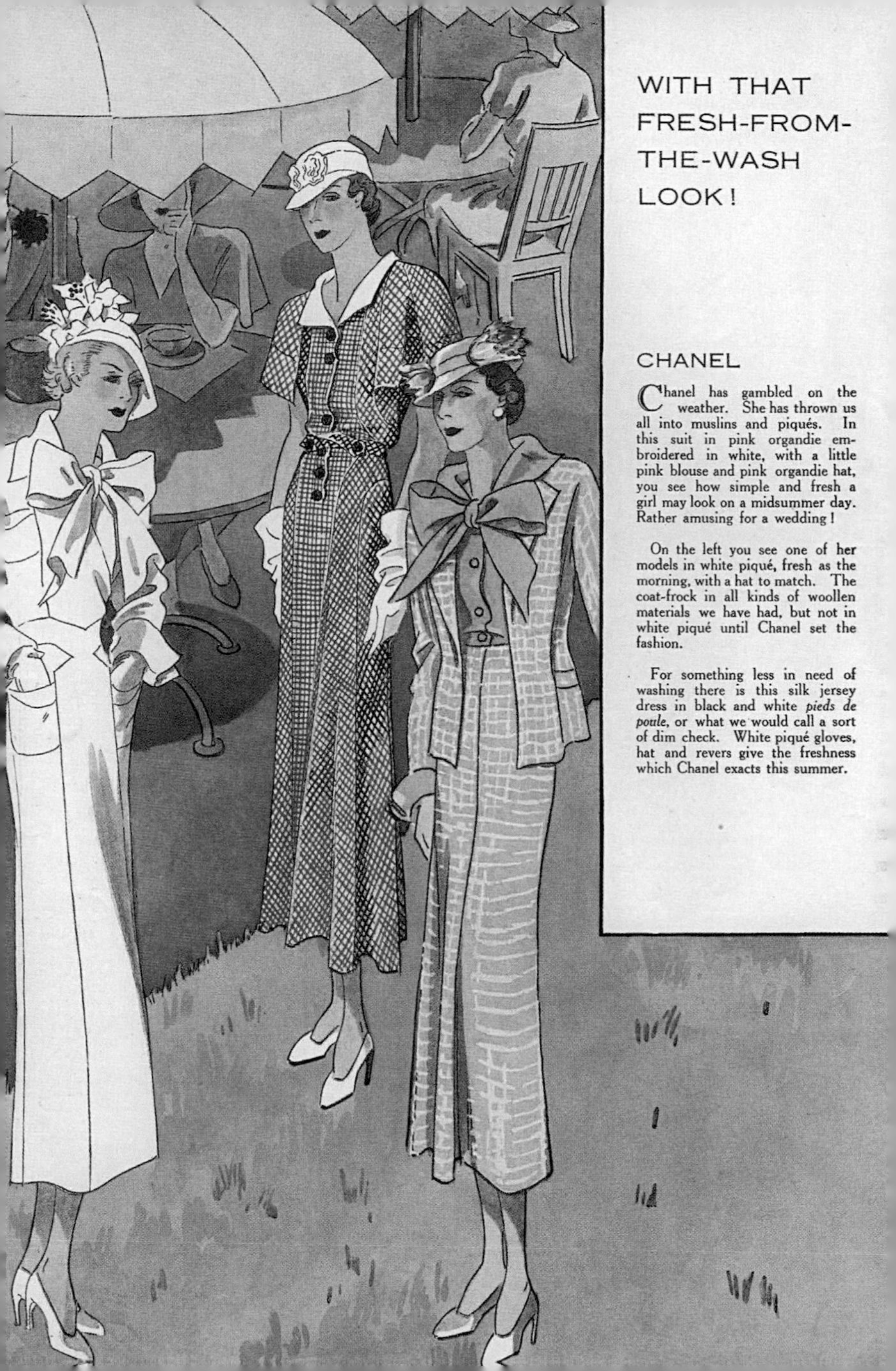

WITH THAT FRESH-FROM-THE-WASH LOOK!

CHANEL

Chanel has gambled on the weather. She has thrown us all into muslins and piqués. In this suit in pink organdie embroidered in white, with a little pink blouse and pink organdie hat, you see how simple and fresh a girl may look on a midsummer day. Rather amusing for a wedding!

On the left you see one of her models in white piqué, fresh as the morning, with a hat to match. The coat-frock in all kinds of woollen materials we have had, but not in white piqué until Chanel set the fashion.

For something less in need of washing there is this silk jersey dress in black and white *pieds de poule*, or what we would call a sort of dim check. White piqué gloves, hat and revers give the freshness which Chanel exacts this summer.

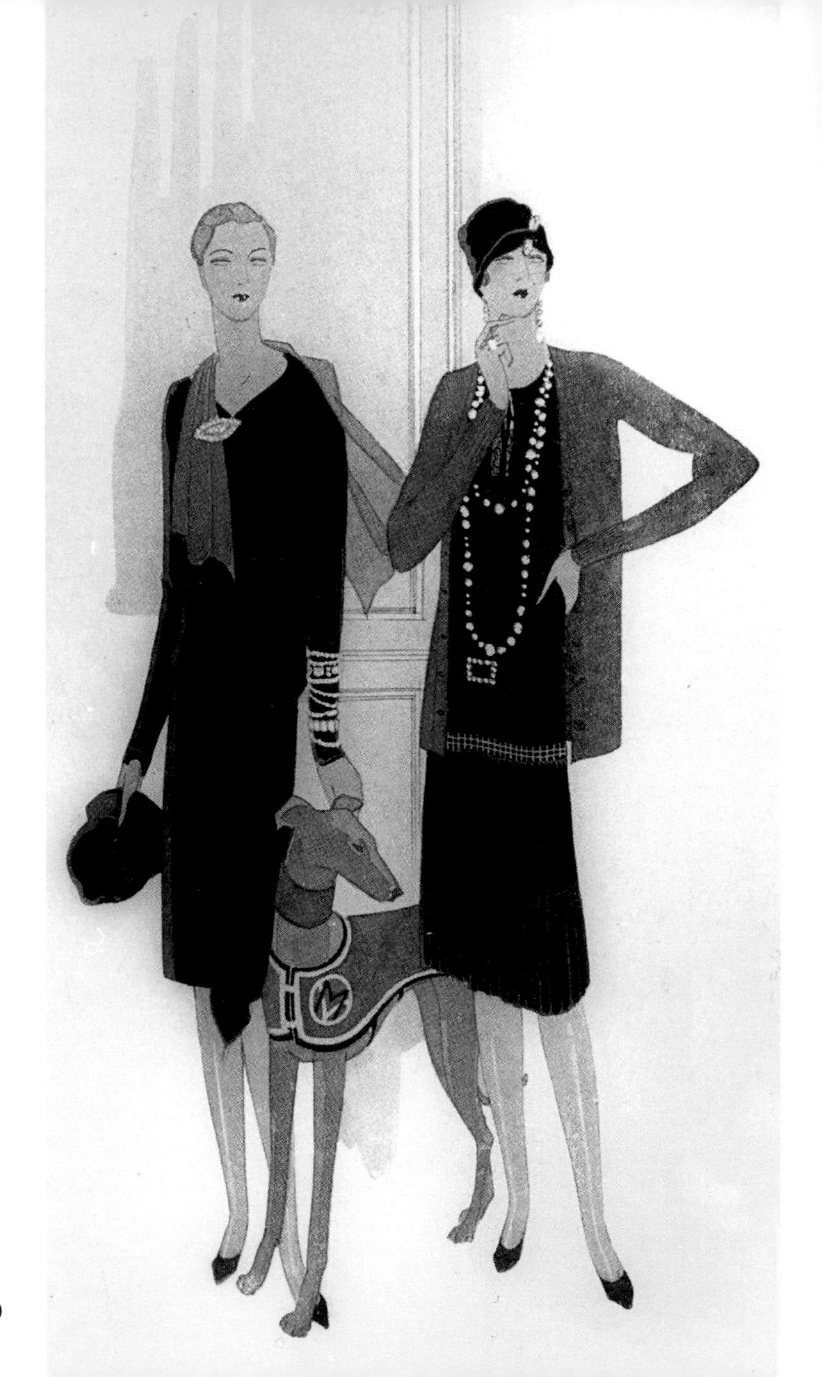

The Little Black Dress

Chanel will also be forever associated with "the little black dress", although if there was a clear moment of inspiration behind the iconic fashion item, it was never revealed. Certainly there was outspoken contempt for the garish ostentatious designs of other couturiers. In her memoirs, as recounted by Paul Morand, Coco declared, "All those gaudy, resuscitated colours shocked me; those reds, those greens, those electric blues, the entire Rimsky-Korsakov palette brought back into fashion by Paul Poiret made me feel ill." She went on to elaborate that while the vivid costumes of the Ballets Russes were perfect for the stage, they were not for couture. Perhaps it came about through a moment of nostalgia related to her childhood in the orphanage at Aubazine, where she spent so much time alone in her miserable dark uniform? Or a reminder of the hellish abyss she fell into after the death of her great love. Boy Capel? Whatever the source, Chanel launched a range of little black dresses in 1926, and like so many of her classic statement pieces it was an item she returned to time and time again to adapt and tweak, endlessly reinventing the ultimate in deceptive simplicity. Chanel was not the only designer to use black, but she was the first to use the colour in such a discreet way, for both day- and eveningwear. Her early dresses were made from wool, or marocain for the day, and dull silk crepe, as well as satin crepe, of which she used both the dull and shiny side, for the evening. The cut was strikingly simple and modern, a sheath dress that hugged the contours of the body without gimmicks or excess of any sort. American *Vogue* in October 1926 dubbed the new black crepe de chine dress "the Ford dress", alluding to the mass-produced Ford motor car and predicting, correctly, that it would become standard uniform for the masses.

Opposite In the late 1920s, fashion followed the sleek, modern lines of the Art Deco movement, and Chanel invented the first of many little black dresses. This illustration from *Vogue* in April 1927 depicts Mme J M Sert in a georgette creation, with her magnificent triple-length chain of diamonds. The overcoat the gazelle hound wears is also by Chanel.

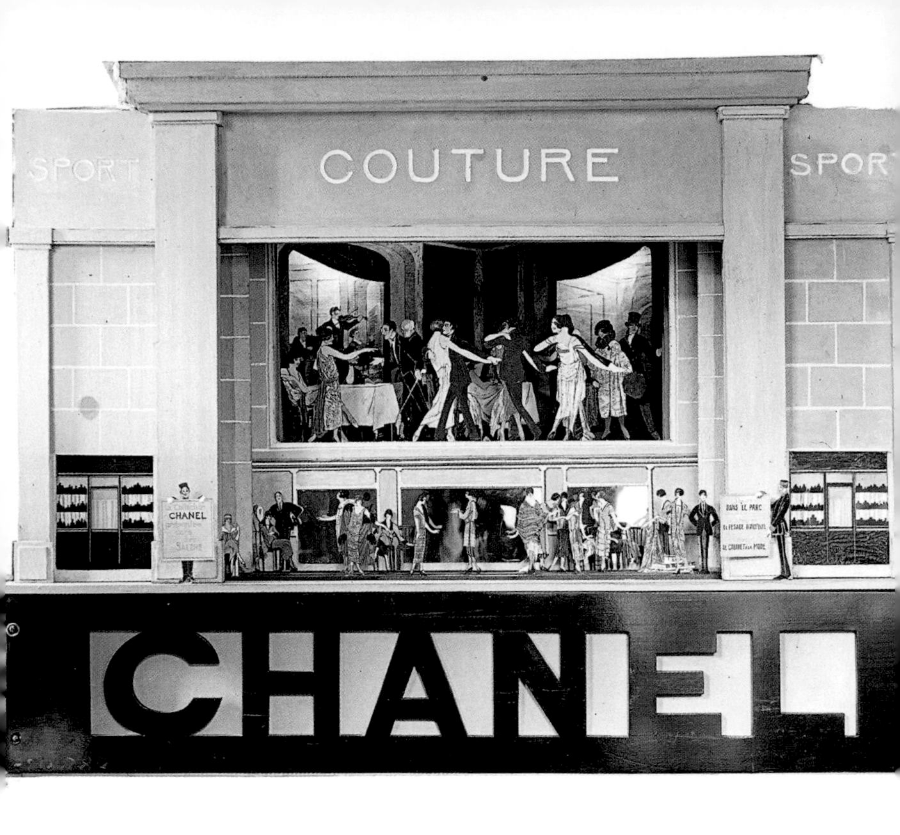

Opposite Published in the American edition of *Vogue* in 1926, this illustration typifies the Chanel look. The model wears a long-sleeved black dress, with detailed tucks that cross in the front, pearl earrings and necklace, and a tall black cloche hat. This angular, unembellished style of dressing caused Paul Poiret to comment that Chanel had invented "Poverty de luxe".

Above From the 1930s, the narrow tubular line of the *garçonne* dress started to flare slightly to allow greater freedom of movement for dancing, as can be seen in this advertisement for the House of Chanel in Paris during this period.

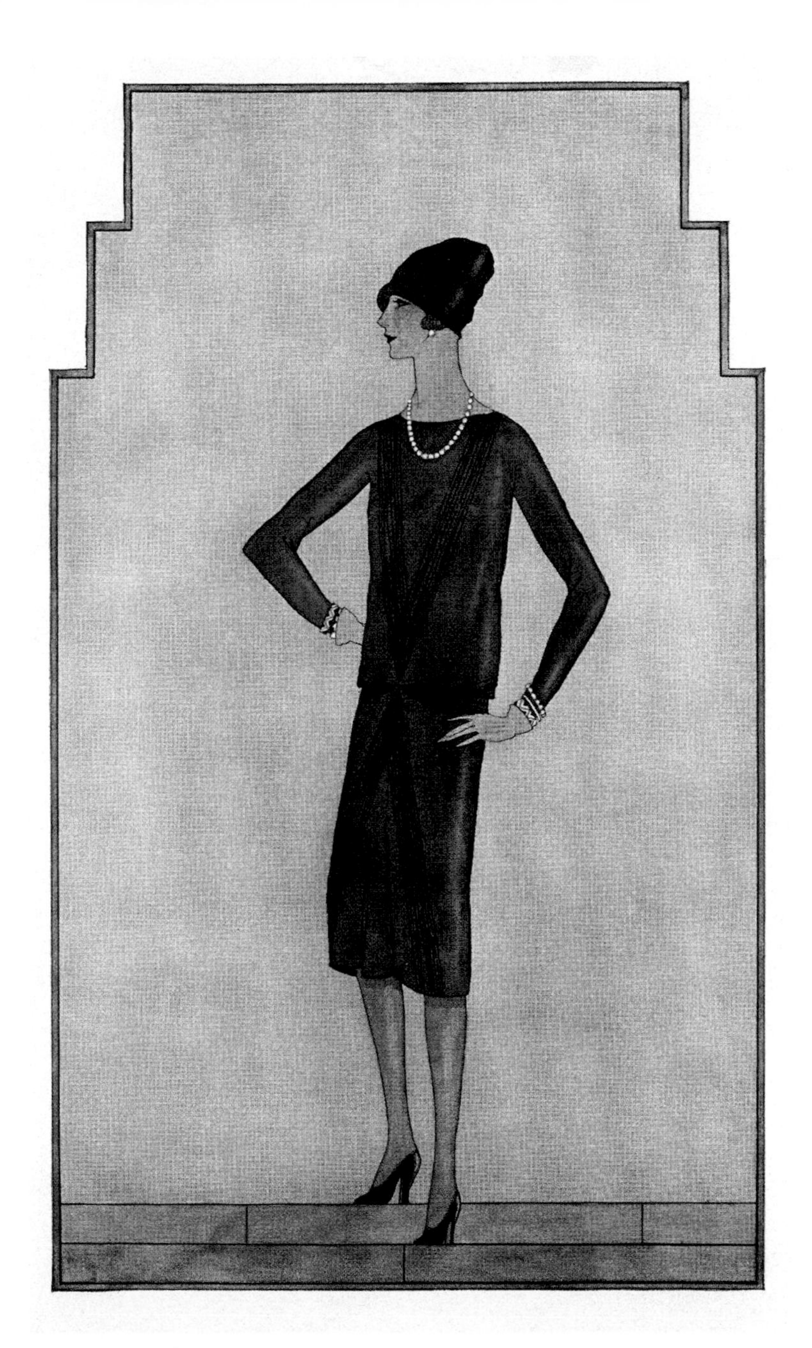

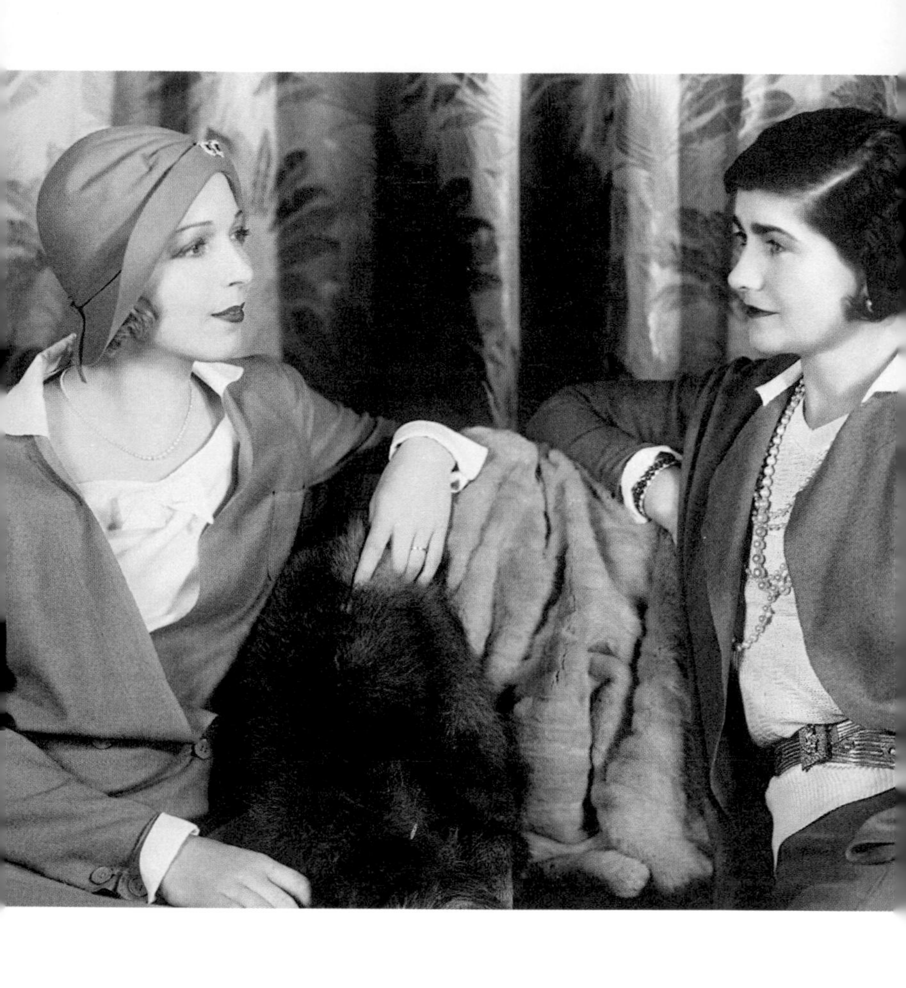

"Look for the woman in the dress. If there is no woman, there is no dress." Coco Chanel

Costume Design

Misia Sert was an extraordinary woman who was capable of bringing out the creative genius in people. She was the only real friend Coco ever had, although their longstanding friendship was not without the occasional explosive outburst. Married to the Catalan artist José-Maria Sert and connected to an impressive circle of writers, musicians and artists, to whom she was both a muse and confidante, Misia acted as a creative conduit within the Parisian art scene. As a couple, the Serts were both instrumental in developing Coco's understanding and appreciation of art, and through their friendship Coco came into contact with Sergei Diaghilev, Léon Bakst, Jean Cocteau, Pablo Picasso, Erik Satie and Ivor Stravinsky, among others.

The prolific and multitalented Jean Cocteau (writer, poet, designer, painter and film-maker) was the first to recognize Chanel's potential as a costume designer, and in 1923 asked her to design for his production of the classical Greek tragedy *Antigone*. It was Coco's first foray into theatre and her geometric prints, based on Greek motifs, and subtle colour palette, highlighted with brick red, cleverly complemented the backdrops, which were designed by Picasso. The play completely baffled audiences but Chanel's costumes received good reviews from the critics.

Her next, and perhaps most famous, theatrical contribution came in 1924 when Diaghilev asked her to collaborate with Cocteau on his idea for the Ballets Russes' *Le Train Bleu*. Diaghilev's groundbreaking production combined ballet with acrobatics, satire and pantomime, resulting in a show described as "danced operetta". A new era of modernism prevailed; the Cubist sculptor Henri Laurens produced the stage sets and Picasso illustrated the programme. Rejecting the idea

Opposite The Hollywood actress Ina Claire (left), pictured here with Chanel in 1931, looked stunning in a Chanel outfit in the 1930 movie *The Royal Family of Broadway*.

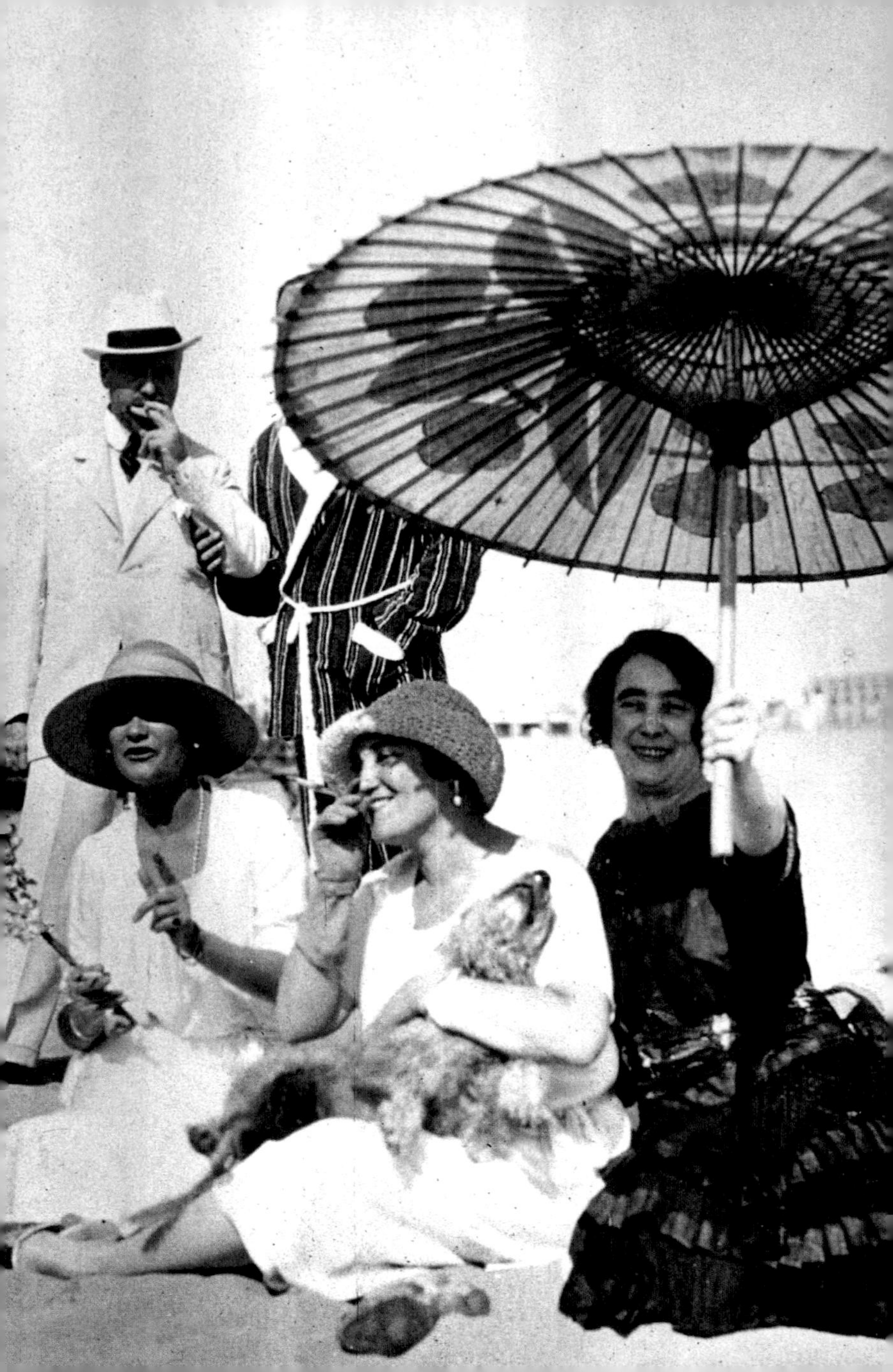

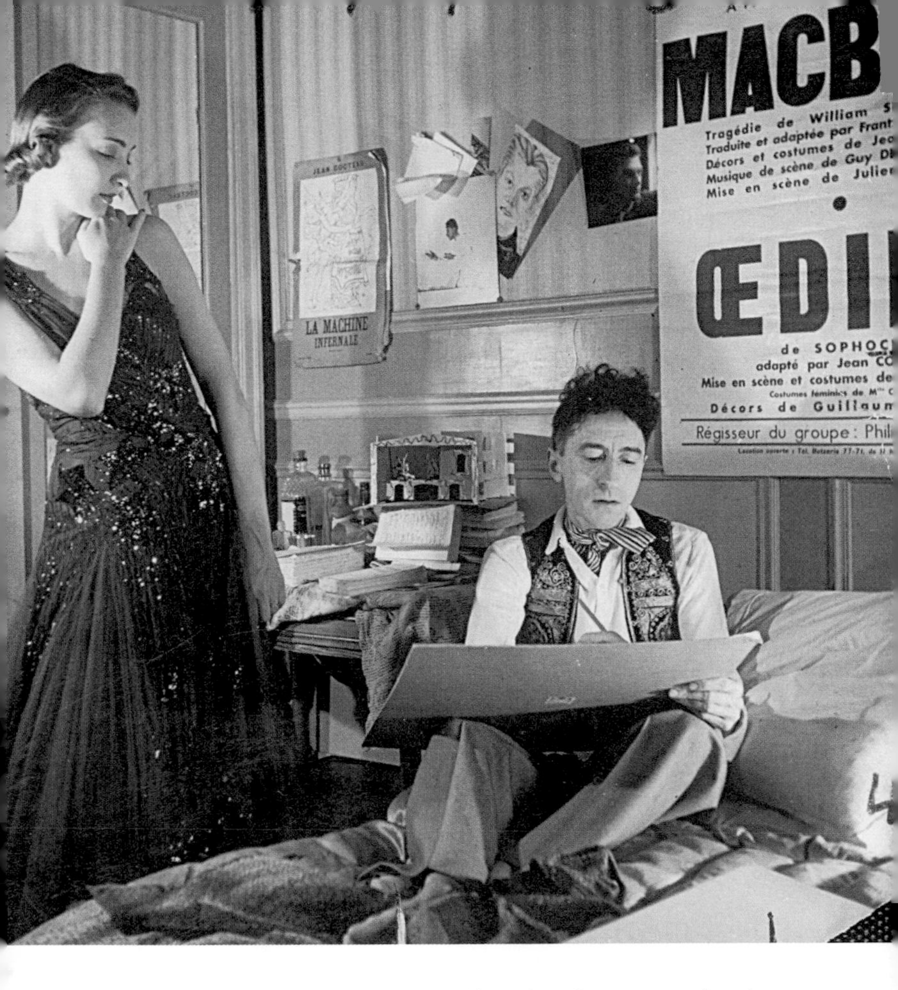

Opposite Chanel is pictured here with her best friend Misia Sert (centre), on the Lido beach in Venice in 1929. Misia acted as a creative conduit for Chanel, introducing her to a wide circle of artistic and aristocratic people.

Above Jean Cocteau, seen here in his hotel bedroom in 1937 sketching the model Elizabeth Gibbons in a sequinned Chanel dress, was introduced to Chanel through their mutual friend Misia Sert. They collaborated on many artistic projects, and Cocteau called her "the greatest couturière of our time".

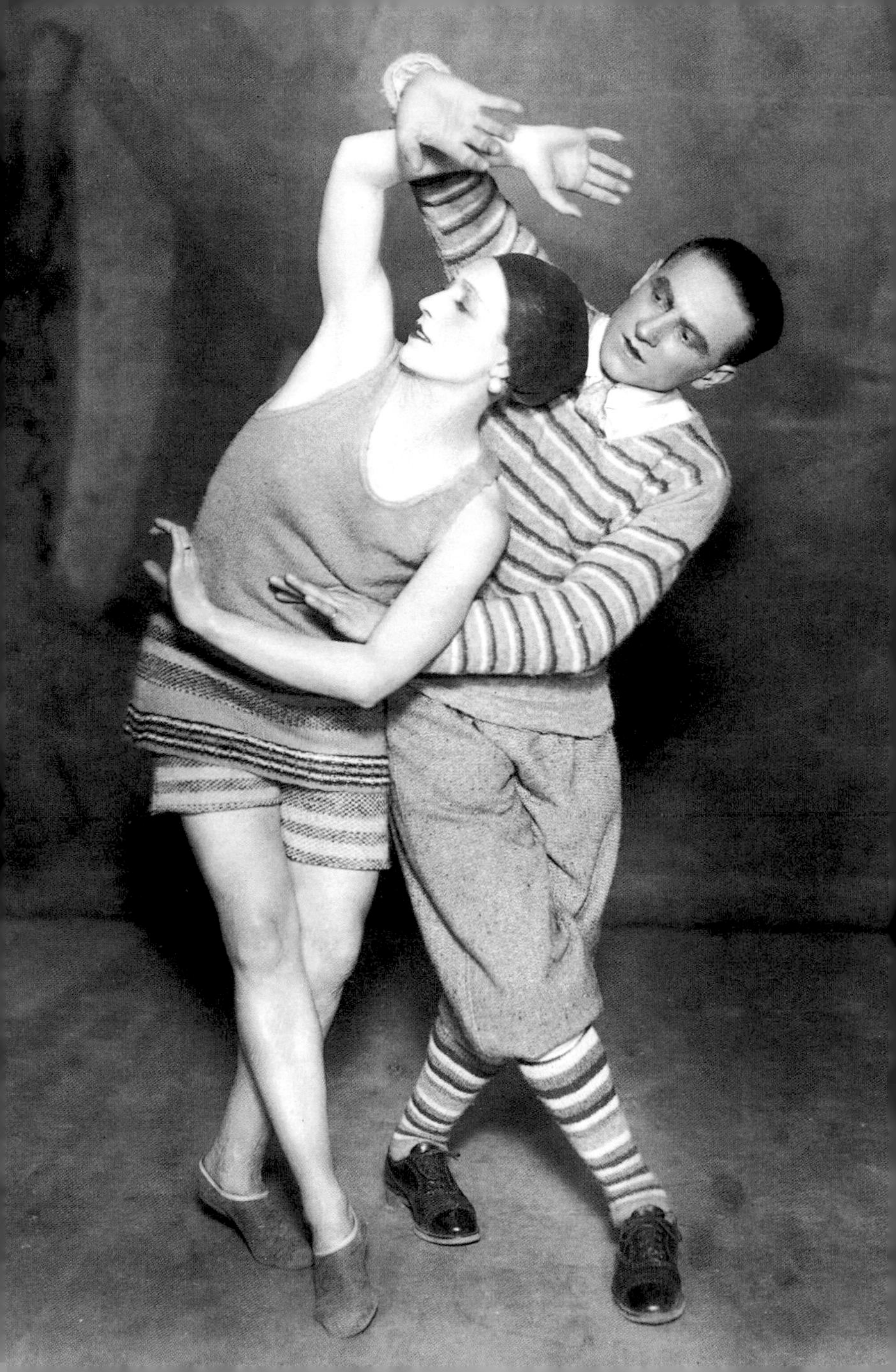

of stage costume, Coco chose instead to put the dancers in real sports clothes from her current collection – swimsuits, drop-waist shift dresses and striped sweaters. She did not adapt the loose-fitting knits (always a Chanel staple) for stage performance and, unsurprisingly, the dancers found it hard to firmly grasp and hold each other during the complex routines. The couturier gave no concession to the artistic requirements of the performers – and even expected them to dance wearing rubber bathing slippers! However, Chanel went on to design costumes for a series of ballet performances called *Les Soirées de Paris* at the Théâtre de la Cigale produced by her old friend Étienne de Beaumont, and would later again collaborate with both the Ballets Russes and Cocteau.

Opposite Ballet dancers Lydia Sokolova and Leon Woizikwsky in the 1924 Diaghilev production for the Ballets Russes of *Le Train Bleu.* Jean Cocteau conceived the story and Chanel designed the knitted costumes, which caused great problems for the dancers who found it difficult to grasp each other.

Right Chanel collaborated with the Spanish artist Salvador Dalí on the ballet he designed with Diaghilev's Ballet Russes de Monte Carlo. Set to the music of Wagner's "Tannhauser", Chanel is seen here putting the final touches to the costume of Mad King Ludwig of Bavaria, who is the central character in *Bacchanale,* which was premiered at the Metropolitan Opera House in New York in 1940.

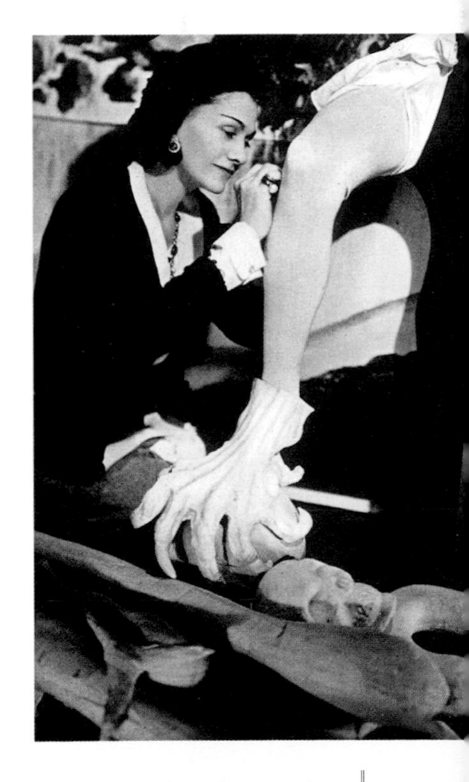

The Hollywood Connection

In the meantime, complicated negotiations with Hollywood were underway. To be connected in some way with the ultra-chic style of Mademoiselle Chanel gave a production an added dimension of glamour, and it was this that the movie magnate Samuel Goldwyn was determined to tap into when, through the Russian Dmitri, he stage-managed a meeting with Coco in Monte Carlo. Goldwyn wanted Chanel to provide some understated Parisian glamour for his leading ladies, but he also wanted her to refine American's tastes in fashion, and planned that all his stars should not only be dressed by Chanel in his movies but also in their private lives. At a time when America was suffering financially, he was furious that his female stars were flaunting conspicuous extravagance, and thought with Chanel on board he could win back public approval. In the 1930 movie *The Royal Family of Broadway*, Ina Claire had already appeared wearing a stunning black Chanel suit with a red fox fur trim, but Goldwyn's new deal for Coco asked for a much bigger commitment on both sides. After many months of protracted negotiations he offered her a guaranteed contract of $1 million dollars, which seemed too good to turn down, and Coco finally set off for Hollywood with Misia in 1931. There she was greeted with much acclaim and introduced to Hollywood royalty: Greta Garbo, Marlene Dietrich, Claudette Colbert and the directors George Cukor and Erich von Stroheim. Her visit was short, and somewhat volatile, as she let it be known that she would not be told what to do by the studio system and that she would be designing everything in Paris, sending a team of assistants to the studios in California to complete fittings. Having worked so hard to gain total independence in her business, Coco found it impossible to put herself up for hire and be subordinate

Right Chanel's association with Hollywood was shortlived, but she was responsible for designing the costumes for Gloria Swanson in *Tonight or Never* in 1931 which also starred Melvyn Douglas.

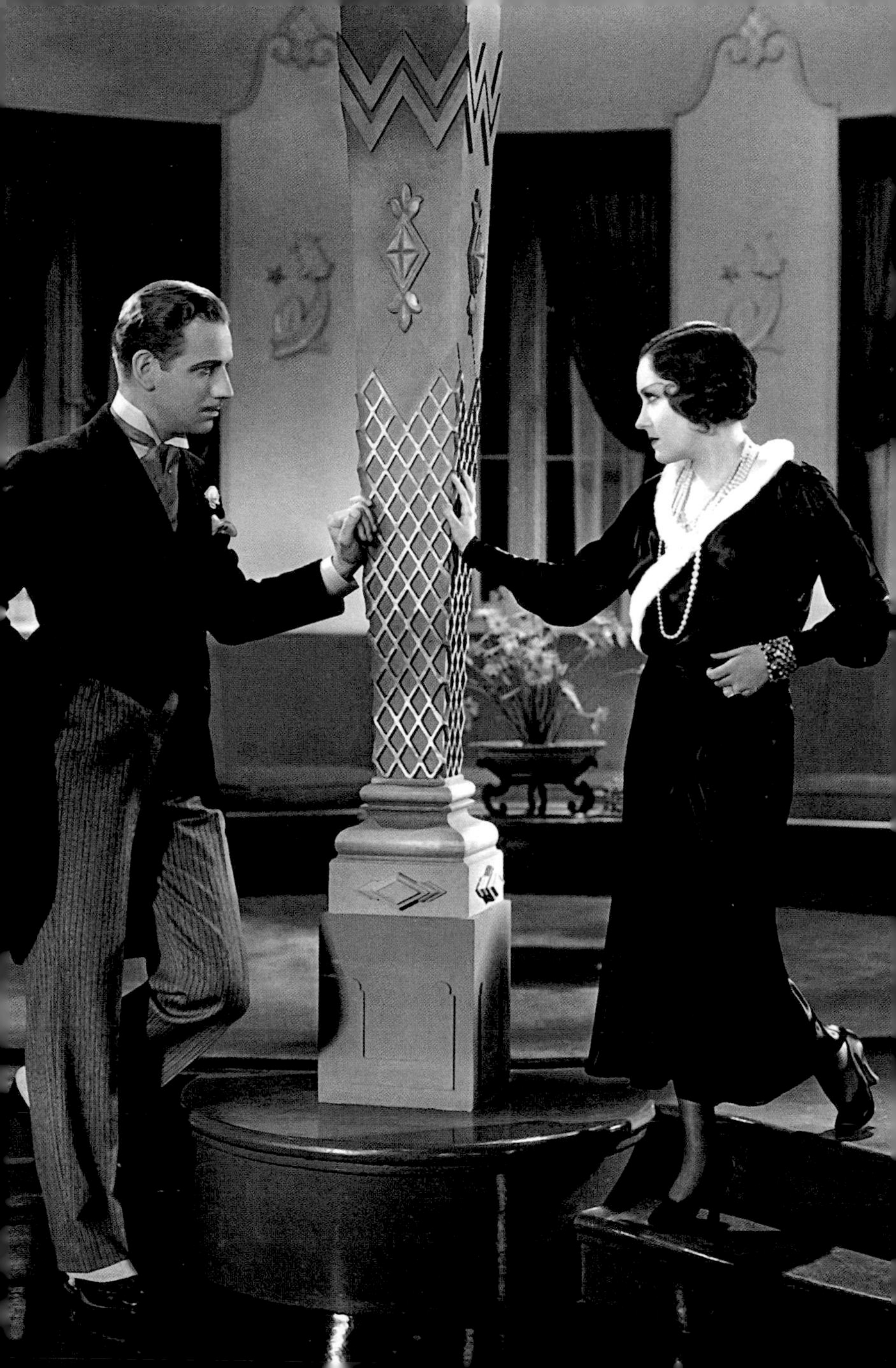

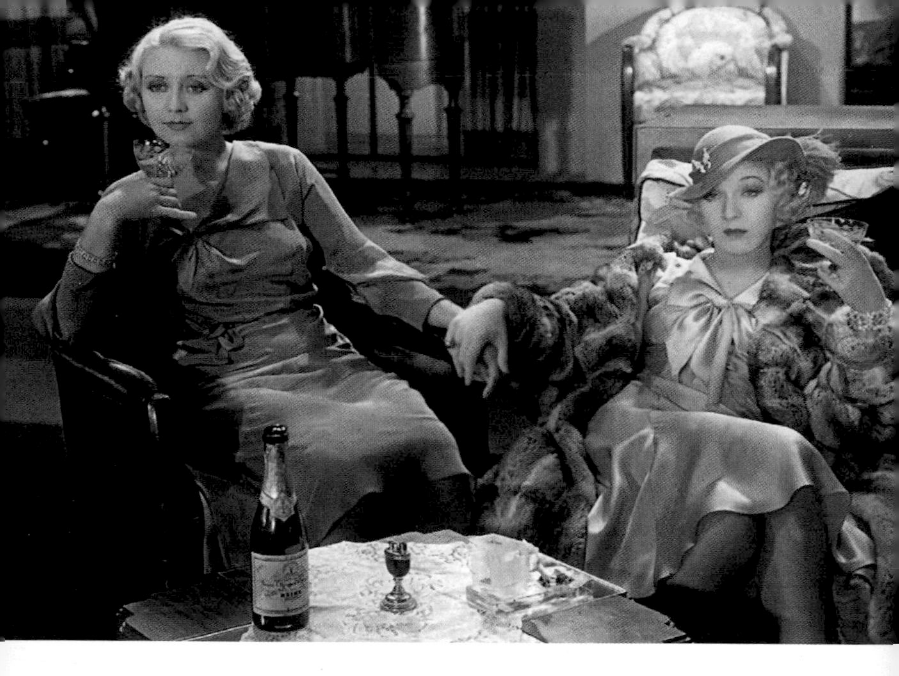

to the female stars of Hollywood, who in turn refused to have her style imposed upon them.

In the end she worked on just three films – *Palmy Days* (1931), *The Greeks Had a Word for Them* (1932), and *Tonight or Never* (1931) starring Gloria Swanson. None were huge box-office hits, although Chanel's creations for Swanson were praised in the press. *The New Yorker* noted her return to Europe by saying her dresses were simply not sensational enough: "She made a lady look like a lady. Hollywood wants a lady to look like two ladies."

Above A still from the movie *The Greeks Had a Word for Them*, which starred Joan Blondell and Ina Claire, both wearing costumes designed by Chanel. This was the last film Chanel worked on, as she found the Hollywood experience restrictive and uncreative.

Opposite *Palmy Days* was the first movie for which Chanel was contracted to design costumes. Starring Charlotte Greenwood and Eddie Cantor, the musical comedy was not a huge hit, and Chanel was required to deliver little more than a few dresses for the leading lady.

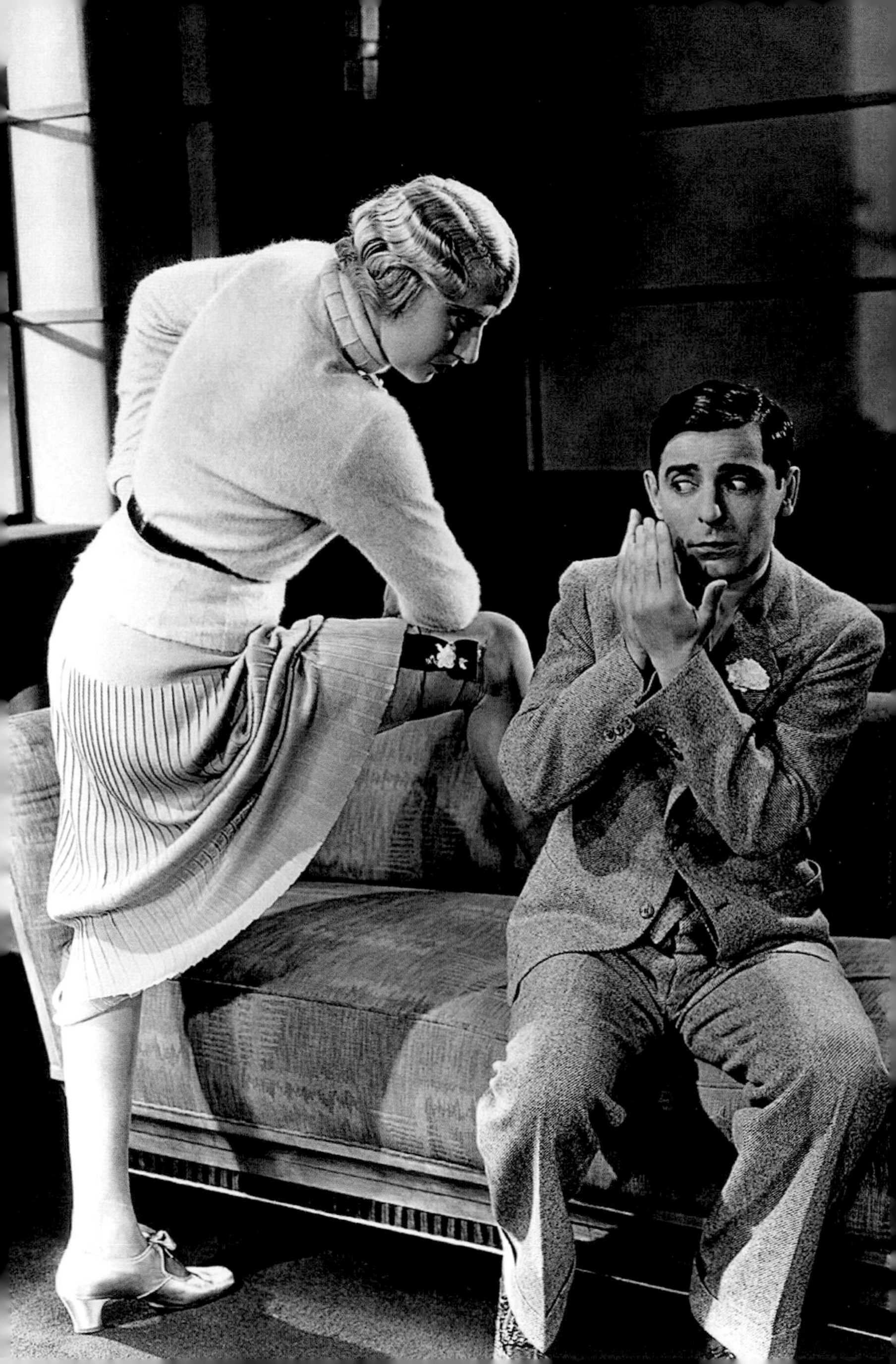

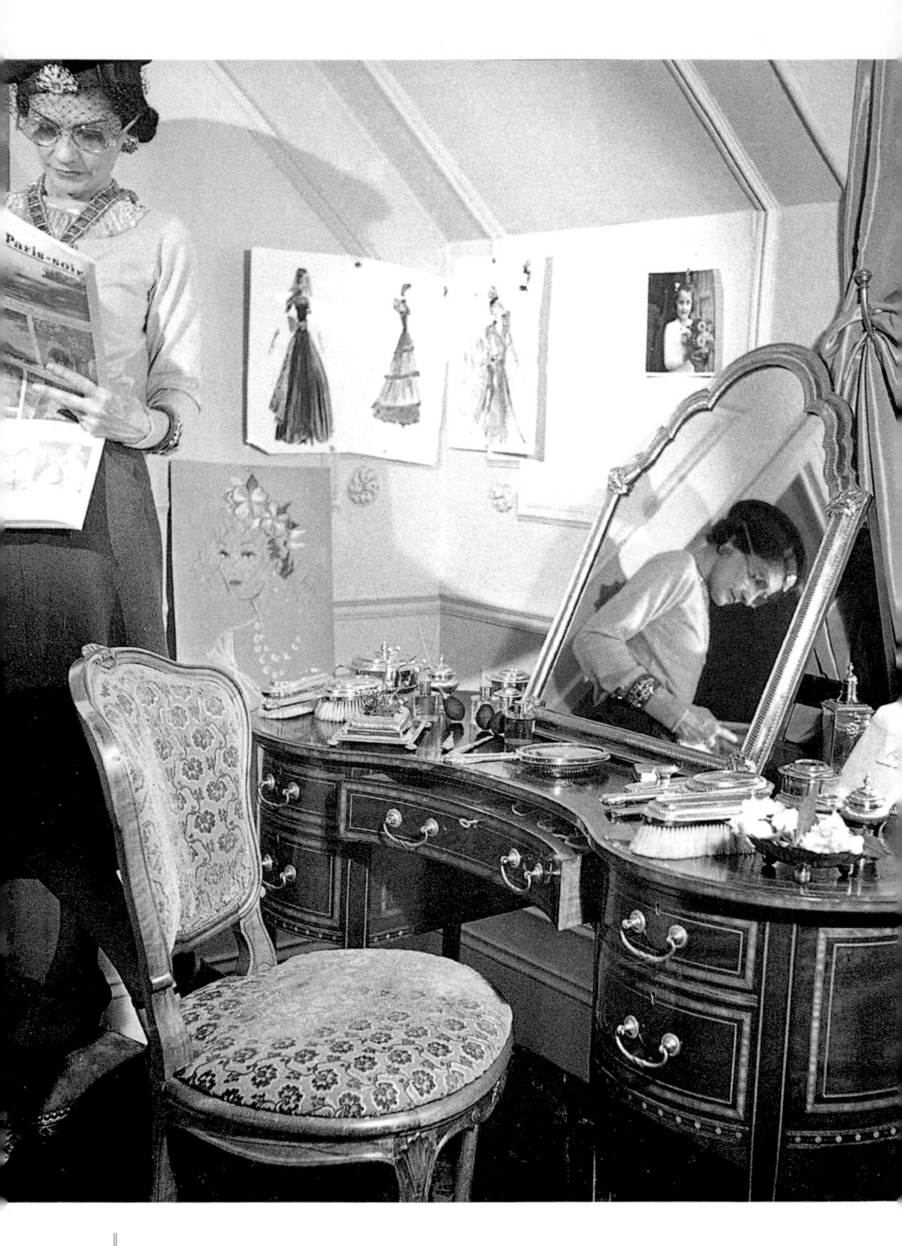
Paris-soir

War & Exile

During the 1930s, the House of Chanel continued to seduce Paris and the wider world, but the decade was not without hiccups. In 1936 Chanel's workforce went on strike to demand more money. Unwilling to negotiate, a furious Coco, who felt betrayed by their disloyalty, fired the whole team. The women who refused to leave had a "sit in" at the Rue Cambon premises until Coco finally capitulated, but the story sparked unwelcome publicity. There was also real competition from the exuberant Italian couturier Elsa Schiaparelli, who was based in Paris. Her witty creations, infused with shocking colour and surreal gimmicks, were diametrically opposed to everything Chanel represented, but while Coco dismissed her as "that Italian woman who makes dresses", the fashion press adored her, and she undoubtedly eclipsed some of Chanel's glory.

Despite ongoing disappointments and tragedy in her personal life, Coco, at 56, showed no signs of retiring, so it seemed a surprisingly knee-jerk reaction to the declaration of war in 1939 to immediately choose to close down the House of Chanel. The government wanted all the couture houses to stay open for French propaganda purposes, and many did, but Coco was unequivocal. She laid off all her employees without notice and decided only the boutique that sold perfume would remain open. She immediately fled the city and took refuge in the south of France for several months, before returning to Paris in the middle of 1940.

Although Coco arrived to find the swastika flying over the entrance to the Ritz Hotel, and all the rooms requisitioned by German military, her connections secured her a room and she still had her

Opposite Chanel, standing next to her dressing table in her apartment in the Ritz Hotel, Paris, in 1937, with fashion illustrations pinned to the wall.

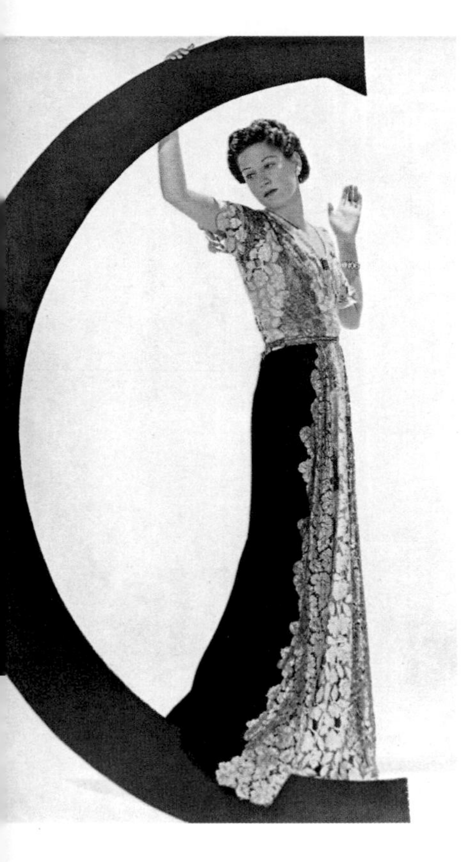

Left Chanel used colour sparingly and usually offset it with black, as here in this dress of high contrasts that has a bodice and centre panel of bright metallized lace in green and candy pink, highlighted over a narrow skirt of dull black crepe.

Opposite A 1938 Jean Cocteau illustration of a stunning Chanel evening gown, made from black Valenciennes lace with decorative flower patterns and trimming made from iridescent paillettes.

private apartment at 31 Rue Cambon. Wartime shortages enforced improvisation, at which Coco was already an expert; she lived discreetly but scandalized Paris by having an affair with a good-looking German who was very much younger than her. Hans Günther von Dincklage (known as "Spatz") was tall, handsome and accustomed to the good life. His exact role in the war remains ambiguous; he was known to work as an attaché to the German embassy in Paris, but persistent rumours suggest he was a spy, working as a double agent for both the Nazis and the British. Despite loud protestations that she did not collaborate with the Germans (Coco always claimed Spatz was

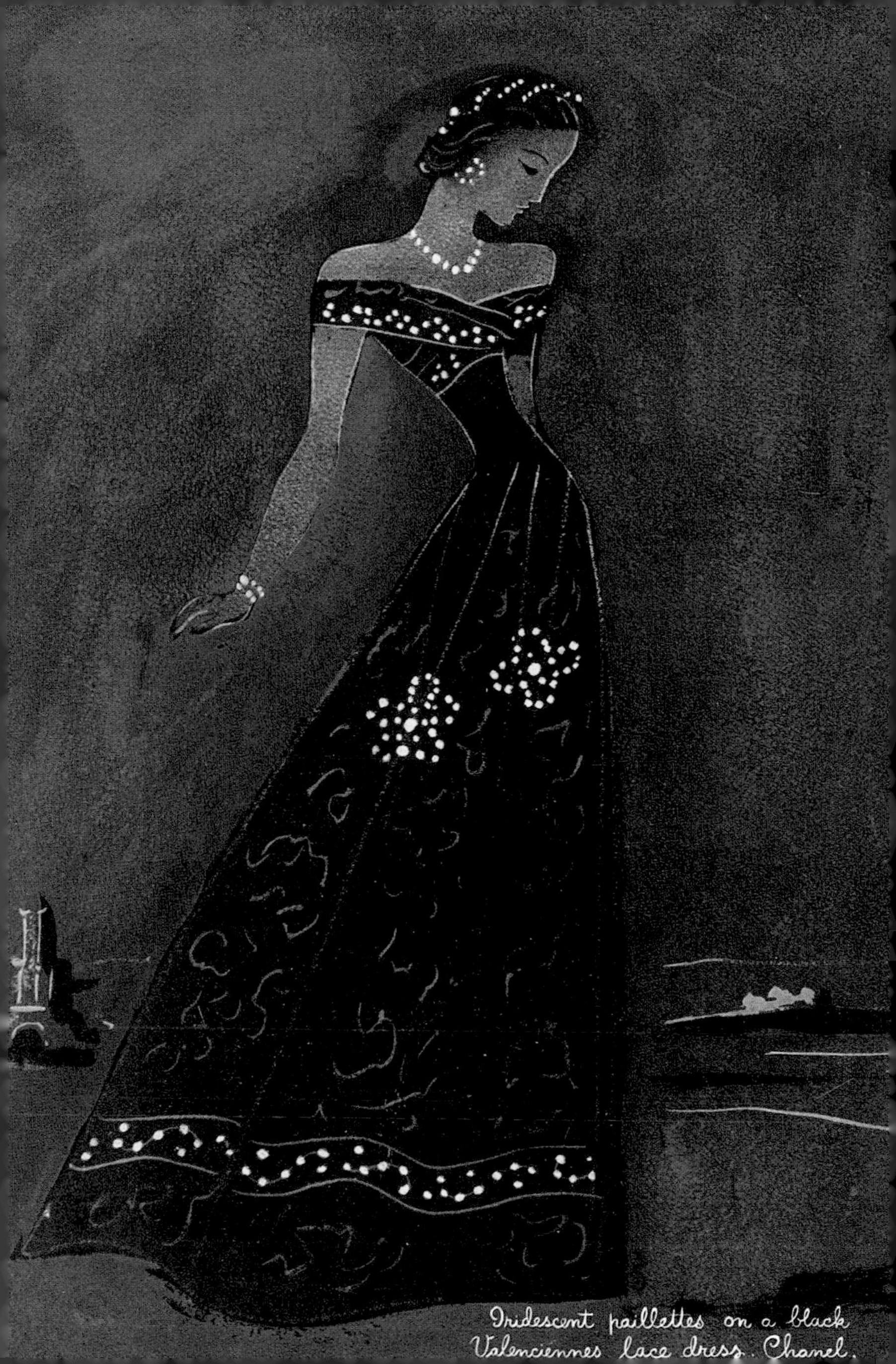

Iridescent paillettes on a black Valenciennes lace dress. Chanel.

English, as they spoke the language to each other and his mother was English), he was not the only German that she had dealings with. British Intelligence papers that are now declassified show that Coco was involved in an extraordinary covert mission called "Operation Modellhut" (fashion hat), which she undertook in strictest secrecy early in 1944. Boasting of her great friendship with Winston Churchill (an acquaintance from the many years she'd spent with the Duke of Westminster), Coco suggested she could act as an intermediary, and use her persuasive powers to encourage Churchill to enter peace talks with the German government. The implausible plan was given the go-ahead, and Coco travelled to Madrid to meet the English ambassador who was to be an integral part of the plot. Whatever her real intentions, Coco's assessment of her relationship with Churchill seems fantastically overstated, and the mission fizzled out.

Two weeks after the Liberation of France, Coco was arrested in her room at the Ritz by the Forces Françaises de l'Intérieur. Punishment for collaboration was brutal, suspects were imprisoned for months, women had their heads shaved and were paraded in the streets; many others were simply shot. Coco was more fortunate. It is thought that intervention from the Duke of Westminster via Winston Churchill saved her, and she was released after just a few hours. The French people were less willing to forgive her romantic liaisons with the enemy and her reputation, which for so long had been untouchable, was now severely damaged. In 1945 Coco left for Switzerland, where Spatz soon joined her. She stayed there for eight long years, an exile who visited the United States occasionally and returned to Paris only for brief visits.

Opposite left Featured in the 1938–9 collection, this was one of the last Chanel dresses created before the outbreak of war. The edge of the silk chiffon and grosgrain bodice is trimmed with red, white and blue grosgrain ribbon, the colour of the Tricolour, worn over a matching red silk chiffon skirt.

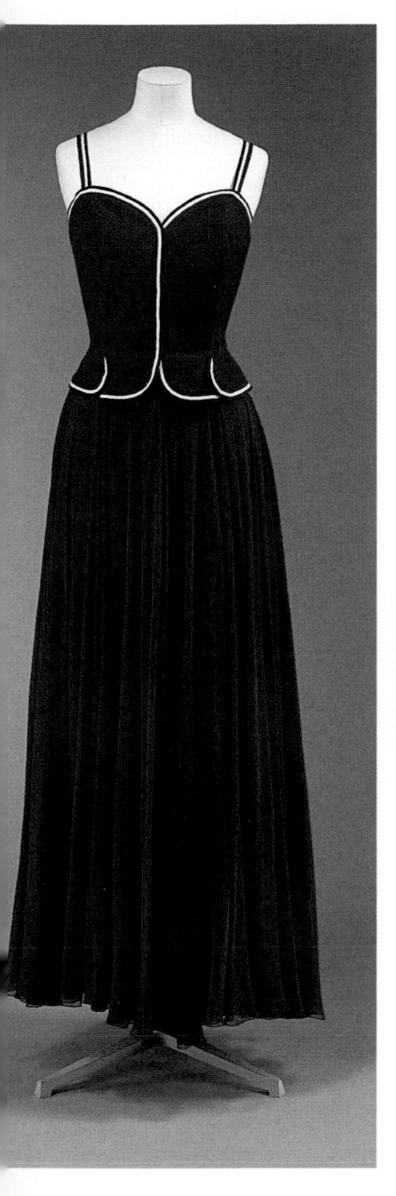

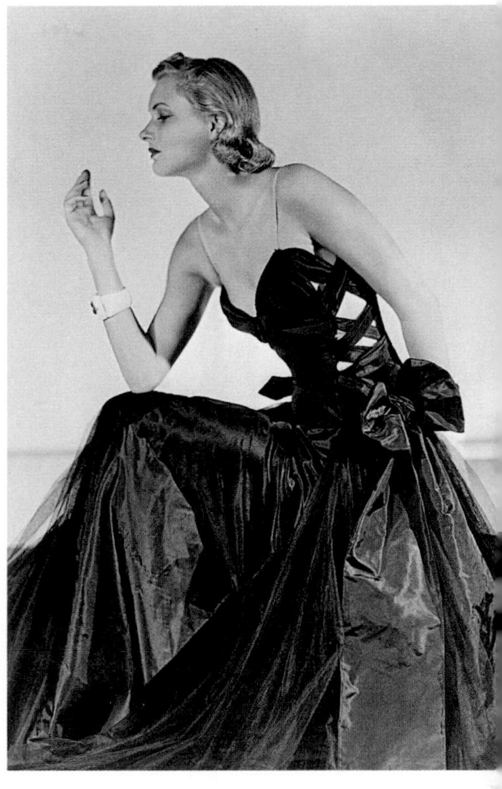

Above A revealing black taffeta evening gown has a fitted corselet bodice strapped with long ribbons that wrap around the body and tie in huge bows at the hips. The bouffant skirt is made from panels of black silk net, but attention focuses on the cutaway straps and a daringly low neckline.

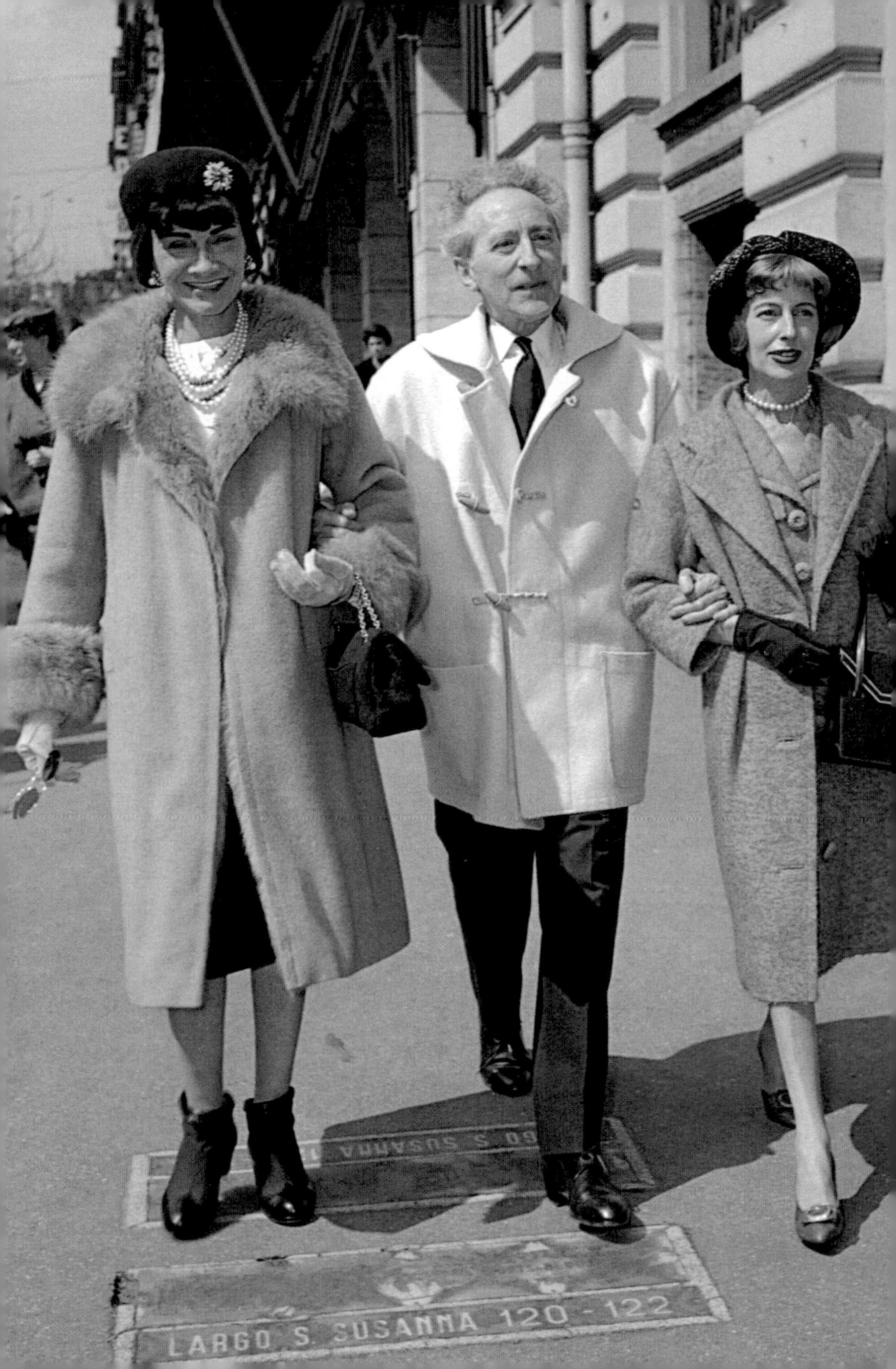
LARGO S. SUSANNA 120 - 122

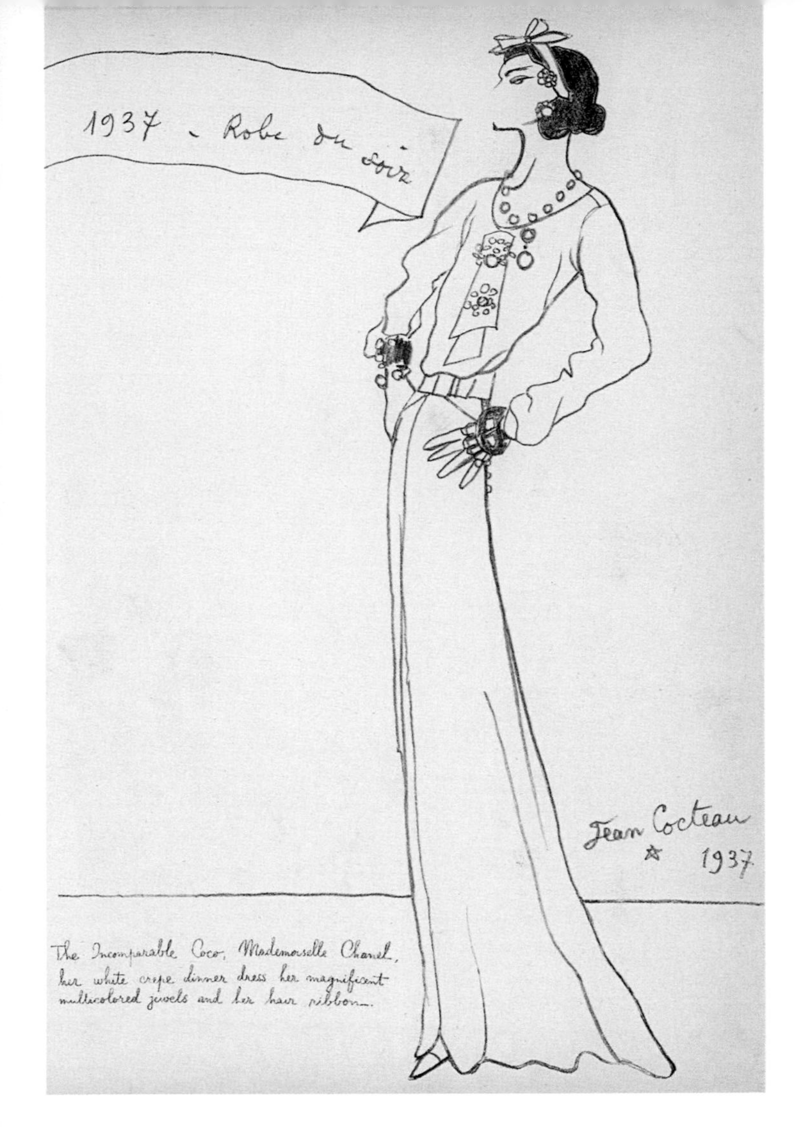

Opposite In Rome with Jean Cocteau and their friend Miss Weiseveiller. Cocteau became one of Chanel's most trusted friends.

Above Illustration by Jean Cocteau of Chanel, 1937, wearing a white crepe dinner dress, accessorized with her trademark enamel cuffs.

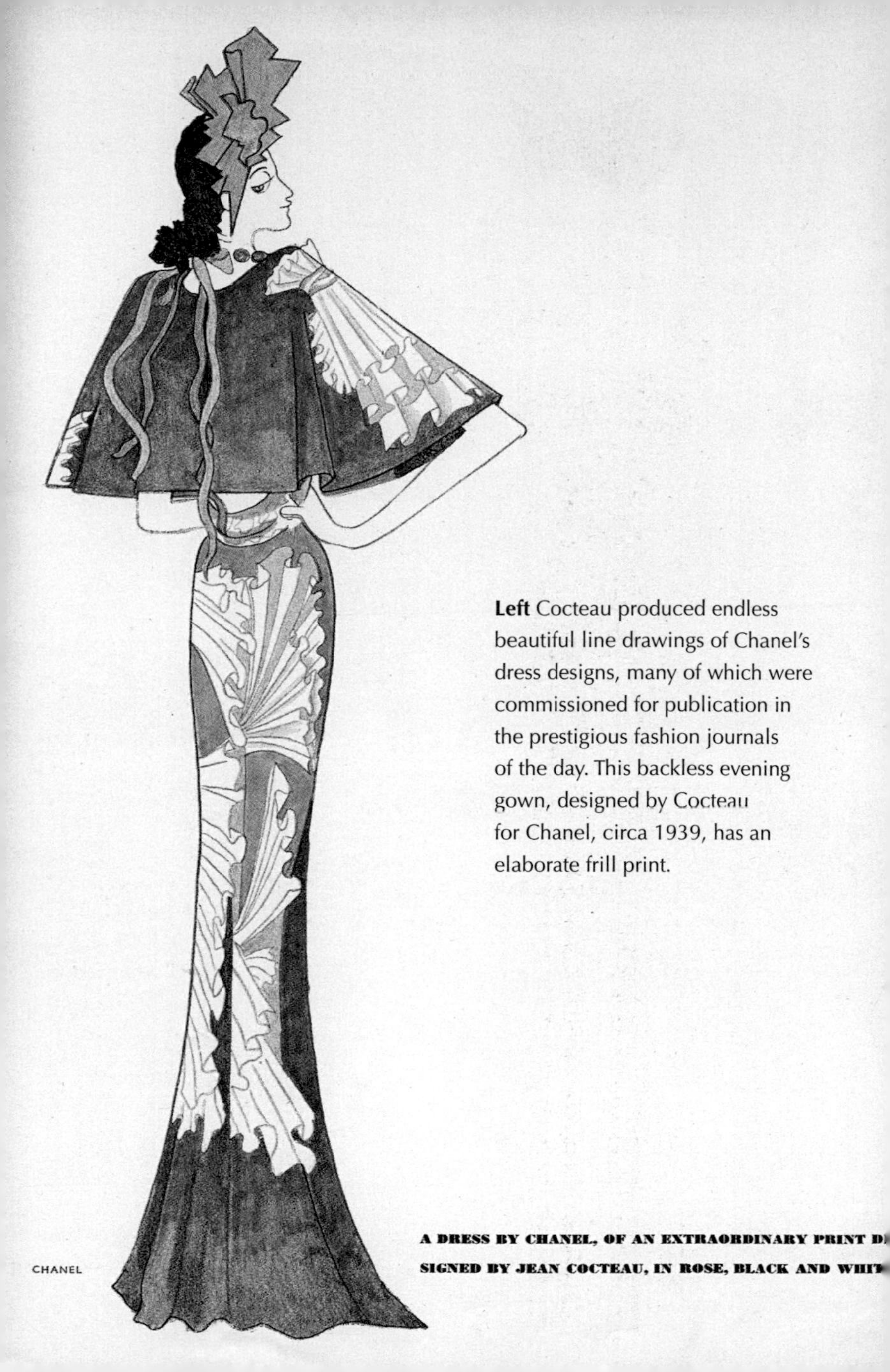

Left Cocteau produced endless beautiful line drawings of Chanel's dress designs, many of which were commissioned for publication in the prestigious fashion journals of the day. This backless evening gown, designed by Cocteau for Chanel, circa 1939, has an elaborate frill print.

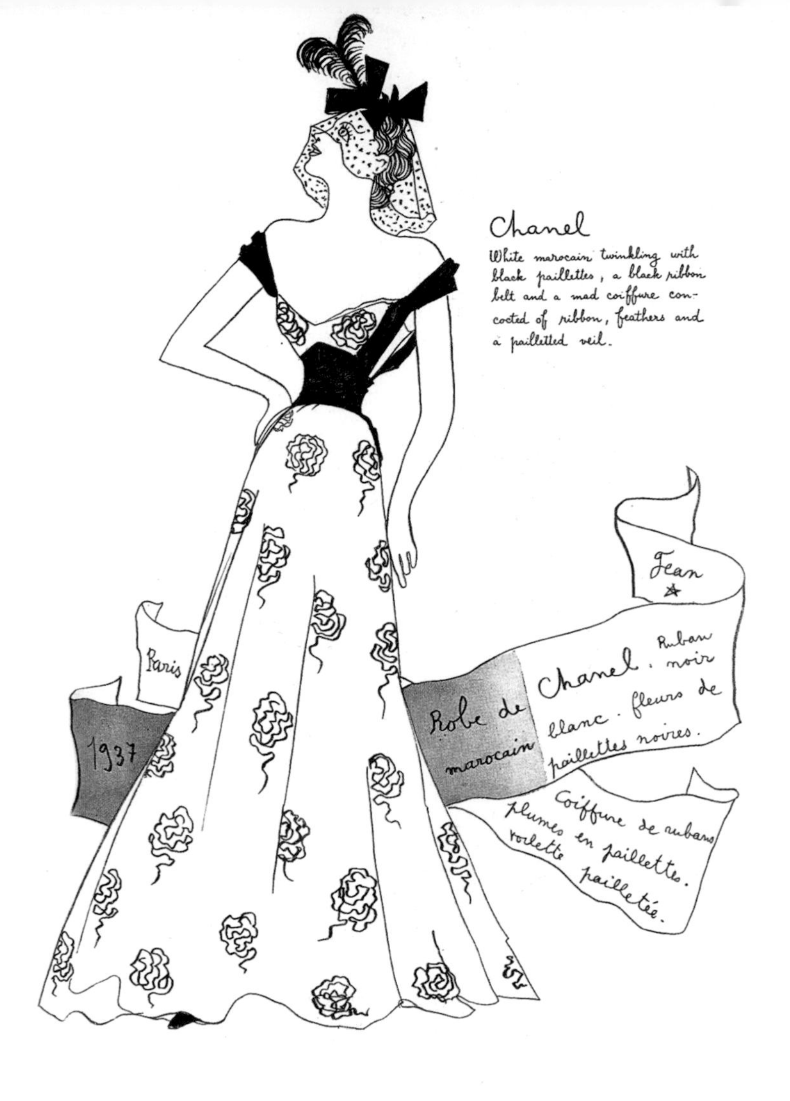

Above In another illustration by Cocteau, this Chanel design from 1937 is made in white marocain and decorated with twinkling black paillettes. The extravagant hairpiece, made of ribbon, feathers and a pailletted veil, is not typical of Chanel's understated style.

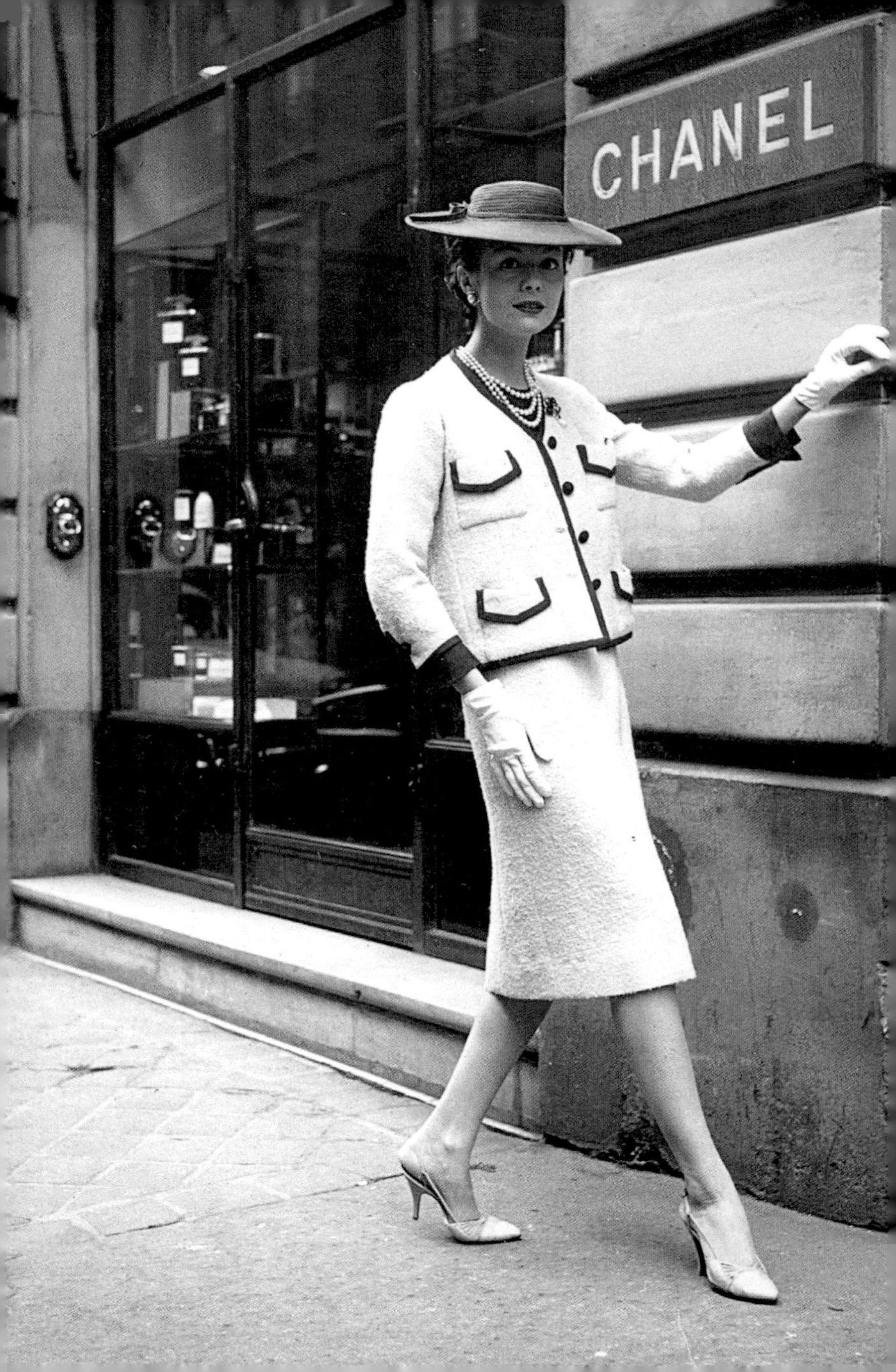
CHANEL

The Triumphant Return

The House of Chanel had been closed for 14 years, and the exceptional success of its founder had long since passed into fashion history, when Coco, who was now over 70, made the momentous decision to relaunch her career. There were many reasons behind her decision: it is thought her time in exile had left her lonely and bored and she desperately missed the work she loved, which she always claimed "consumed her life". Sales of her perfume *Chanel No. 5* were in decline and needed a publicity boost, and perhaps more pertinently she was horrified at the postwar success of Christian Dior's "New Look". Coco was outspoken in her views, having worked so hard to release women from the tyranny of theatrical dress, and it infuriated her now to see Dior being worshipped for his restrictive silhouette that once again subordinated women's bodies to a male view of femininity. She felt the time was right to reinstate her original ethos: to provide clothes that simplified choice, offered women comfort and understated elegance and which liberated the female body.

In 1953, in preparation for her new collection, Coco went back to 31 Rue Cambon, where she refurbished the boutique that sold her perfume as well as reinstated the workrooms and her famous third-floor apartment. She presented her new collection of 130 models on 5 February 1954 (the date was significant because five was always her lucky number).

The fashion press anticipated fantastic things from the House of Chanel – and then damningly delivered their verdict. Almost unanimously the European papers derided her collection as dull and disappointing, the reviews savage in their condemnation: "a Fiasco"...

Opposite That instantly recognizable classic, the Chanel suit, is photographed outside the boutique in Rue Cambon in 1959. The trademark accessories of pearls, white gloves, flat hat and slingback shoes complete the look.

"a melancholy retrospective"... "a flop". Lesser women would have been crushed by the criticism, but not Coco, who was back at her workroom within a few days with a renewed determination to go on and prove her point. Europe may have dismissed her, but the American press showed enthusiastic support by running features on the new collection in the March issues of both American *Vogue* and *Life* magazines. The American public liked what they saw, and orders from the states flooded in. Women were responding to what Chanel offered them: less-conspicuous "fashion" and instead a rather more modern attitude to functional style. As each new collection appeared, the essence of the Chanel phenomenon gathered speed. She remained faithful to the neutral colour palette she loved – beige, black, white, red and navy – and used the same classic fabrics: tweeds, jersey, satin brocades, velvet and lamé for evening. Her 1950s suits were significantly more tailored than her earlier cardigan suits, and she was now incorporating the styling details that would ultimately come to define the "Chanel look".

By 1958, with Dior dead, British *Vogue* proclaimed: "Chanel is the major fashion influence in the world. Her jersey suits and blazer jackets are copied all down the line to the local high street, and she is responsible for the popularity of men's shirts, jewelled cufflinks and medallions, gilt and pearl earrings, Breton sailor hats, and slingback shoes with contrasting toe-caps."

Opposite A Chanel suit from the year Coco made her comeback in 1954. The outfit in navy blue jersey, with its plain white shirt, man's bowtie and Breton-style sailor hat, embodies much of the androgyny that Chanel championed for women.

Overleaf left White organza and silver strapless dress with a layered skirt dates from the mid-1950s. Silver leaves edge the neckline of the bodice and the tiers of the skirt.

Overleaf right Cocktail dresses, like this one in black lace, featured regularly in Chanel's collections in the late 1950s and early 1960s. The strapless, boned dress, from 1958, has a trumpet-shaped skirt with a triple flounce.

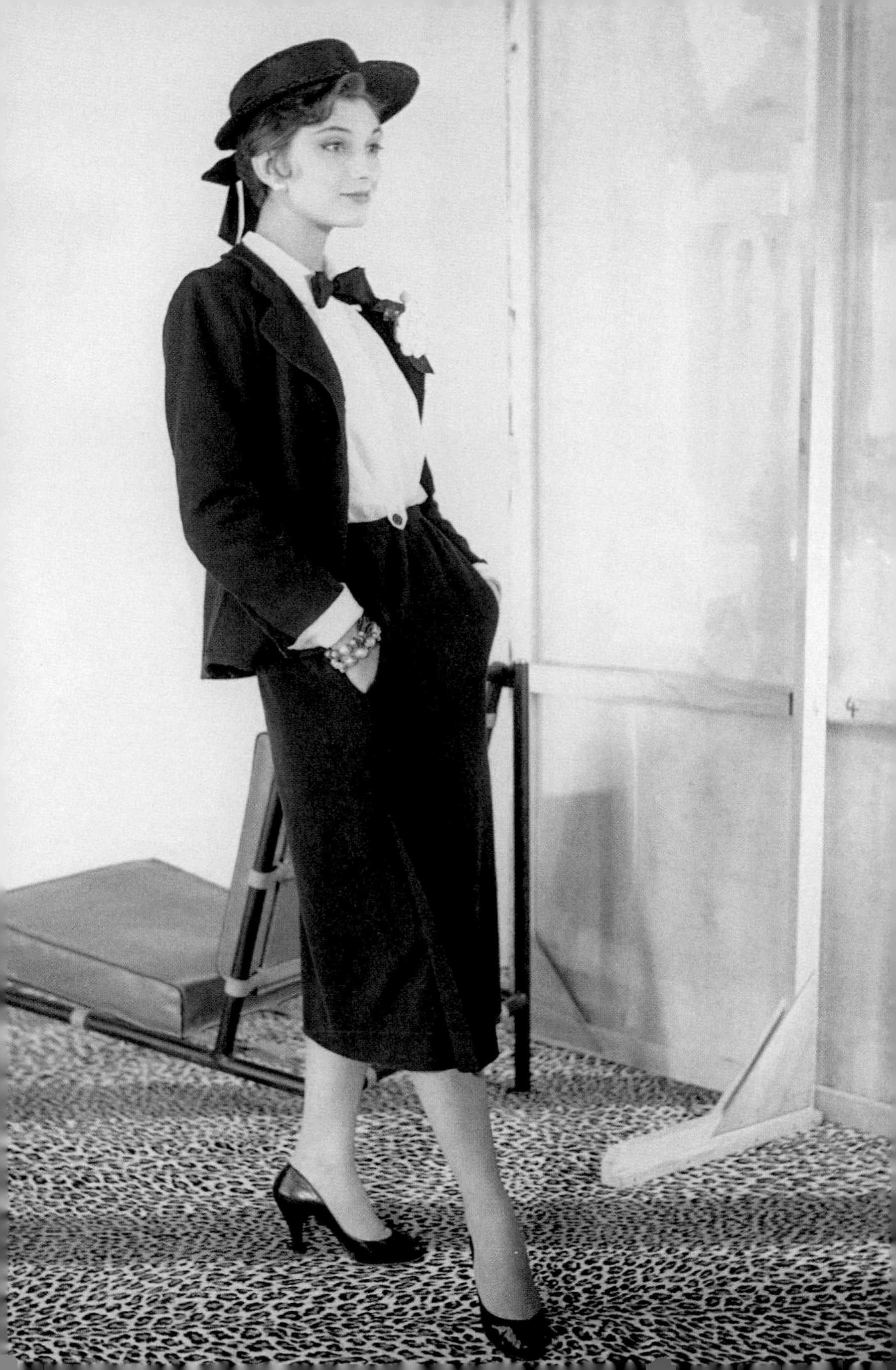

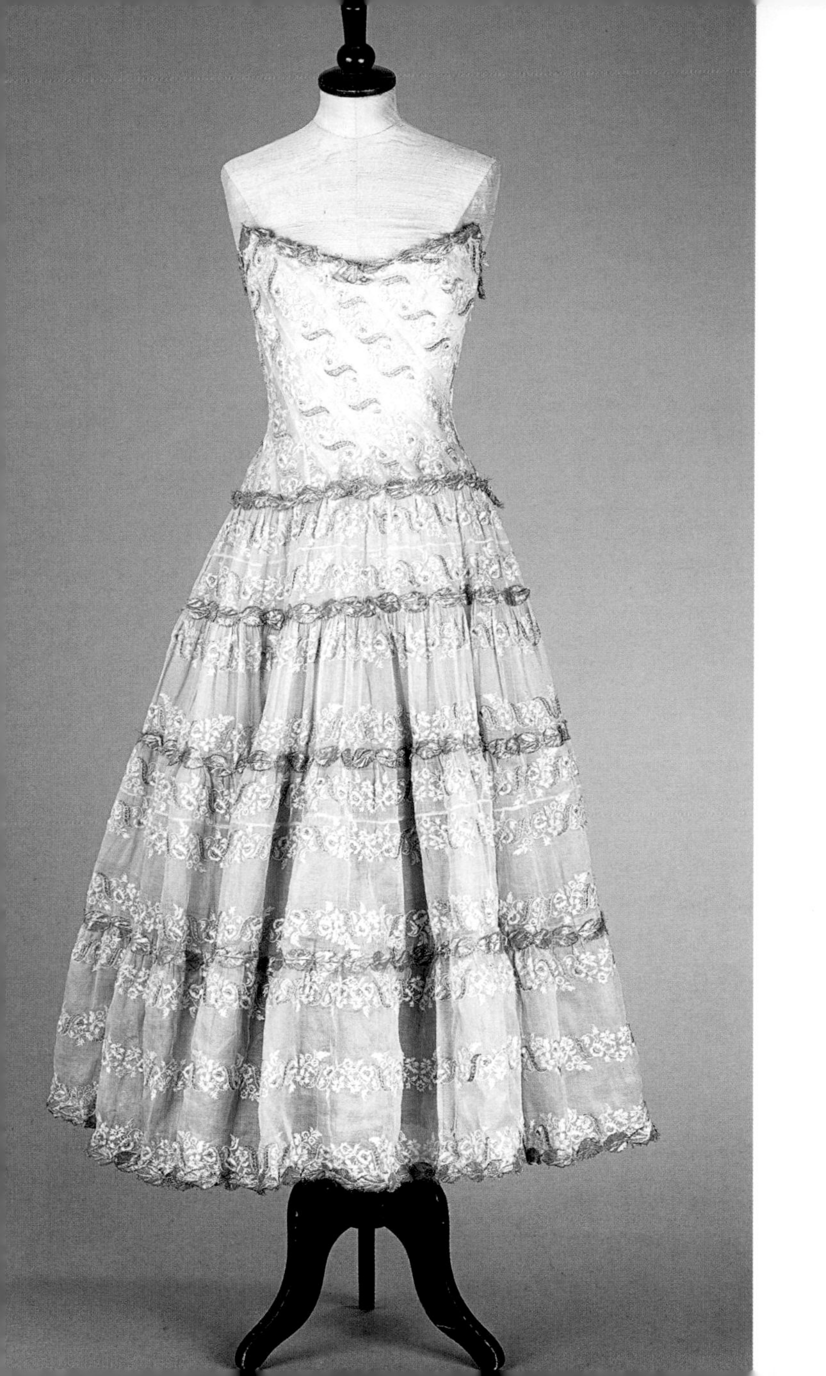

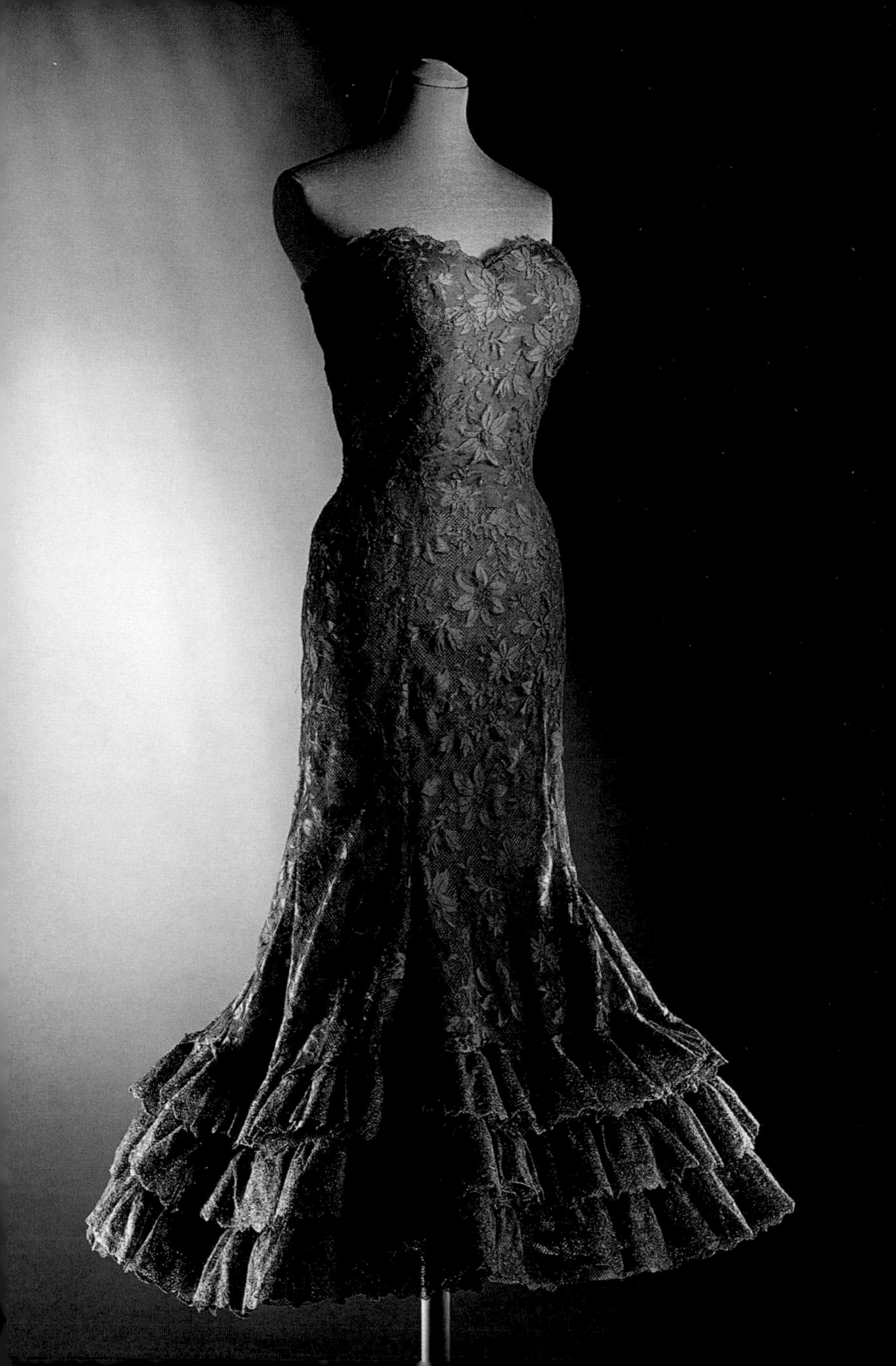

The Chanel Suit

The head-to-toe look, which was instantly recognizable, flew in the face of "fashion" and remains utterly timeless, began with the Chanel suit. Whatever the detailed variations, proportions are visually balanced. The soft boxy jacket was easy to wear, unstructured and yet had so many trademarks. It was always identifiable by the gold chain stitched to the hem of the lining that guaranteed a perfect hang, the overstitching of the lining that ensured the inside of the jacket was just as elegant as the outside, and the buttonholes, which were never fake. In keeping with her personal taste, all the embossed buttons were made to be functional as well as decorative, often designed to look like jewellery. Gilt buttons were particular favourites; they could be traced with the double-C logo or a lion's head, which originated from Coco's astrological star sign Leo.

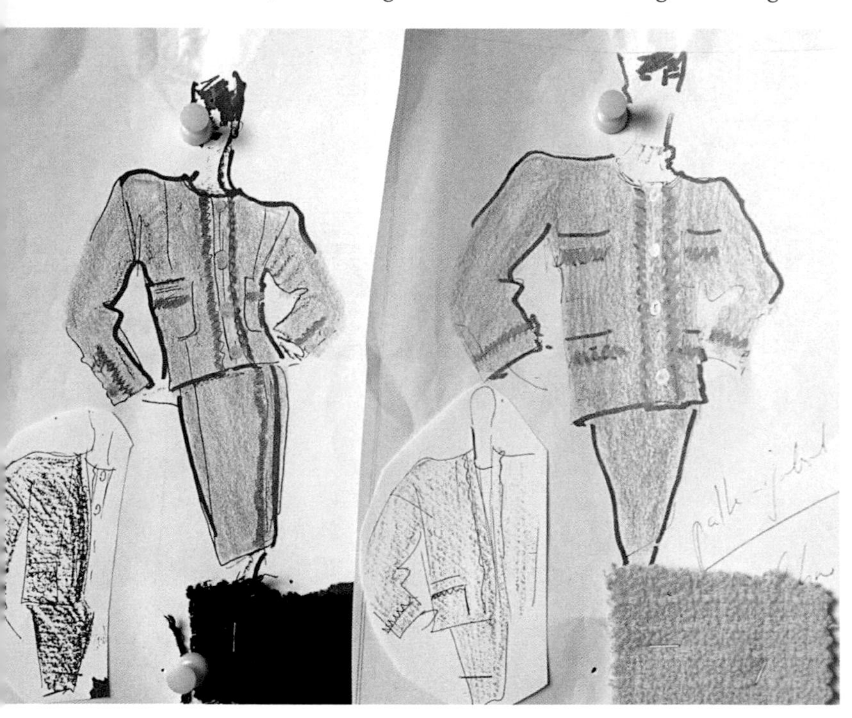

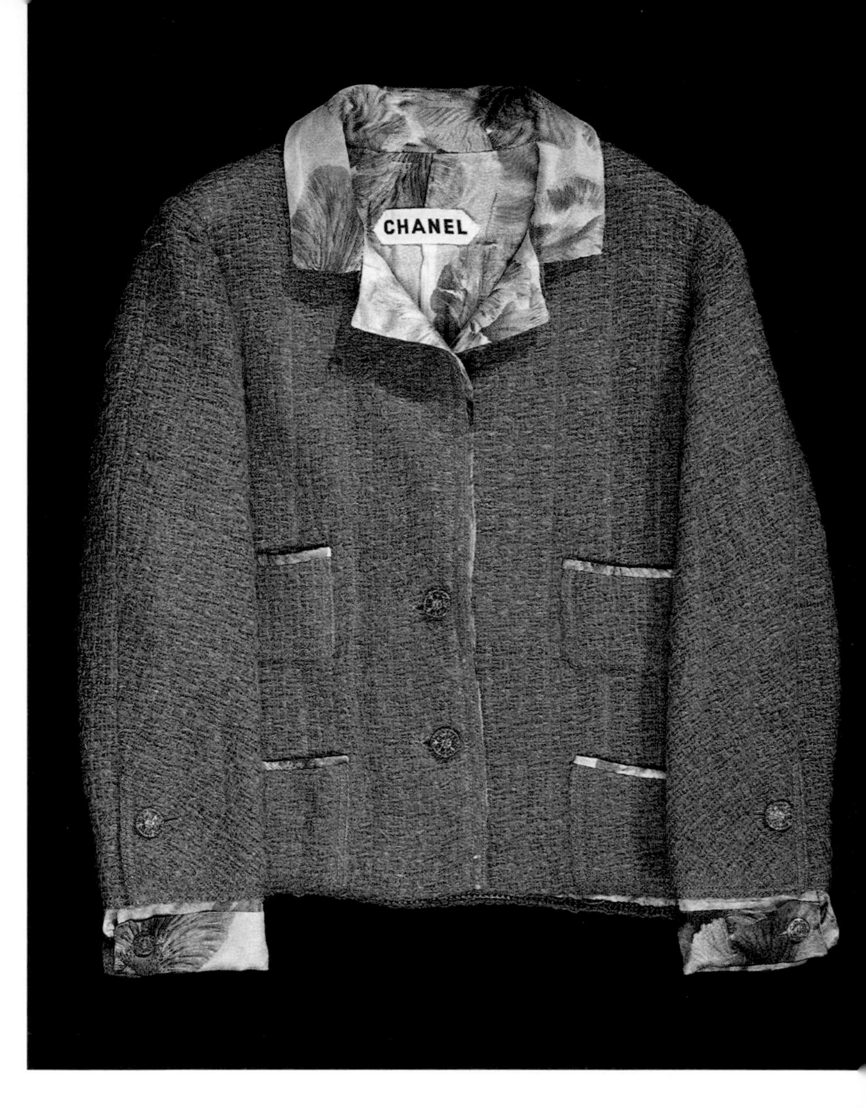

Opposite Fashion illustrations for the iconic Chanel tweed jacket by Karl Lagerfeld.

Above A 1964 Chanel mauve tweed jacket with double pockets has a silk floral lining, turned over to trim the collar, patch pockets and front opening.

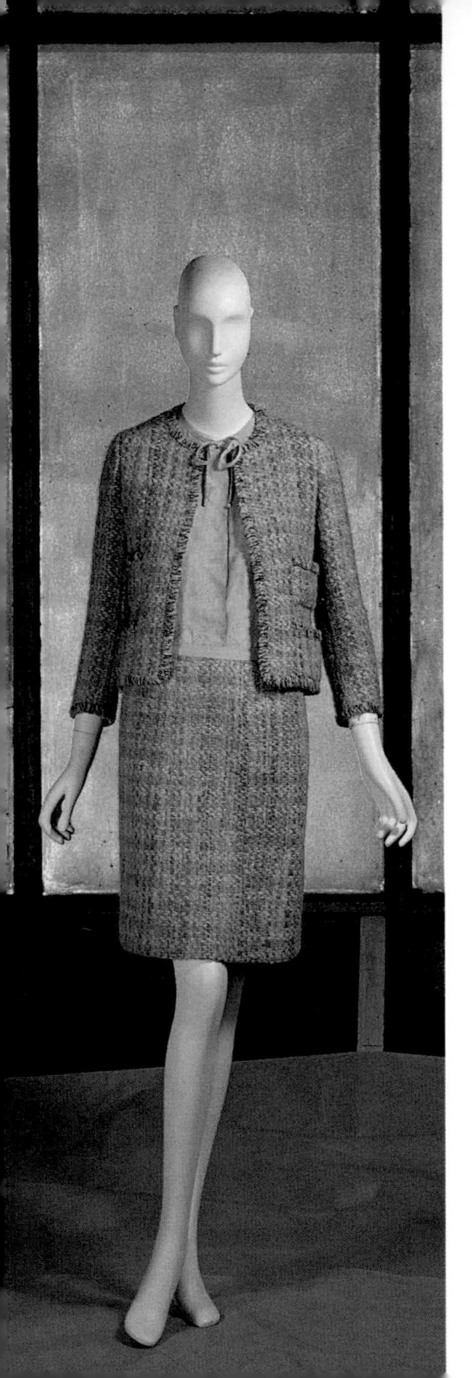

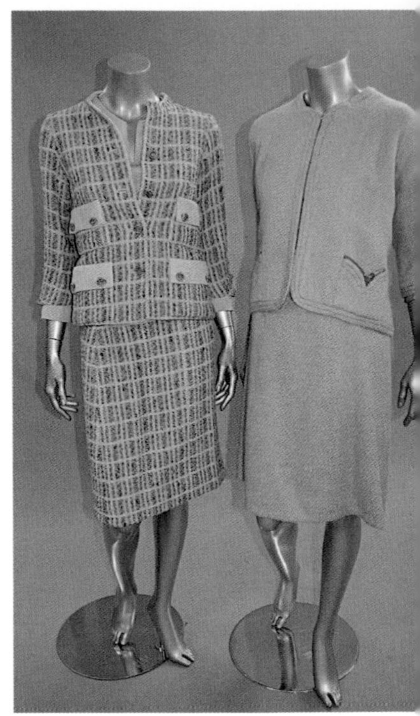

Left Chanel dismissed the Youthquake antics of 1960s fashion, and carried on honing her style. This signature suit from autumn/winter 1965 has a collarless boxy jacket, with three-quarter-length sleeves and numerous pockets; the skirt length has crept up to above the knee.

Some jackets were collarless, others had neat narrow lapels or stand-up Nehru collars – and the fit of the sleeve was paramount. Coco maintained the sleeve was the most important part of the garment, and would spend hours repositioning the shoulder and sleeve seams to achieve perfection. Her suit jackets always included real pockets because they were needed to hold Mademoiselle's cigarettes. Coco added braid to the jackets of her suits and very often utilized the same fabric for other details, edging a pocket, adding a fake cuff, trimming a button or lining the suit.

This winning formula of a short, square, collarless jacket worn with a slightly flared skirt that cut across the knee became the signature piece for the House of Chanel, and while no two suits were exactly the same, she repeated this particular concept endlessly, subtly reworking through the same style themes to provide her customers with a classicism that went beyond that season's fashion. Added to this were the trademark finishing touches that continually reinforced Coco's personal signature: layers of jewels, glass stones or pearls, sometimes just a few neat strings around the neck, occasionally more flamboyant; the gently rounded two-tone slingback shoes with a delicate heel and black cap toe, designed to visually shorten the foot, and the perfectly placed hat, usually small with a simple ribbon tied into a bow at the back or a camellia perched on the side. These are the essential elements that together add up to the success of the look.

Opposite top The soft tweed couture suit (left) is lined in quilted cream cotton jersey and worn with a cream wool sleeveless bodice underneath the collarless jacket, which has double pockets on both sides, decorated with Chanel buttons. The salmon pink dress and jacket (right) is lined in pink chine taffeta, which is also used for the piping detail on the pockets and cuff. Both circa 1960s.

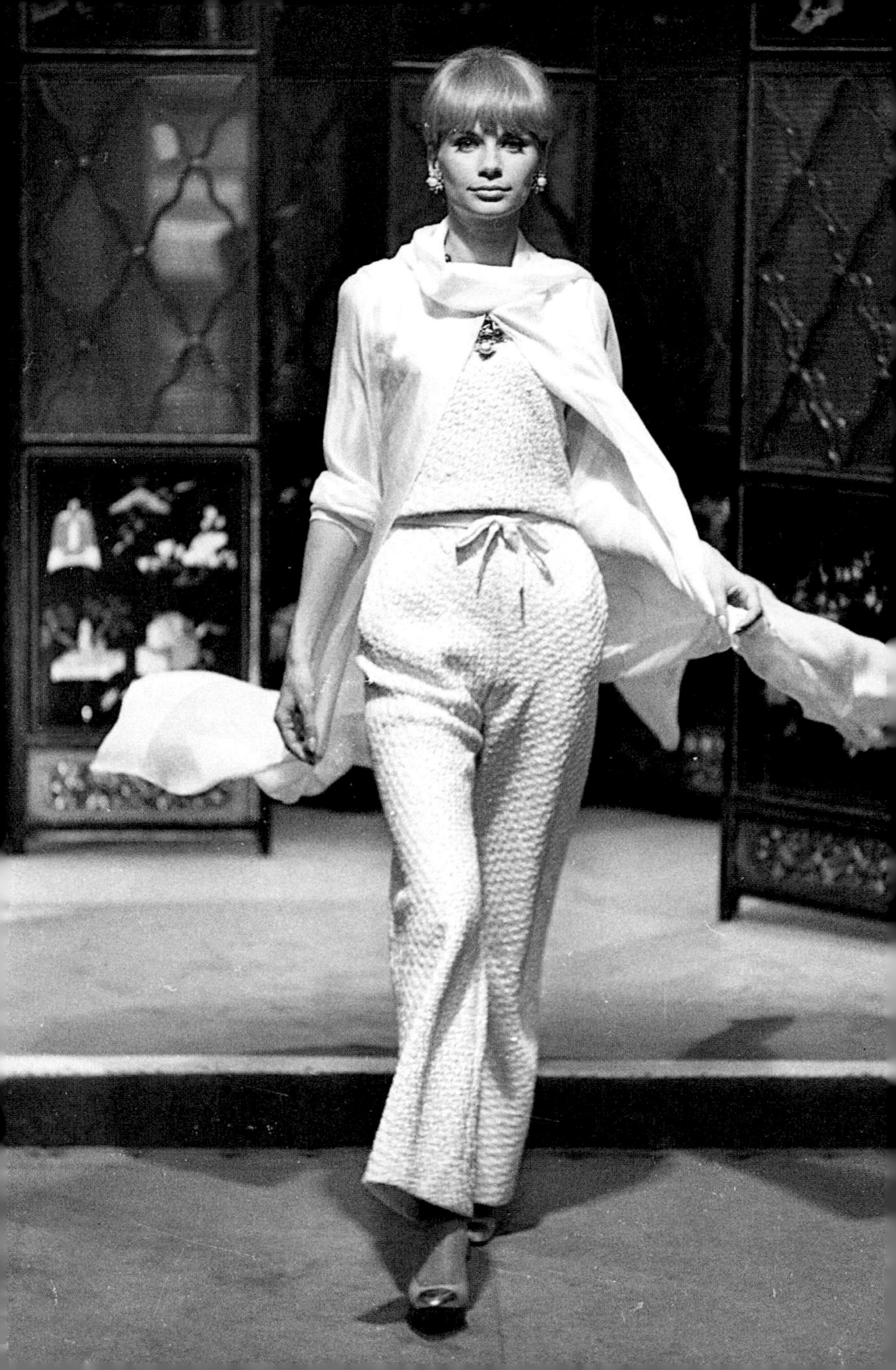

Opposite Chanel was one of the first couturieres to put women in trousers. Here, in a mid-1960s ensemble, she successfully mixes textures, using soft white wool for the sleeveless vest and trousers, with an oversized diaphanous shirt.

Right The masculine lines of this 1960s black trouser suit are softened by the ice blue silk used to line the jacket and create the blouse. Chanel often designed fake cuffs for sleeves, using the same fabrics she had used for other details; here, the blue silk is used as a tie to belt the trousers, wrapping into a decorative bow.

Overleaf left By the mid-1960s a Chanel jacket was coveted by fashionable women the world over who wanted to buy into her "casual chic", like this pink and blue tartan jacket with fringed collar and fringed sleeve seams, photographed for *Queen* magazine.

Overleaf right A salmon pink and cream woollen dress, cut to the knee, is worn with the matching collarless jacket. Complementary shades are used to trim the jacket edges, sleeve opening and for the chevron-shaped pockets. Gilt buttons fasten the opening.

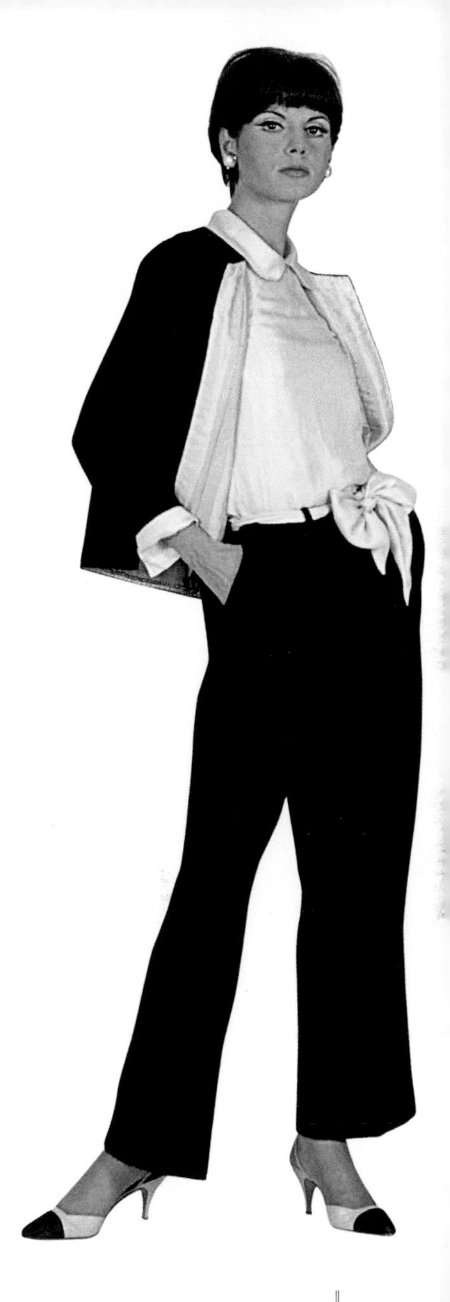

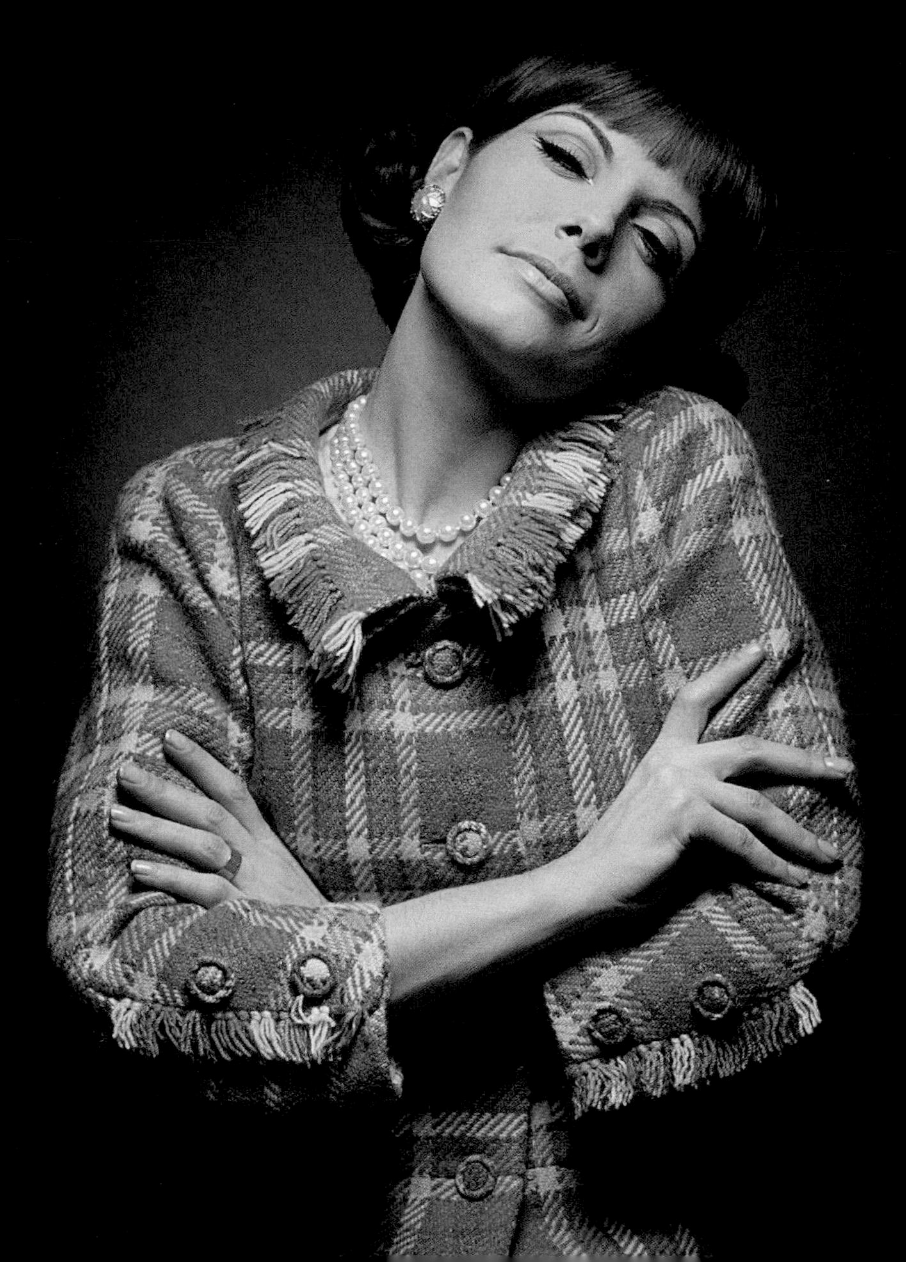

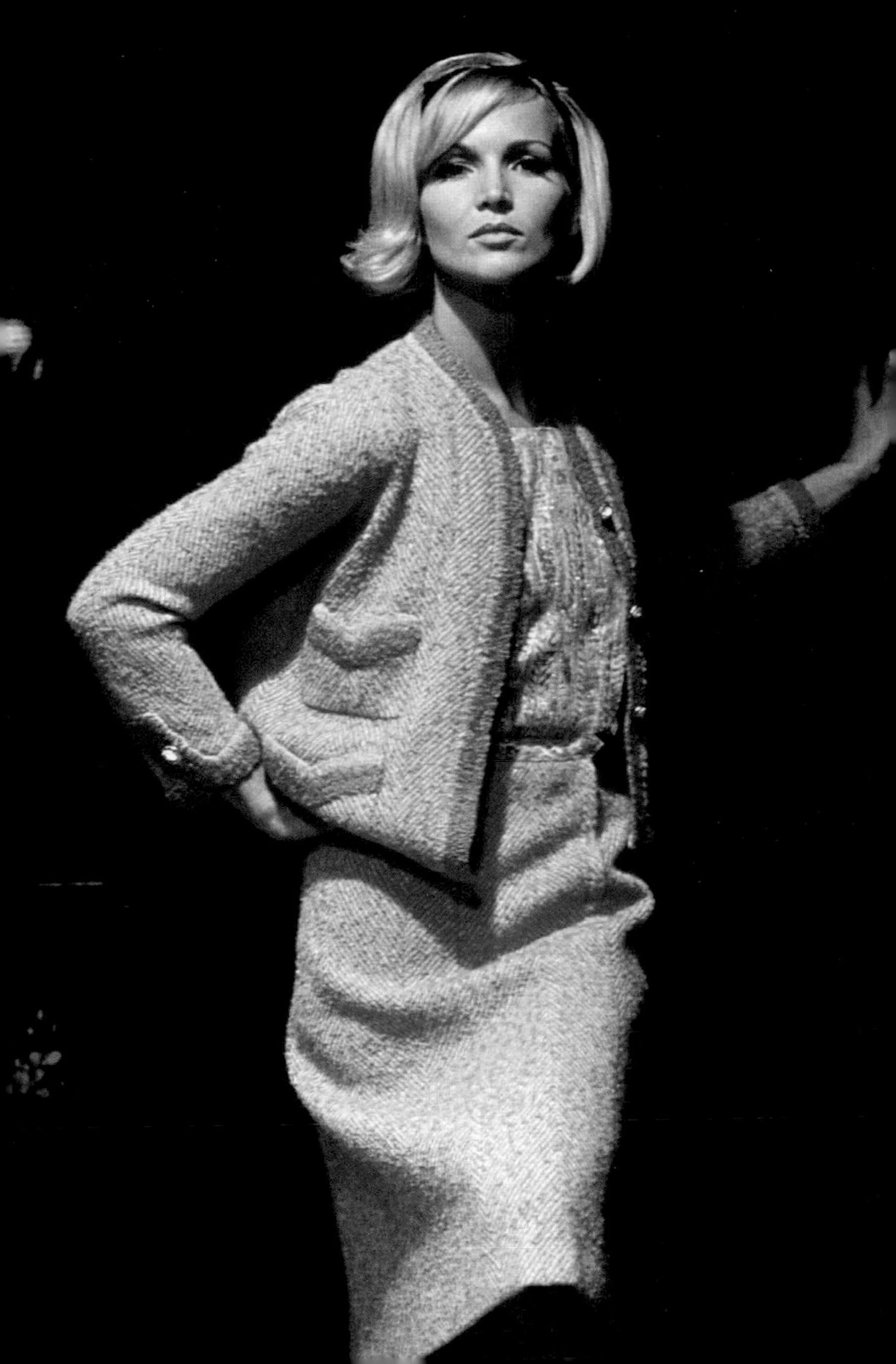

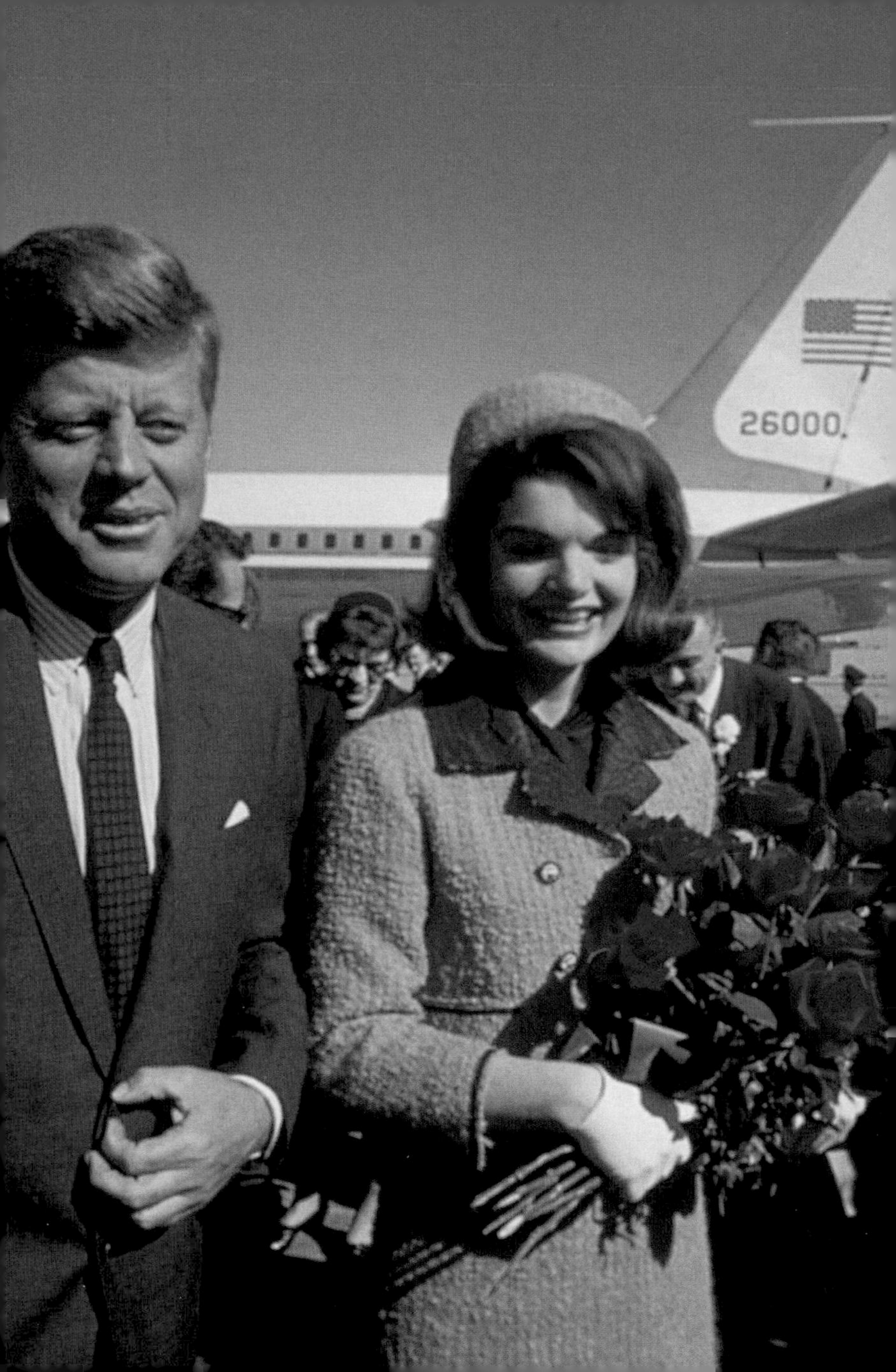
26000

Celebrity Connections

The postwar suit became *the* stylish uniform for elegant women of a certain age who needed Parisian panache. Jackie Kennedy was already a customer of Chanel (as well as many other French couture houses) before her husband became President of the United States, having ordered from Chanel from 1955 onwards. On the fatal trip to Dallas with JFK in November 1963, she was wearing a favourite Chanel suit that she had worn before. Made to order from the autumn/winter 1961 couture collection, the vivid pink suit made from textured wool had a short double-breasted jacket with three-quarter-length sleeves, double pockets on the front, edged with navy taffeta and gold buttons. Jackie was sitting alongside her husband in the open-top limousine when three bullet shots rang out and the president was killed. The First Lady, covered in blood and gore, stayed in her Chanel suit all day, and the pictures broadcast around the world remain the enduring image of a tragic day.

Chanel was now the label that everyone wanted to be seen in, and it was not just the chic European stars that flocked to Rue Cambon. Great French beauties like Jeanne Moreau, Brigitte Bardot and Anouk Aimée all endorsed her signature style; the film director Luchino Visconti (whom Coco knew from a brief affair in the 1930s) introduced her to a young ingénue called Romy Schneider, who she dressed for Visconti's section of the 1962 film *Boccaccio '70*. On the other side of the Atlantic, the big names in Hollywood were just as keen to flaunt the label, as a Chanel outfit implied chic glamour without screaming "showbiz". Elizabeth Taylor never looked so good as when she appeared in a tailored Chanel suit. Lauren Bacall, Grace Kelly, Ingrid Bergman, Marlene Dietrich – these were women who were regularly named as the best-dressed women in the world, and their choice of designer was Chanel.

Opposite Jackie Kennedy in a pink wool Chanel suit and hat, with her husband President John F Kennedy, arriving at Dallas airport on that tragic day in November 1963.

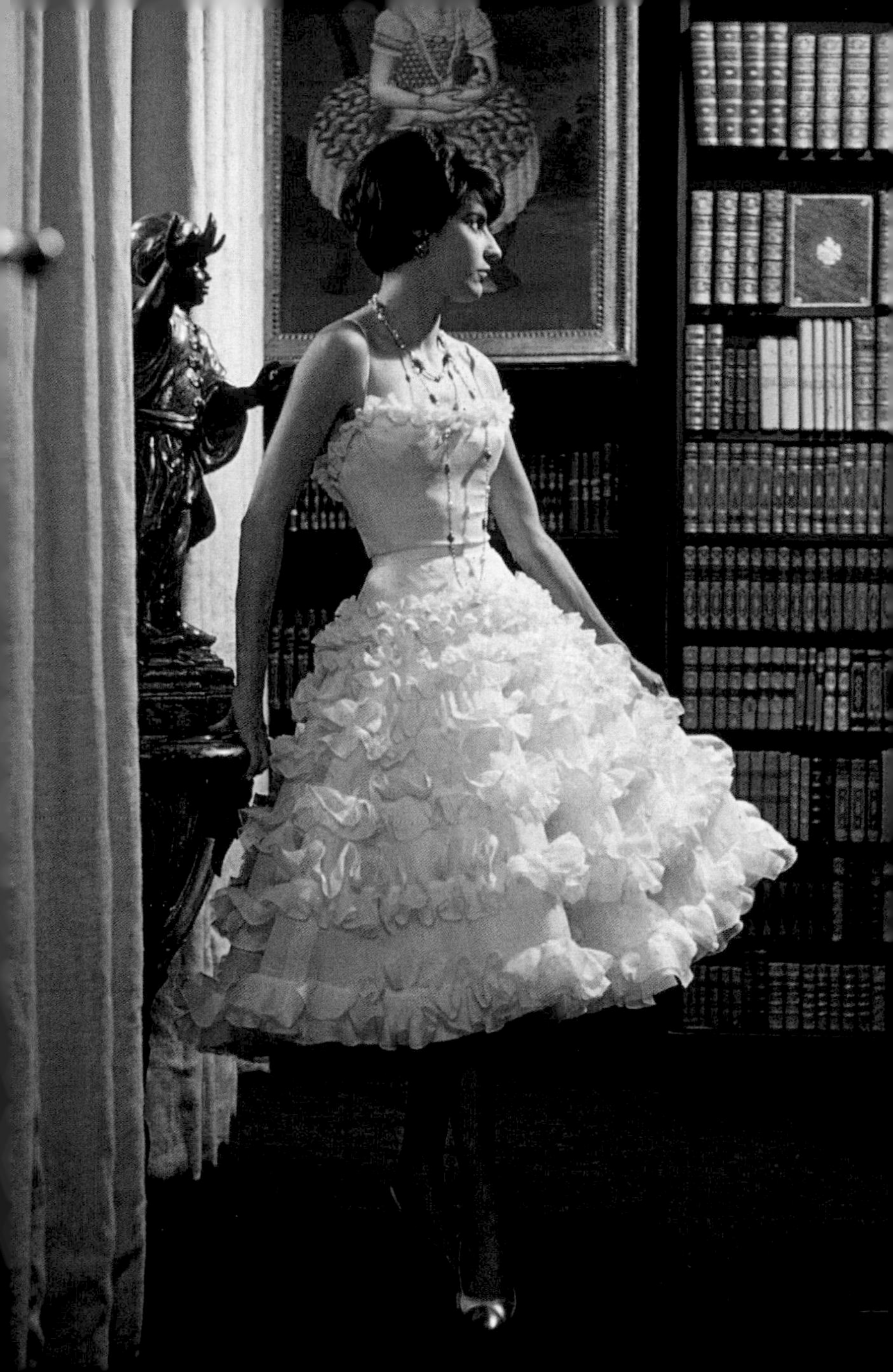

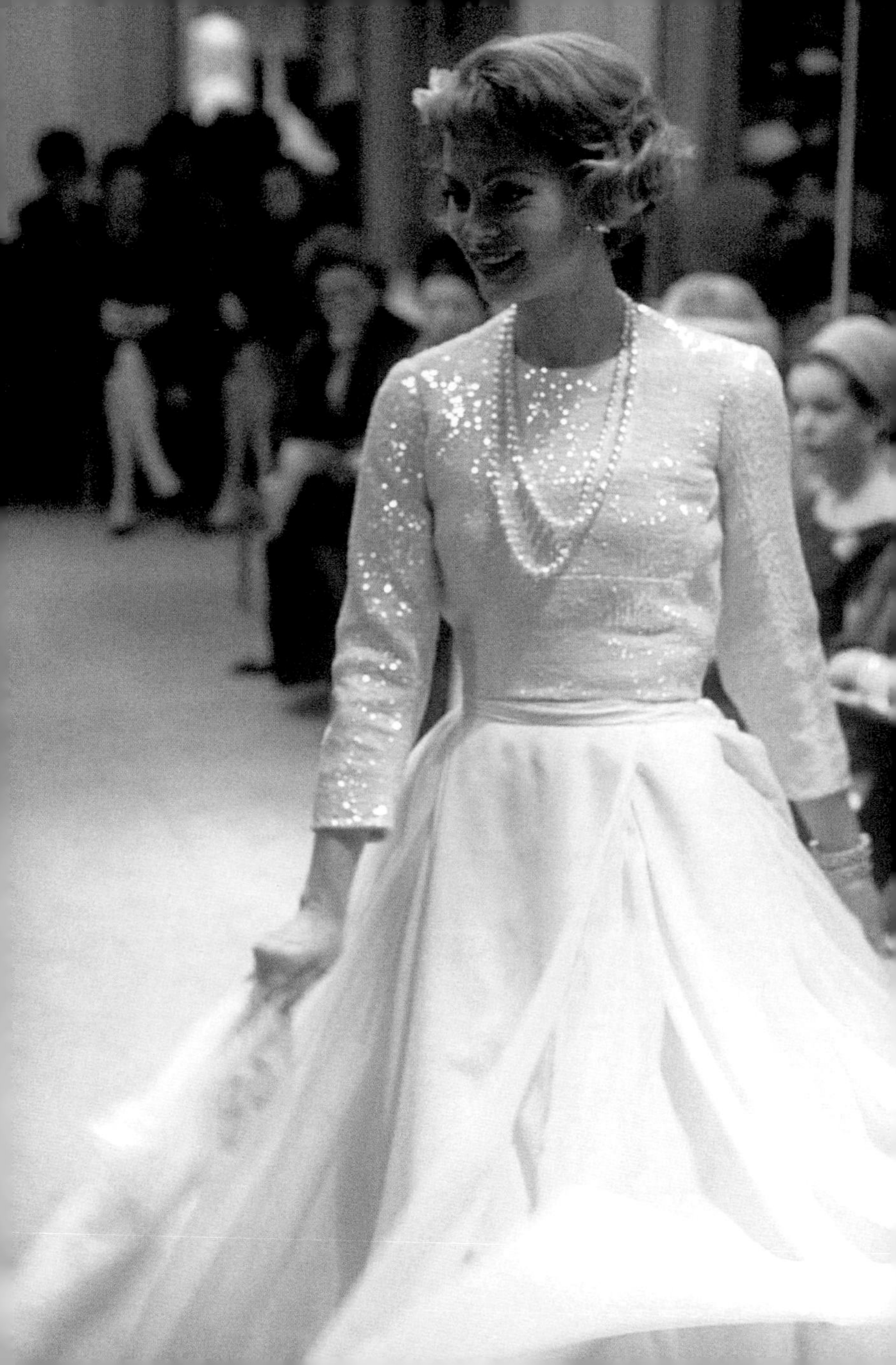

Previous page left White was used to great effect for short cocktail dresses and eveningwear throughout the 1960s: Chanel herself said, "Dress women in black or white at a ball. They will catch the eye". Here the boned bodice fits the body like a glove, and then flares out dramatically from the hips with a full skirt with horizontal layers of ruffles, designed to emphasize the shape.

Previous page right Silver and white were colours that dominated the early 1960s. Chanel captured the mood for evening by using contrasting textures of shiny sequins, iridescent pearls and frothy layers of white tulle.

Right For much of her life Chanel lived in a three-roomed apartment above the shop at 31 Rue Cambon, surrounded by her precious books, the lacquered Coromandel screens and the crystal chandelier she designed herself. A Greek marble dating from the fifth century BC on the mantelpiece and two Chinese bronze deer, dating from the eighteenth century, both are indications of the designer's wealth. She is pictured here in 1965.

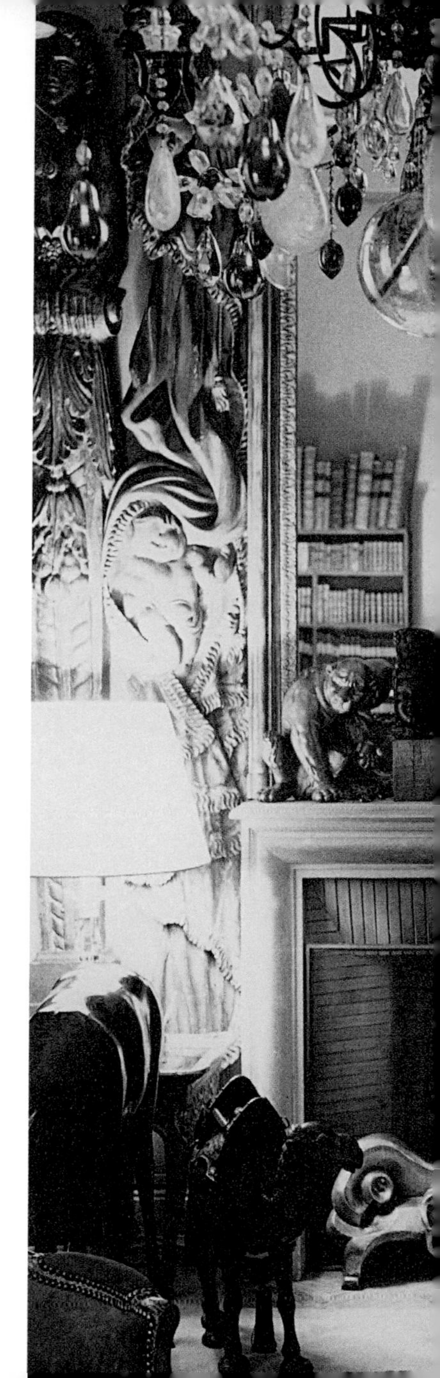

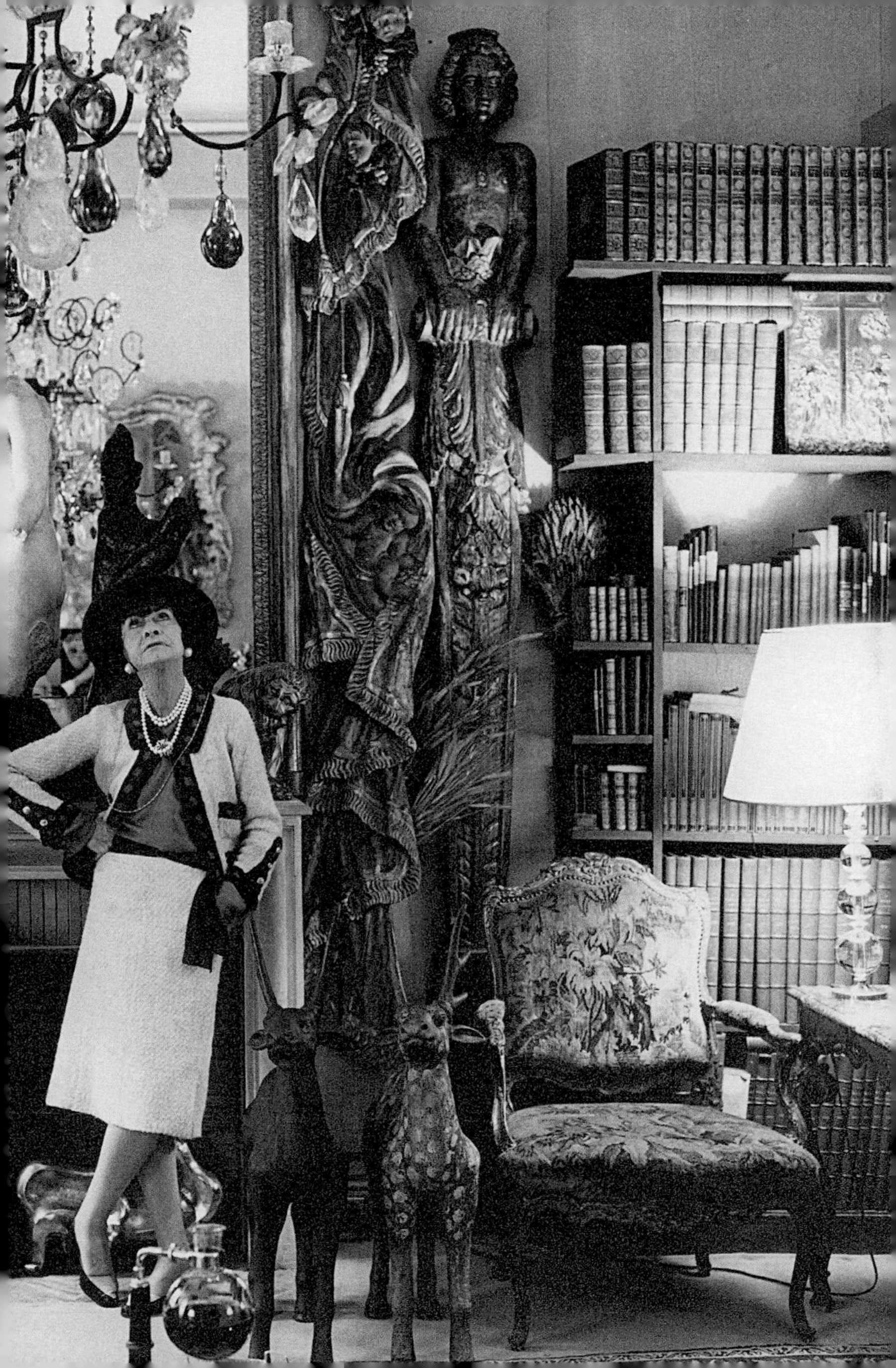

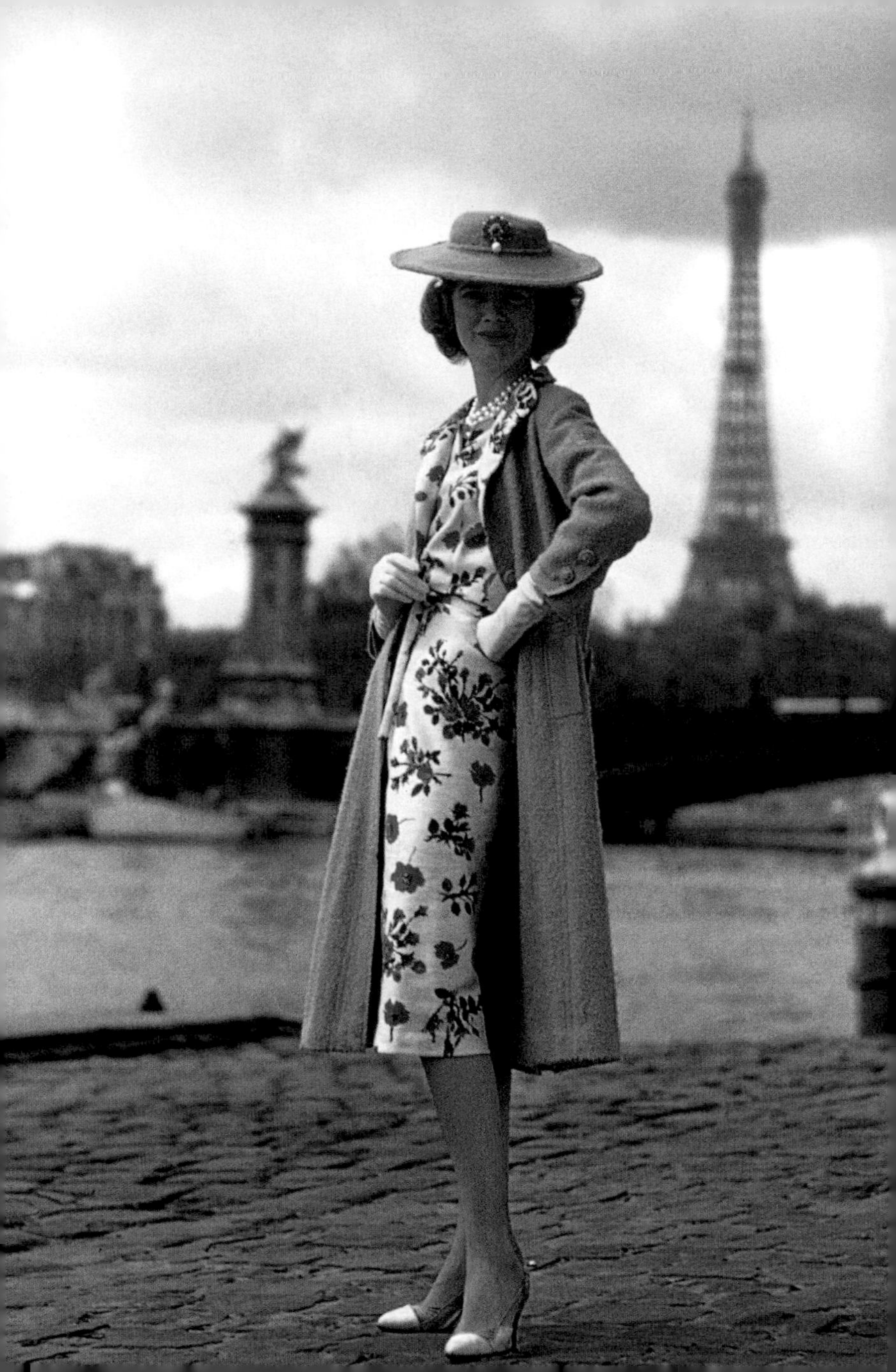

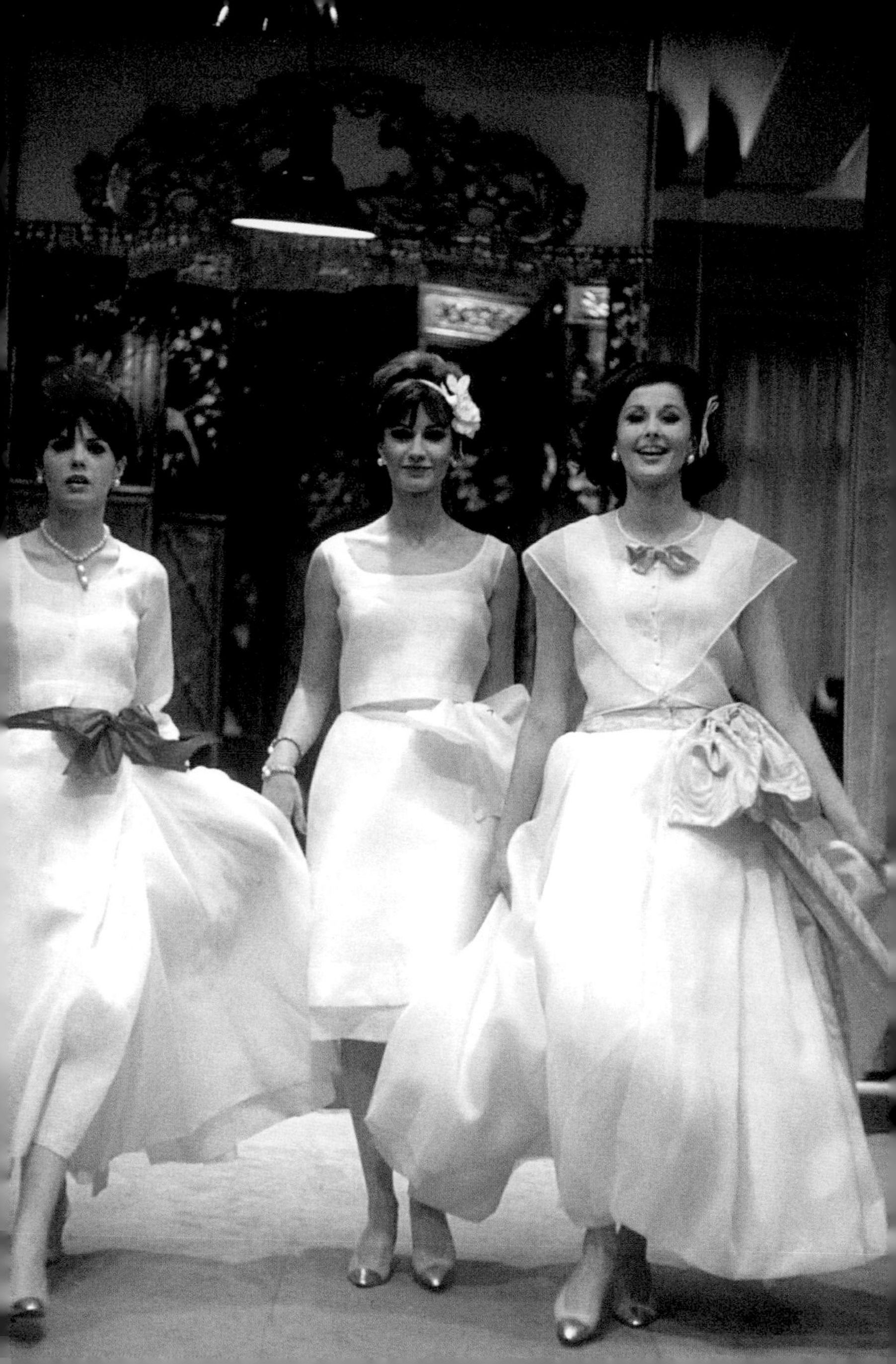

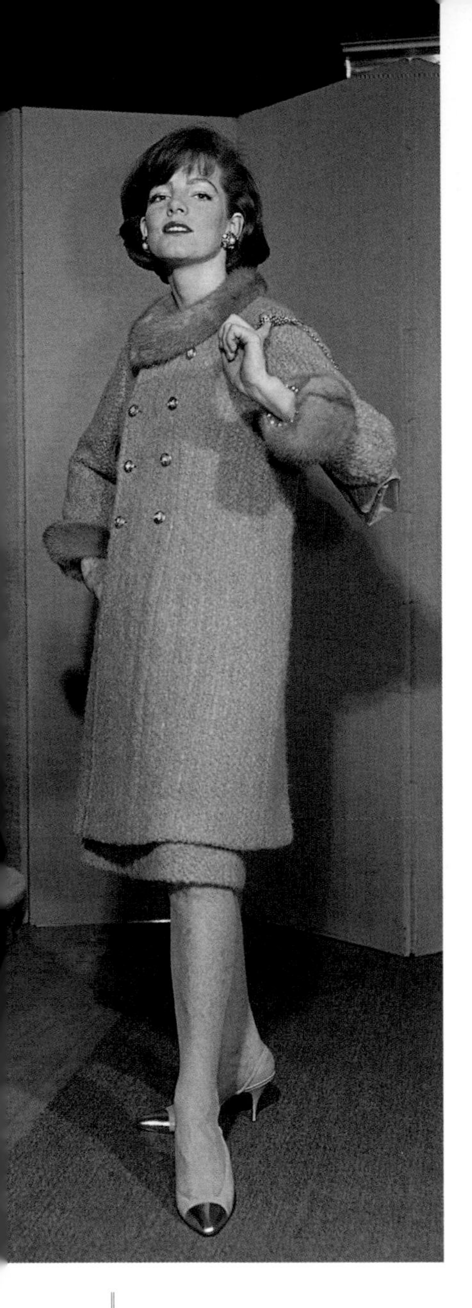

Previous page left Through the years, the signature style remained elegant and inevitably incorporated the essential details that Chanel had made her trademark. The cream floral-print fabric from the shift dress re-appears in the lapels and coat lining, while the flat hat is made from the same dusky pink wool as the coat.

Previous page right Variations on a white theme from the mid-1960s. Layers of crisp organza are offset with a silk taffeta sash and bow in contrasting colours and silver cap-toe shoes.

Left New proportions for the suit in 1963: a slim skirt cut to below the knee with straight seven-eighths coat made in bright wool. Luxurious grey mink trims the collar and cuffs, and two rows of small gilt buttons are used for the double-breasted opening.

Opposite Brown cape and dress ensemble, with a matching hat, from the 1960s. Mink lines the cape and trims the collar and brim of the hat. The model wears pearl stud earrings and one of Chanel's innovative pieces of costume jewellery the pendant cross, set with pearls and heavy glass stones.

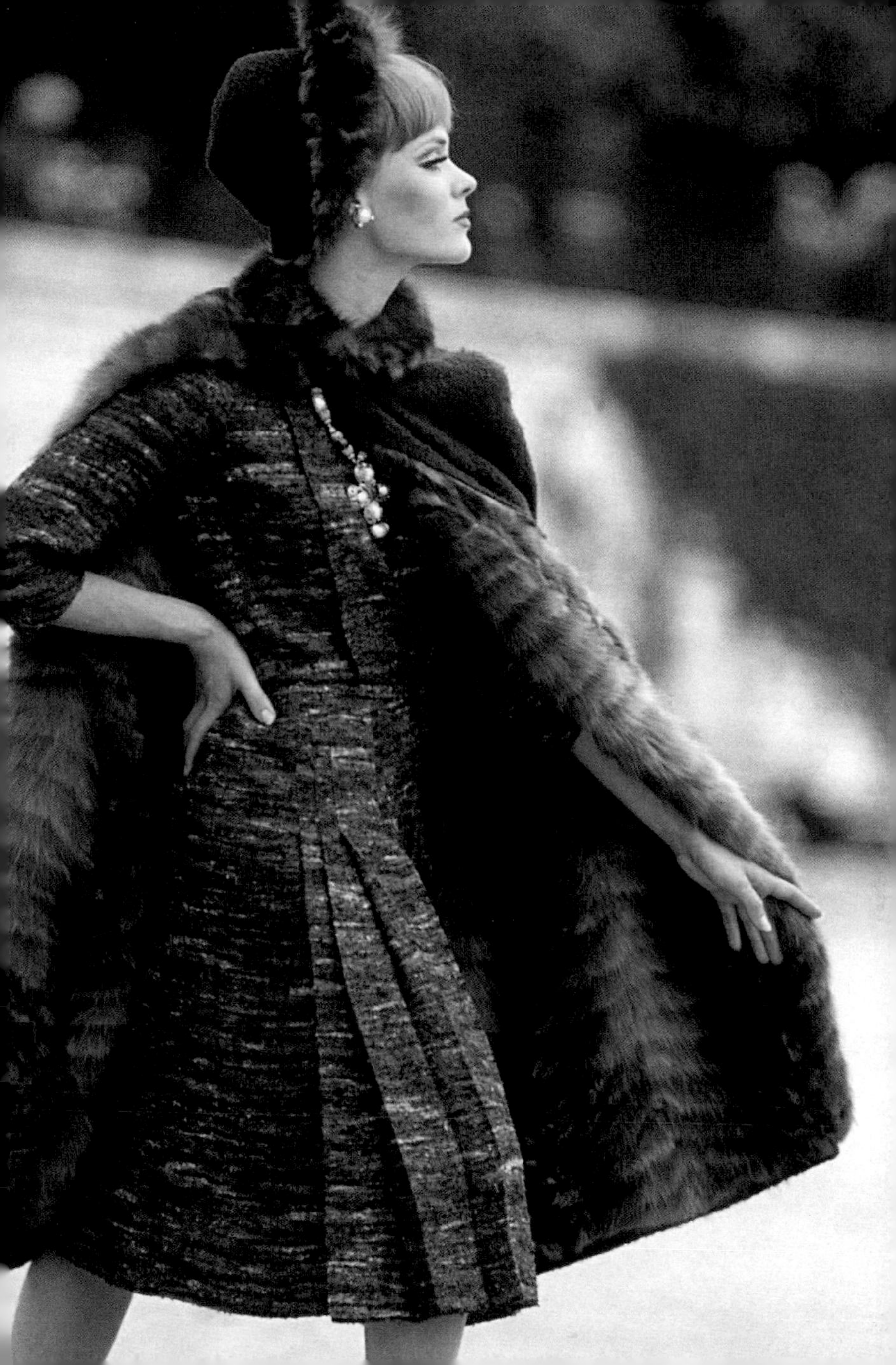

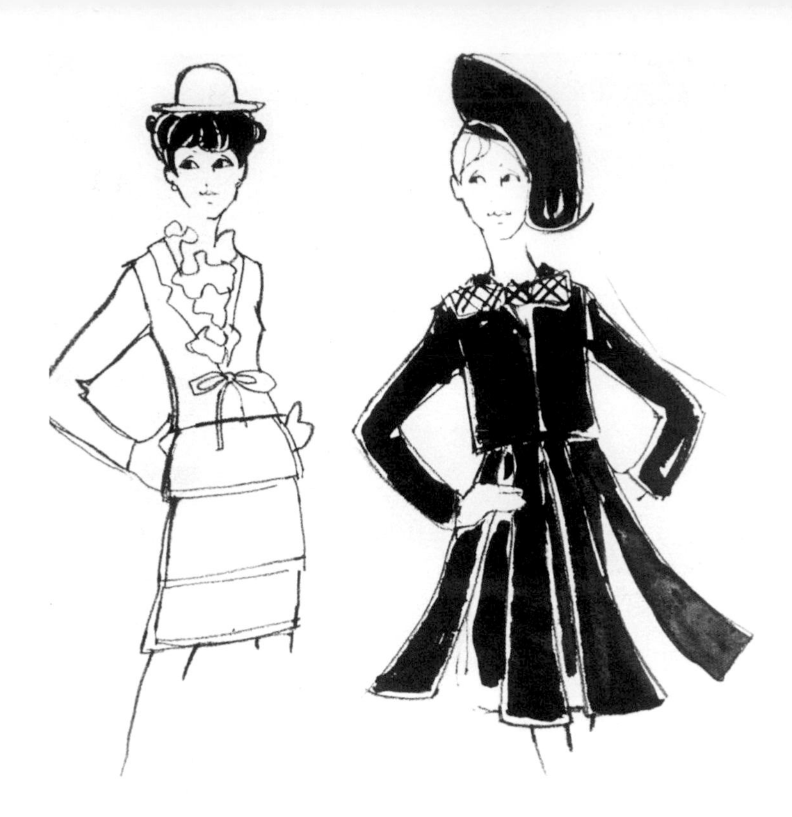

Above Illustrations of two of Chanel's dress designs from around 1965 both show a shorter silhouette in response to the changing times.

Opposite A vibrant turquoise and pink, silk, print dress, worn with an off-white wool jacket, uses matching fabric for pocket, cuffs and lining. The Breton-style hat is reminiscent of the very first styles Chanel wore as a young girl.

Overleaf left Coco Chanel, celebrating backstage after a show surrounded by models, all of whom were chosen because they resembled Mademoiselle and exemplified the house style.

Overleaf right In the workroom Chanel was rarely seen without a pair of long scissors hanging on a ribbon around her neck. Models were expected to stand for hours while she scrutinized the fit and eliminated any flaws.

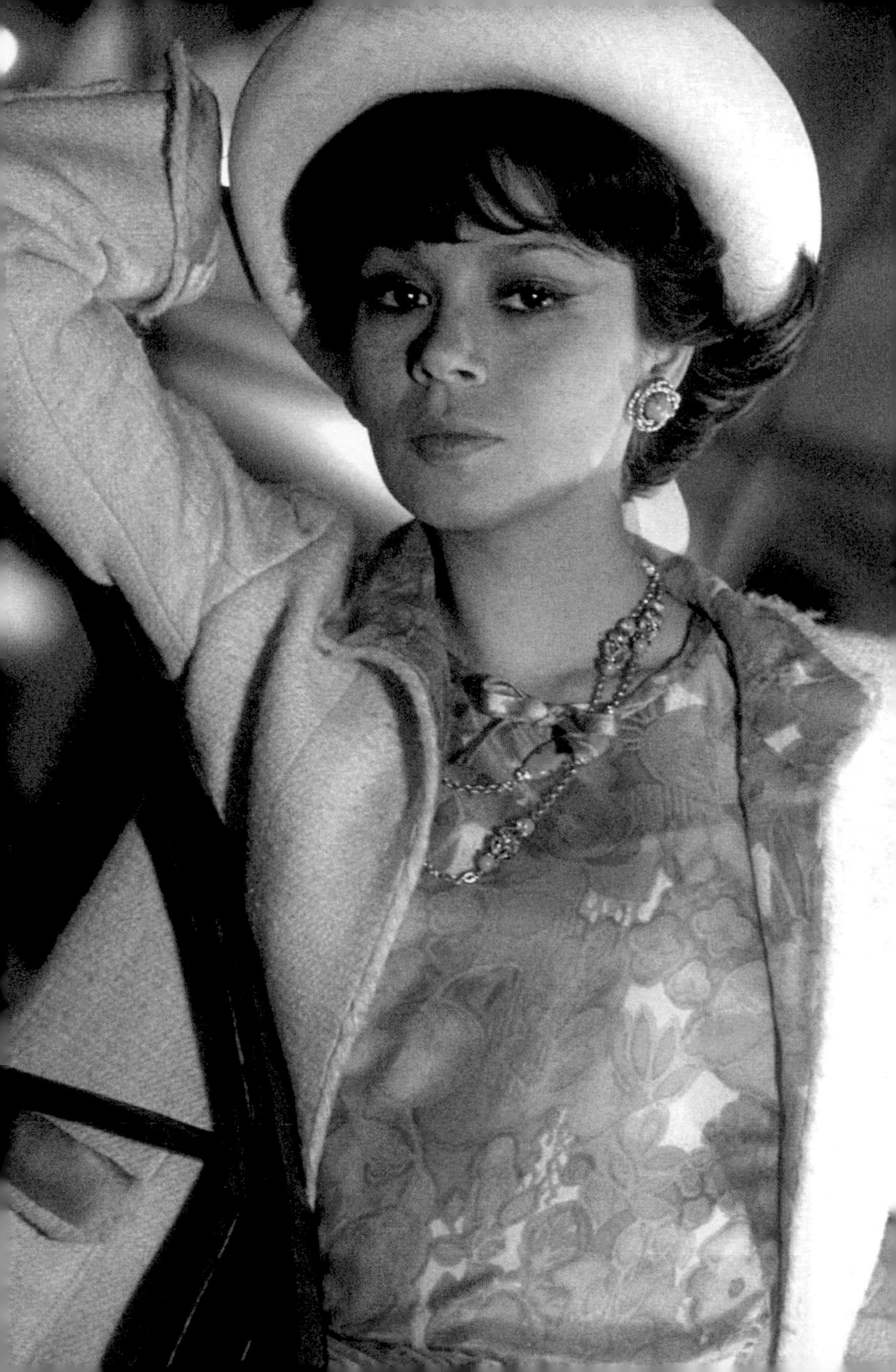

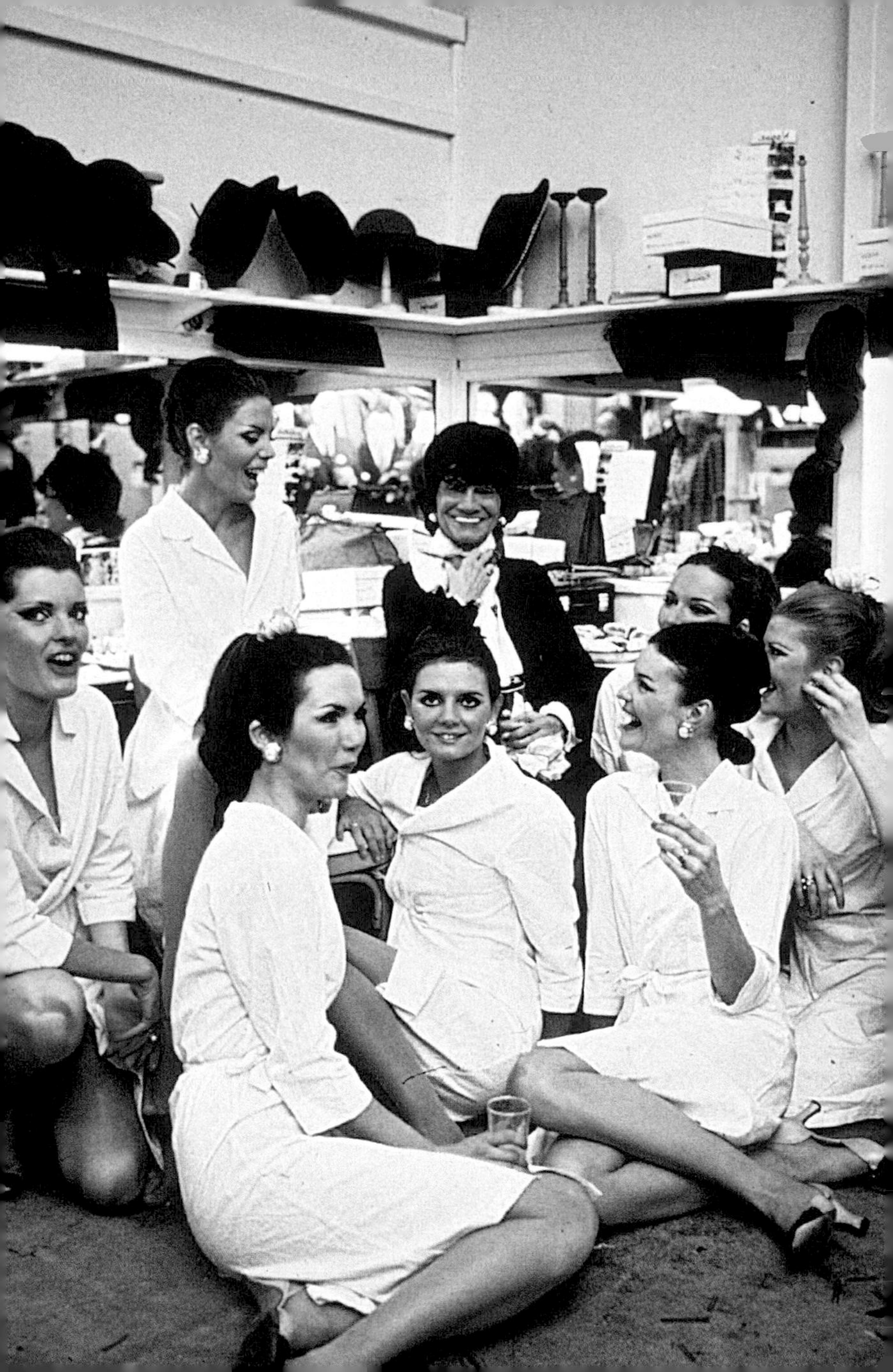

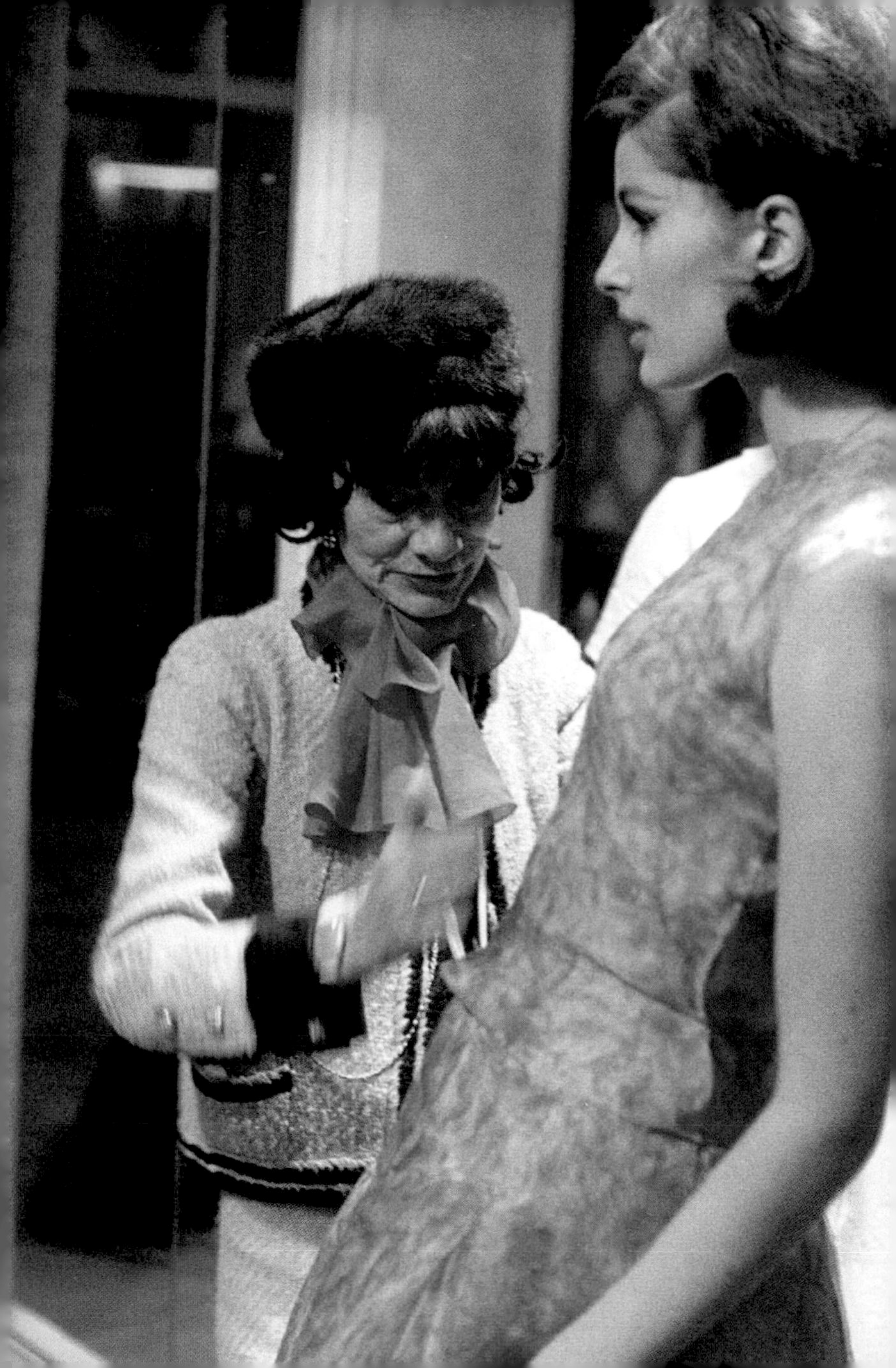

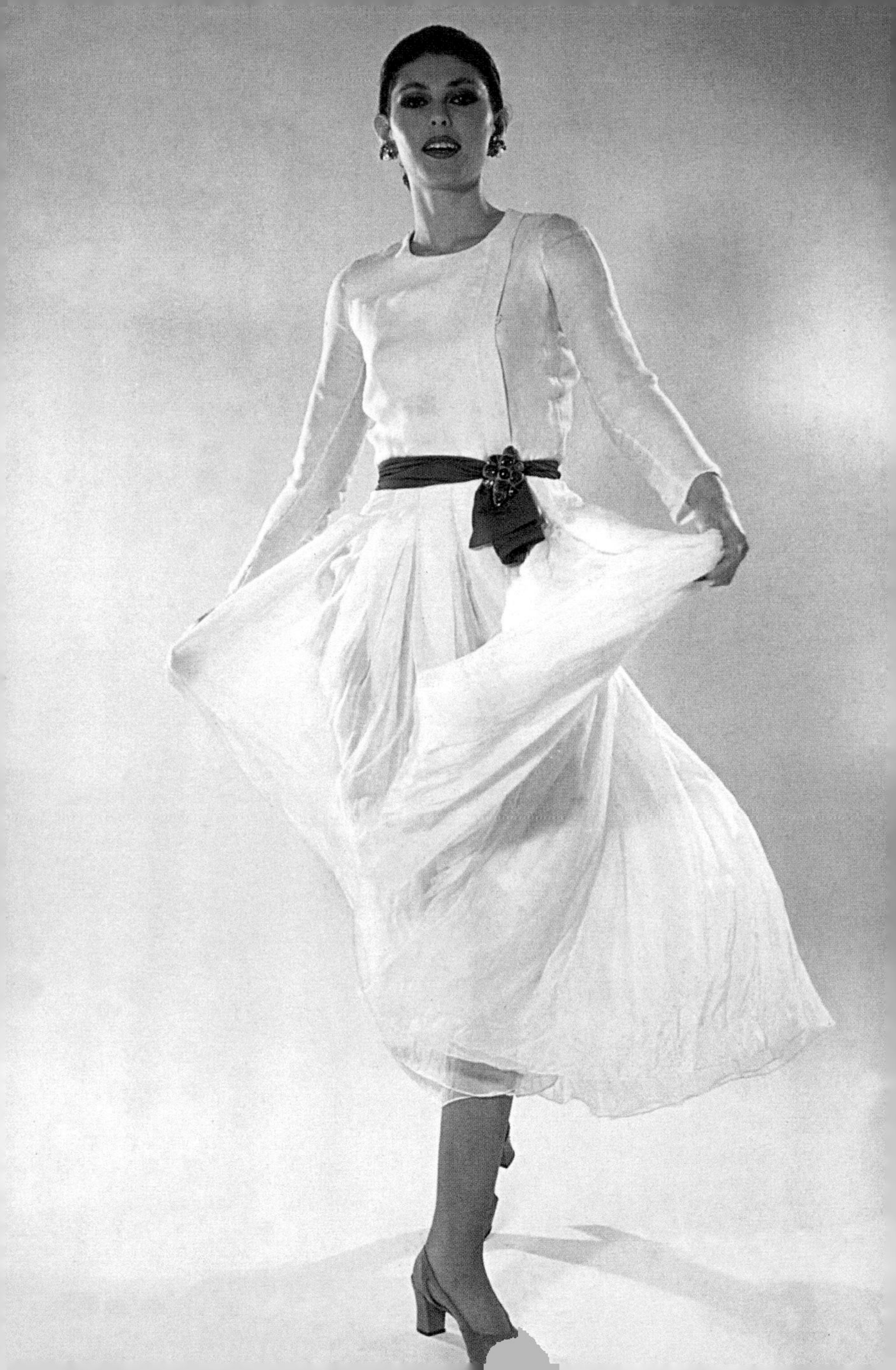

The End of an Era

Coco kept working up until the very end. The Swinging Sixties seemed an irrelevance to someone who had carved out such a distinguished career based on elegant modernity as opposed to fashionable trends; she simply ignored the obsession with youth and carried on in her own indomitable way. In the final years, Coco had a small retinue of staff to look after her in her rooms at the Ritz Hotel; she was extraordinarily wealthy, but having sacrificed her personal life to work, and with so many of her friends gone, she became increasingly isolated and lonely. Coco Chanel died in her room at the Ritz on Sunday, 10 January 1971. She was 88 years old. The funeral service, which was attended by all the great and the good of the fashion world including Yves Saint Laurent, Pierre Balmain and Cristóbal Balenciaga, as well as Salvador Dalí and Jeanne Moreau, took place at L'Eglise de la Madeleine, the grandest church next to Rue Cambon. As her final resting place she requested the cemetery in Lausanne, Switzerland.

Opposite This long white evening dress from 1970 was the last dress Chanel ever made for herself. Understated in its simplicity, it was made from white silk chiffon, worn over a fine white silk knit strapless petticoat. She wore it on several occasions before she died.

Overleaf Models from the House of Chanel were among mourners who attended the memorial service at L'Eglise de la Madeleine. Chanel died in her bedroom at the Ritz Hotel, 10 January 1971.

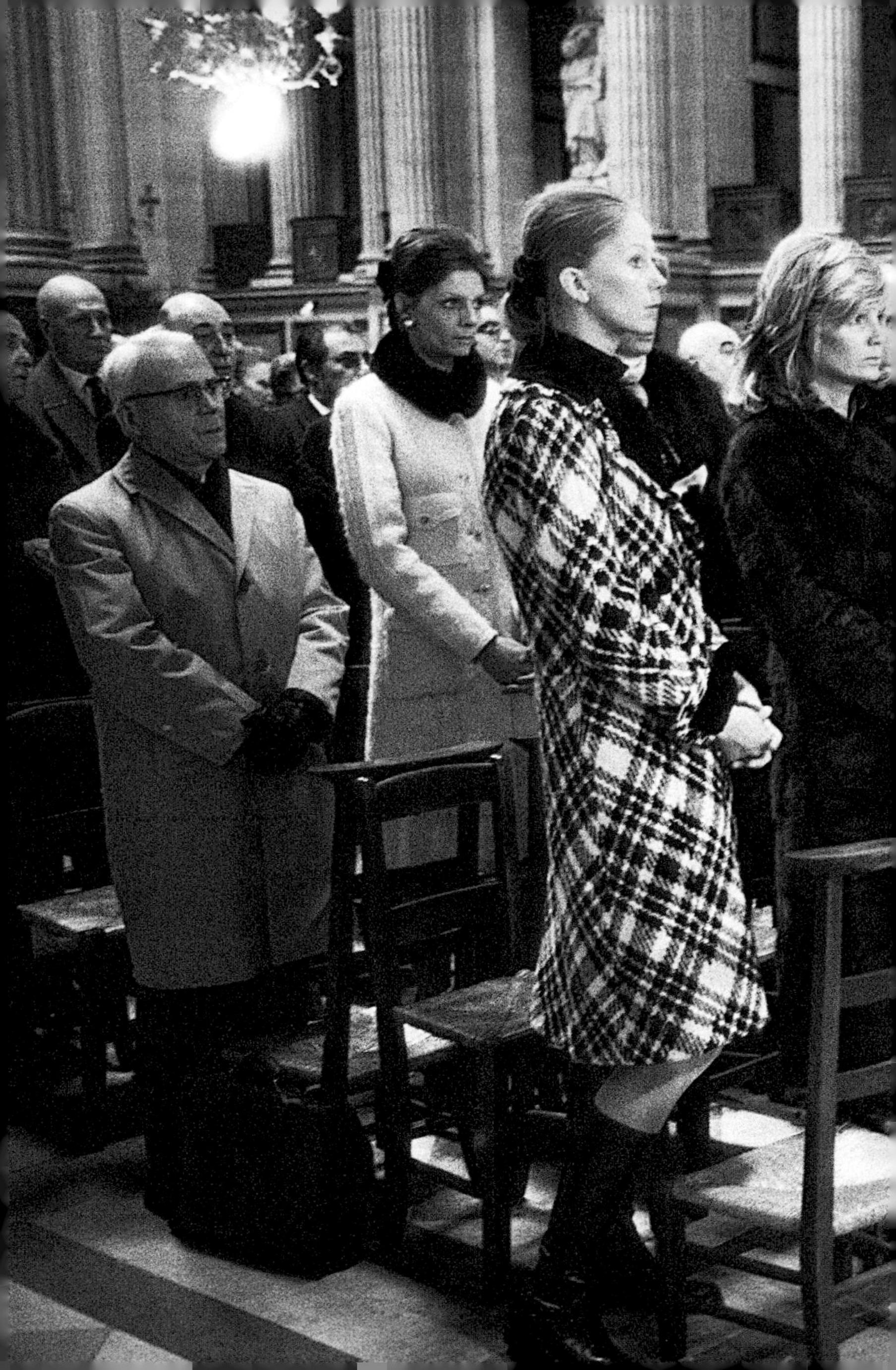

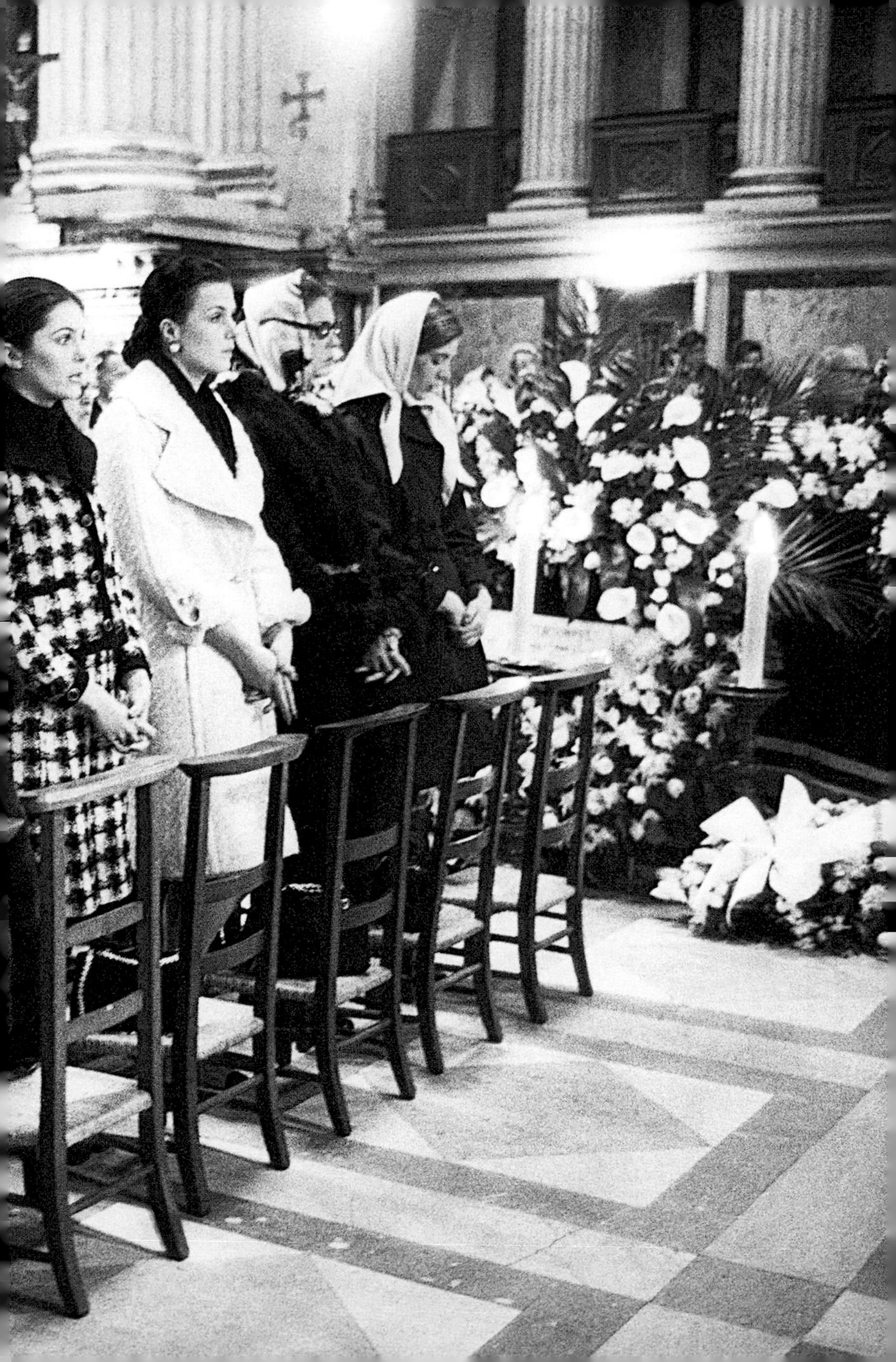

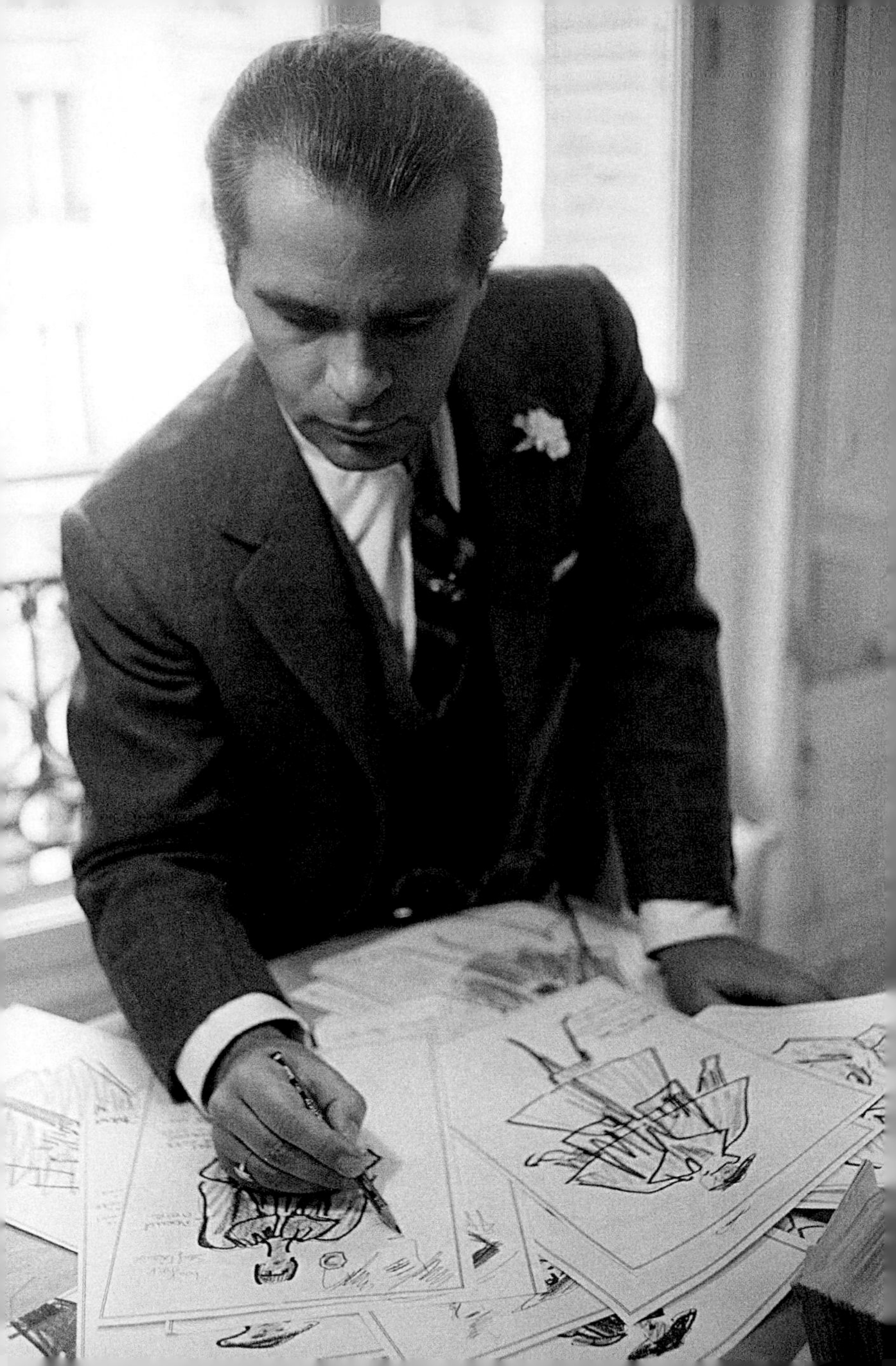

The Lagerfeld Years

"Coco always borrowed from the boys. She took their jackets, and made them into uniforms for women." Karl Lagerfeld

With the death of Coco, the House of Chanel stagnated for a while. Without the commander-in-chief, the empire lurched onwards, lacking direction but still supported by a continually ageing clientele who remained faithful to Chanel's classic style. It was not until 12 years later, with the arrival of Karl Lagerfeld in 1983, that the House of Chanel once again emerged as a creative and extraordinarily influential force. The prolific German fashion designer, who also worked for Chloé, Krizia and Max Mara, and produced collections for Fendi, his own label Karl Lagerfeld, and both haute couture and ready-to-wear for Chanel, was an inspirational choice to continue the legacy that Coco worked so hard to establish.

Affectionately known in the fashion press as "King Karl", Lagerfeld breathed new life into the memory of Coco Chanel for nearly 30 years. Under his masterful leadership Chanel rose phoenix-like to a position of worldwide dominance. His genius lay in incorporating a younger funkier edge into the collections, to broadening the mass appeal of the brand, while simultaneously retaining the established slightly older market who expected the label to be synonymous with impeccable quality, elegance and understatement.

Opposite Karl Lagerfeld seen here at work, sketching designs, in his studio in Paris, April 1983.

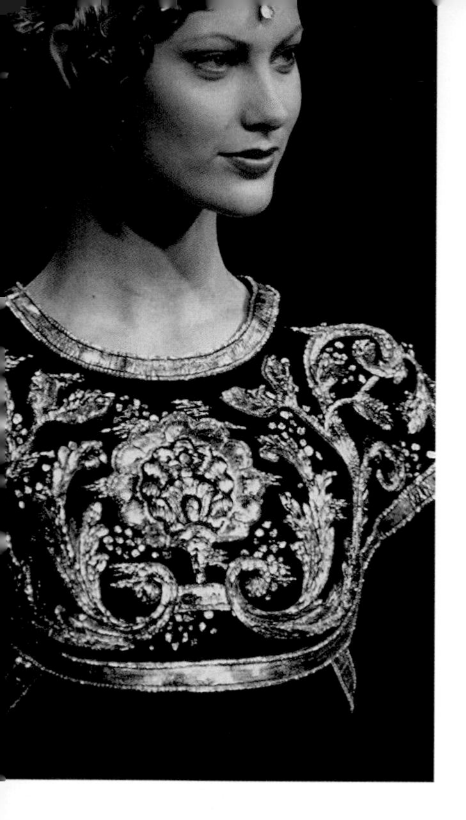

Left Lagerfeld incorporated all the iconic Chanel symbols into his work, taking inspiration from the motifs he found on the famous Coromandel screens and reworking them with exquisite embroidery for autumn/winter 1993–4.

Opposite Karl Lagerfeld with the model Stella Tennant, dressed in a lavishly embroidered black evening coat depicting the intricate images of birds of paradise, waterfalls, temples and cherry blossom, all found on the Chinese Coromandel screens that Chanel kept in her apartment. From the haute couture autumn/winter 1996–7 collection.

Lagerfeld's mission statement was to work around the elements of Chanel's original concepts, using what he found in the archives as a springboard to reinterpreting and rejuvenating what had, in truth, become safe and predictable. Initially he made scrapbooks that contained every visual reference to anything that was connected to Chanel's history (see page 113). He used these as a point of reference, acknowledging the spirit of the past, and then absorbed and rejected as necessary, with the ultimate intention of producing something disconcertingly new. Lagerfeld didn't do nostalgia. Rather, he had the ability to skilfully juggle the connective threads between the past, present and future. While acknowledging the founding principles on which Coco based her vision, he was also known to have quoted the words of the German writer and poet Goethe: "Make a better future by developing elements from the past".

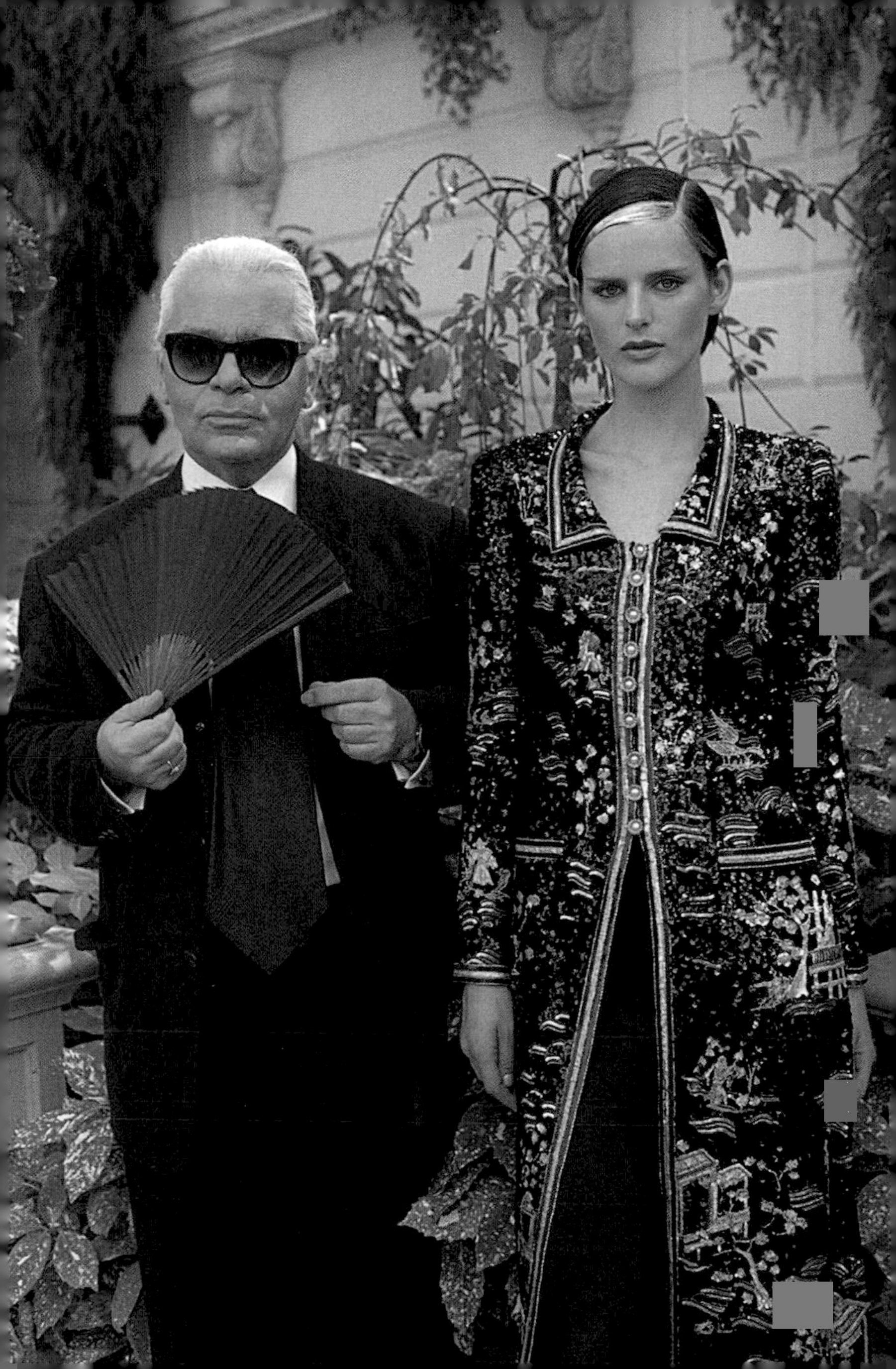

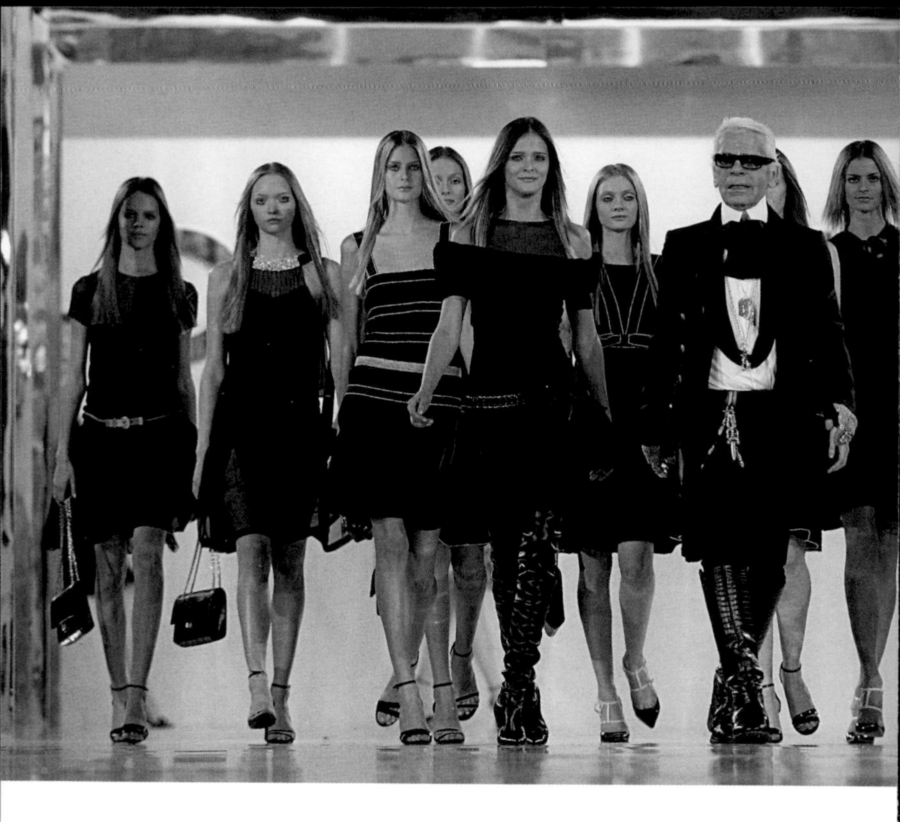

The intention was to reinvent Chanel, and when Lagerfeld made his debut in the early 1980s he took the staple pieces – the tweed suit, the rope of pearls, the quilted bag, the cap-toe shoes – and manipulated the elements before representing them in a sensational way that may have surprised the purists. Early on he showed a succession of beautiful black evening dresses that took motifs directly from the Coromandel screens which decorated all of Chanel's homes. The dresses, which combined a 1920s drop-waist style with a more fitted body-conscious silhouette, were covered in lavish embroidery and delicate beading in the form of exotic camellia, foliage and oriental symbols: pure Coco with a King Karl twist. The iconic "Little Black Dress" that was so quintessentially Coco has remained a constant in the modern era, with Lagerfeld unleashing new ideas like fireworks: chiffon, lace, layers of tulle, embroidery and sequins, all to match the spirit of the times. Then he dipped into Coco's details to

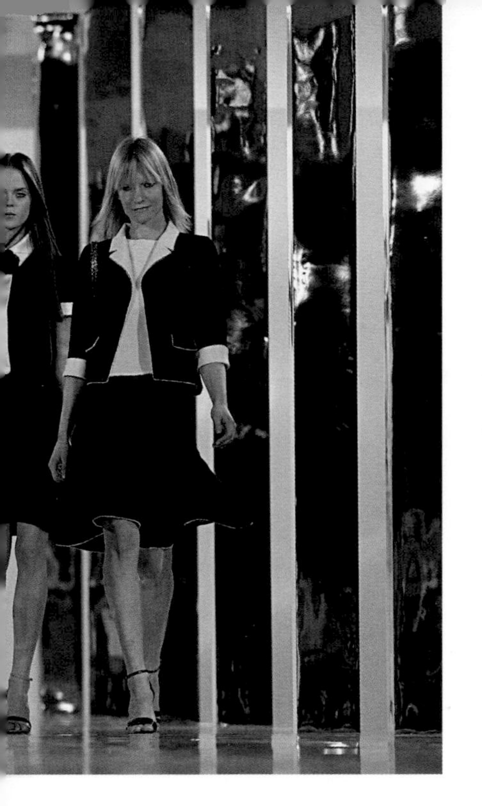

"One is never over-dressed or underdressed with a Little Black Dress."

Karl Lagerfeld

define the look: strings of giant pearls, ropes of chainmail, crisp white contrasts in the collar and cuffs, or a perfectly placed camellia. Lagerfeld took his bow at the end of his 2005 autumn/winter prêt-à-porter collection, surrounded by models wearing updated interpretations of the versatile LBD.

While Coco reappropriated items of menswear and sporting uniforms for her collections, Lagerfeld also looked elsewhere, taking inspiration from the dress codes and unique styling details of urban sub-cults. For spring/summer 1991 Lagerfeld took Chanel to Californian surf school. His body-conscious sequinned jackets in vibrant primary colours were matched with black Lycra running shorts and sunglasses, and instead of the ubiquitous designer handbag the girls strolled down the catwalk with the ultimate beach accessory: a surfboard emblazoned with the double-C logo.

For autumn/winter 1992–93 he contrasted the toughness of the heavy biker boys uniform with the tenderness of a floaty ballerina skirt. Boxy black leather jackets with chunky gilt buttons and quilted sleeves were juxtaposed with pretty pastel evening gowns that fell to the floor in soft folds. Flat biker boots, leather caps and an overload of gilt chains hung from the neck, the waist and the wrists. While not readily identifiable as typical Chanel (understated simplicity) each new collection keeps enough traces of the trademark signatures (buttons with the double-C insignia, the iconic quilting, the camellia, the gilt chains) that allowed the house to progress in a modern idiom, assuring them of commercial success.

Lagerfeld was driven by curiosity for change, and was never unduly reverential in his role; as he said, "Absolute respect would have been fatal to creativity." The double-C insignia has adorned everything from high-top trainers to bra tops, Wellington boots and hot pants, and while

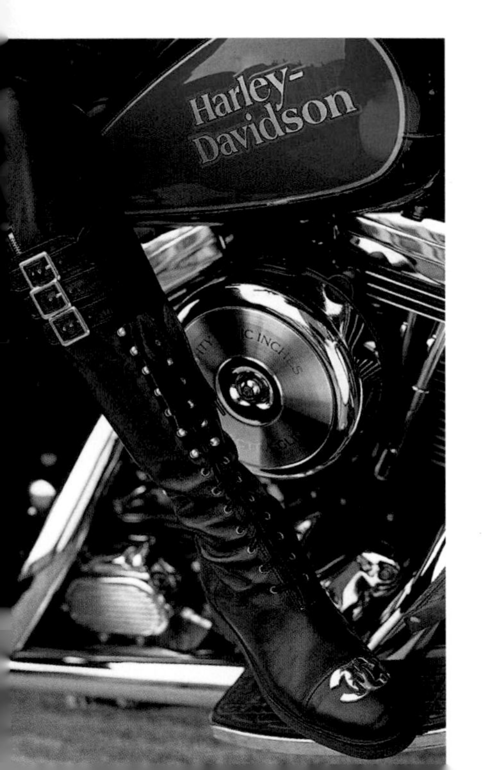

Previous pages Lagerfeld takes to the catwalk surrounded by models, all showing a variation on the versatile Little Black Dress, from autumn/winter 2005–6.

Left Knee-length leather biker boots get a Chanel makeover with the addition of the double-C logo, stamped in metal on the toecap.

Opposite Lagerfeld's inventive imagination allowed him to endlessly reinvent the Chanel suit without losing its original identity. His sketches show detailed variations on proportions and a wide range of fabric samples, from pastel tweeds, to leather.

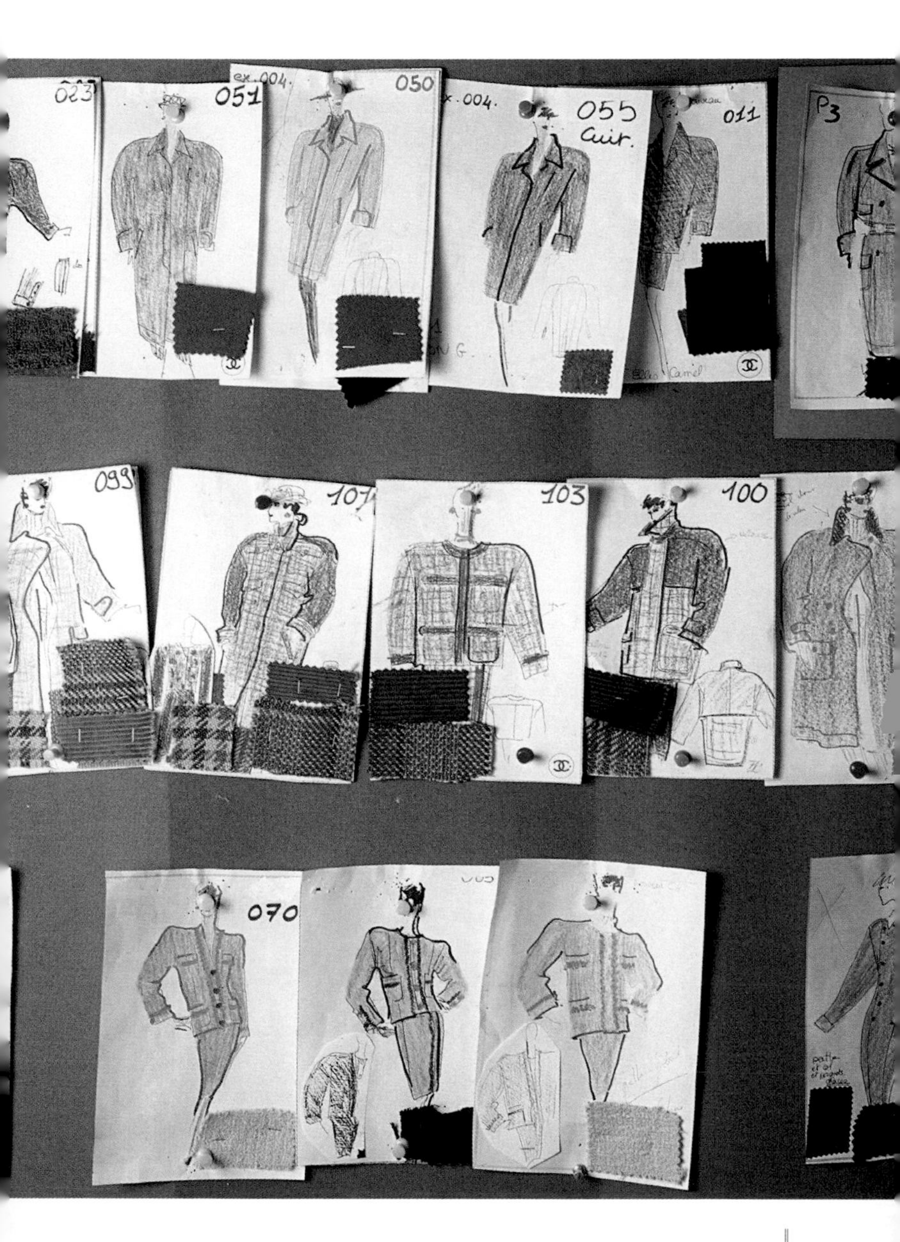
023
051
ex.004.
050
ex.004.
055
Cuir.
011
P3
099
103
100
070

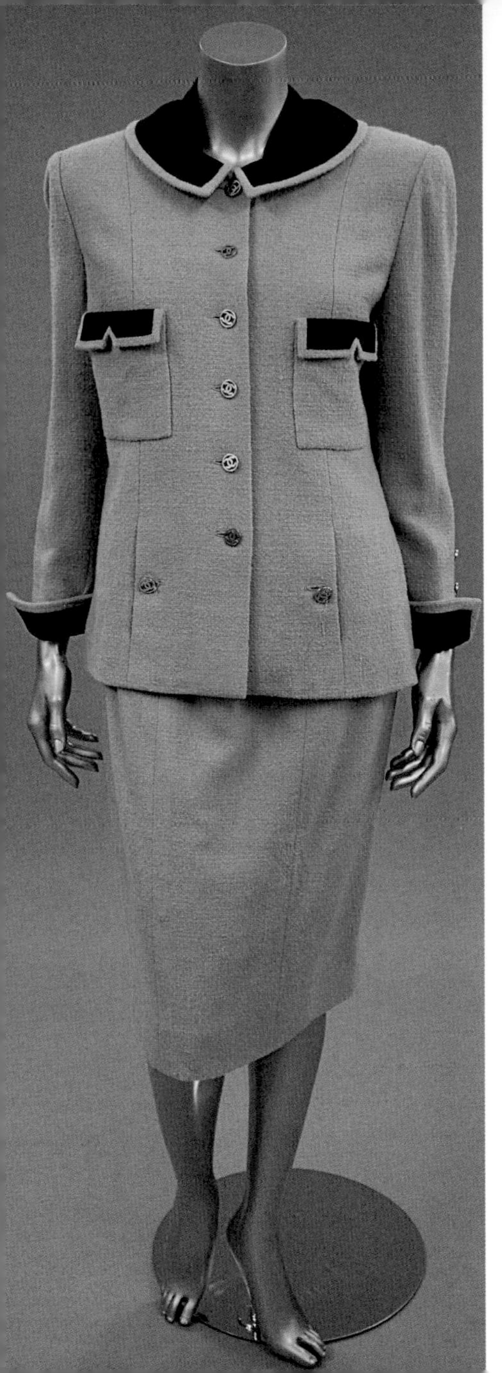

Left A Chanel Boutique suit from the 1980s, made from green bouclé wool with black silk trim on the jacket collar, cuffs and pocket flaps. The single-breasted jacket has gilt buttons embossed with the double-C logo.

Opposite Bright red bouclé wool suit from 1983, the year Lagerfeld produced his first collection for the House of Chanel. The fitted jacket, with rows of gilt buttons and chain belt, together with the quilted cuff bracelet, take the iconography of Coco and re-present them as classic 1980s power dressing.

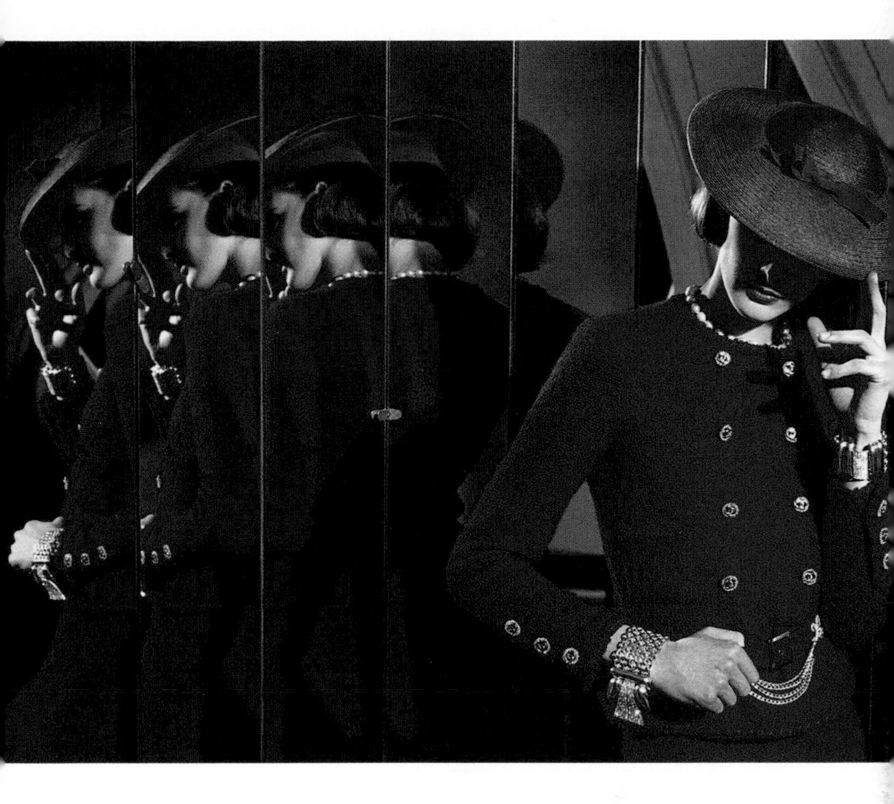

these things may be conceived as sensationalist elements designed to grab the headlines, it is still the Chanel suit that remains paramount to each collection, a re-imagined version of which will always be first down the catwalk.

During his tenure Lagerfeld upended the traditional twice-yearly fashion shows, a fixture of the house since the early 1930s. Tapping into a new age of social media, celebrity culture and an unparallel appetite for innovative imagery, Chanel now produce up to five shows each year, which by 2018 turned the company into a $10 billion luxury brand. With his impeccable sense of the cultural zeitgeist, and an inexhaustible compass of ideas, Lagerfeld created contemporary fashion that referenced technology, politics, humour as well as old-fashioned glamour, while still embracing the signature codes of Gabrielle Chanel.

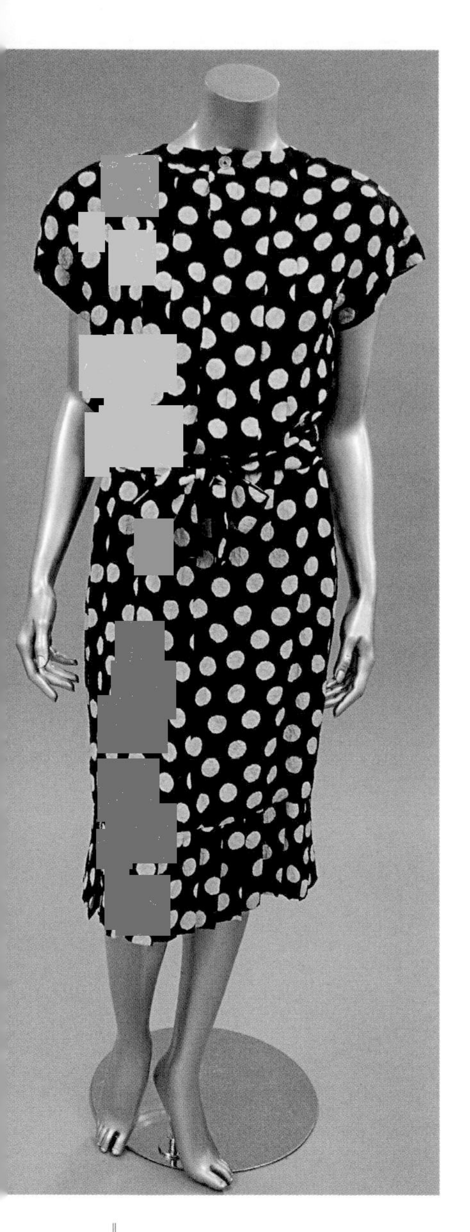

Left A 1980s textured dress for the Chanel Boutique, printed with large cream polka-dots on black silk. The bodice is loosely cut with large pleats down the front, while the skirt has two pockets with gilt buttons embossed with the double-C insignia.

Opposite This advertising still for the Chanel Boutique, dating from the 1980s, was placed in magazines for the British market.

CHANEL

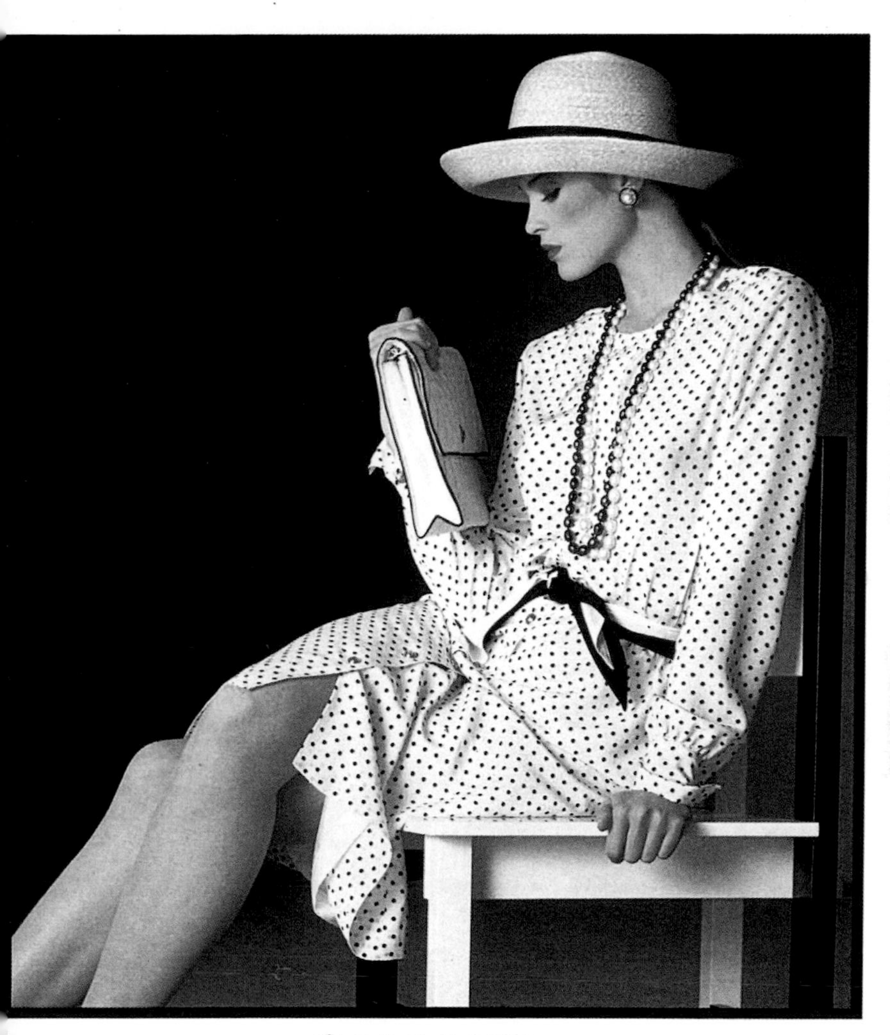

CHANEL

BOUTIQUE

26 OLD BOND STREET – LONDON W1

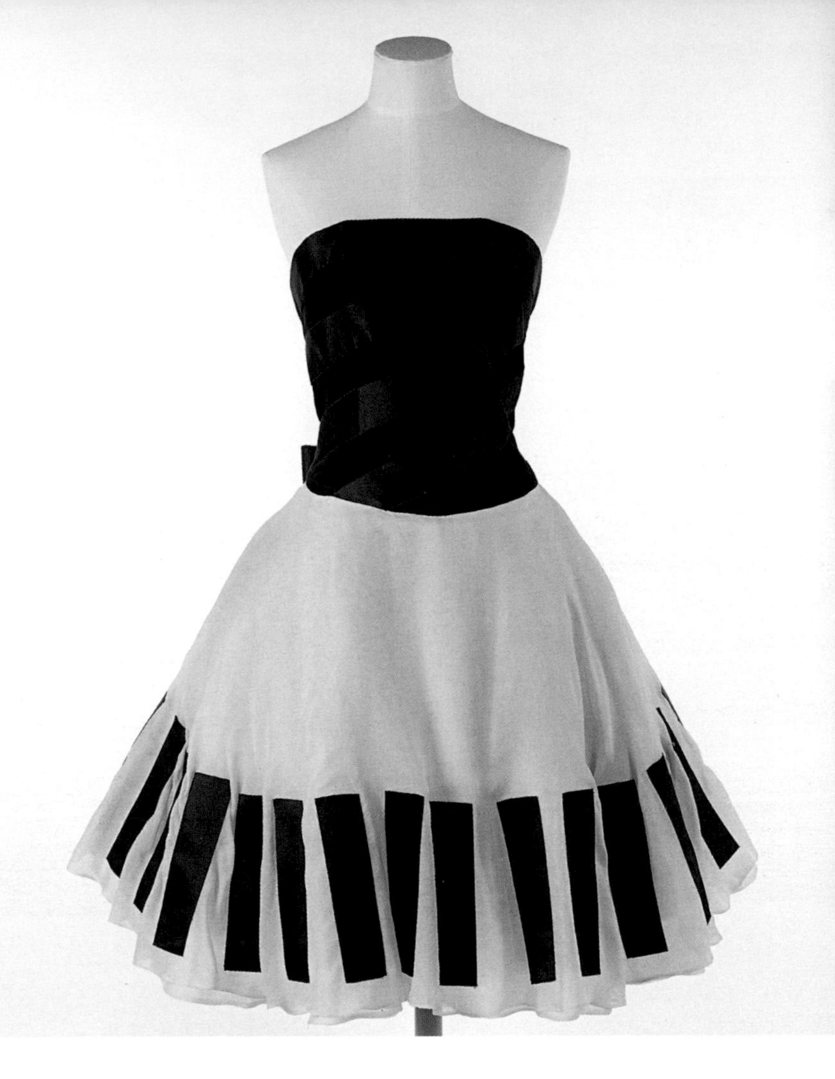

Above The black strapless bodice in silk organza flares out into a white knee-length skirt, with appliquéd "piano keys" at the hem. The dress, from 1985, has a ribbon sash with a camellia at the centre back.

Opposite Canadian supermodel Linda Evangelista wears a white sequinned sheath dress with dramatic black bows and black accessories for Chanel's spring/summer 1987 collection.

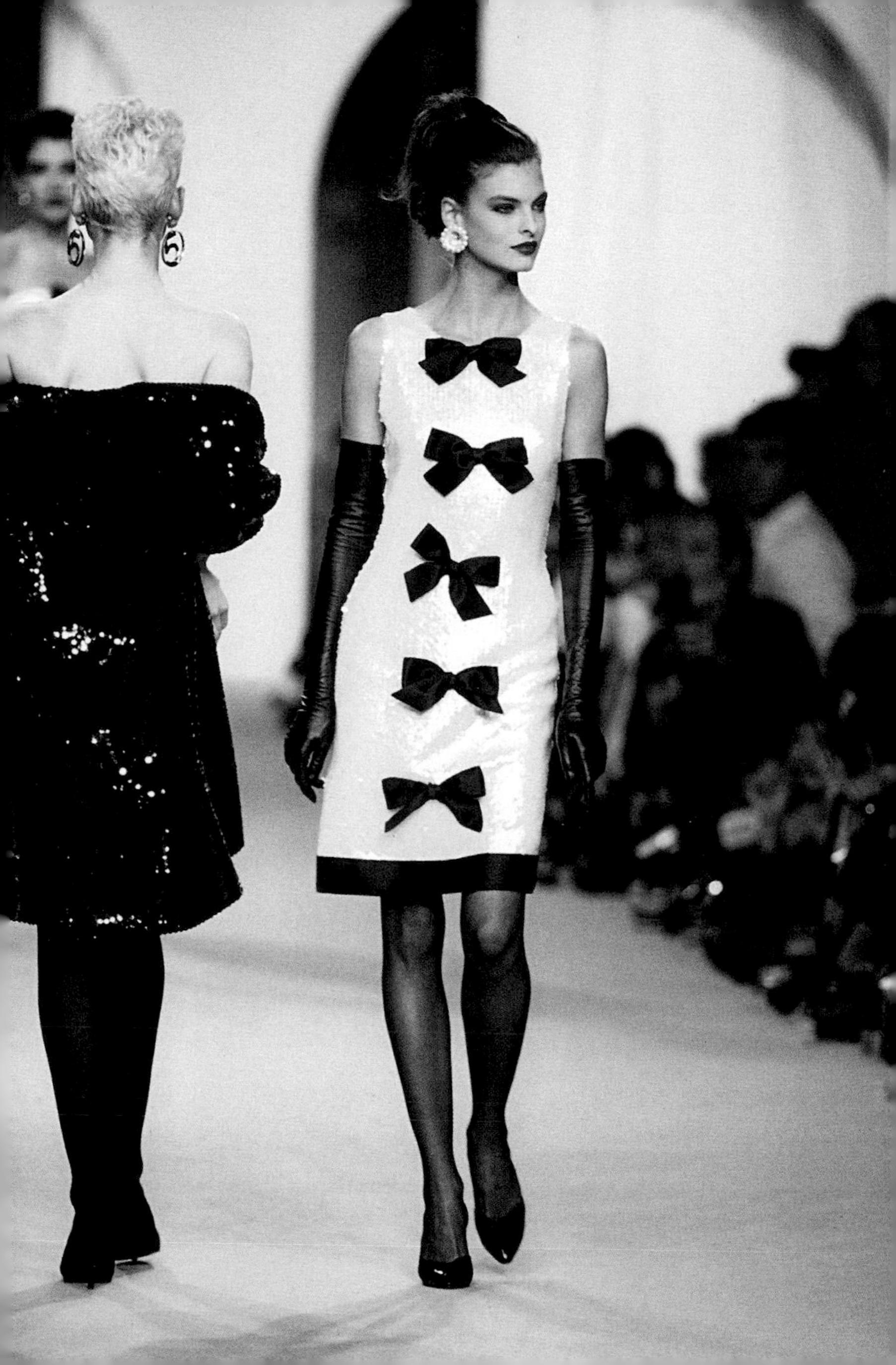

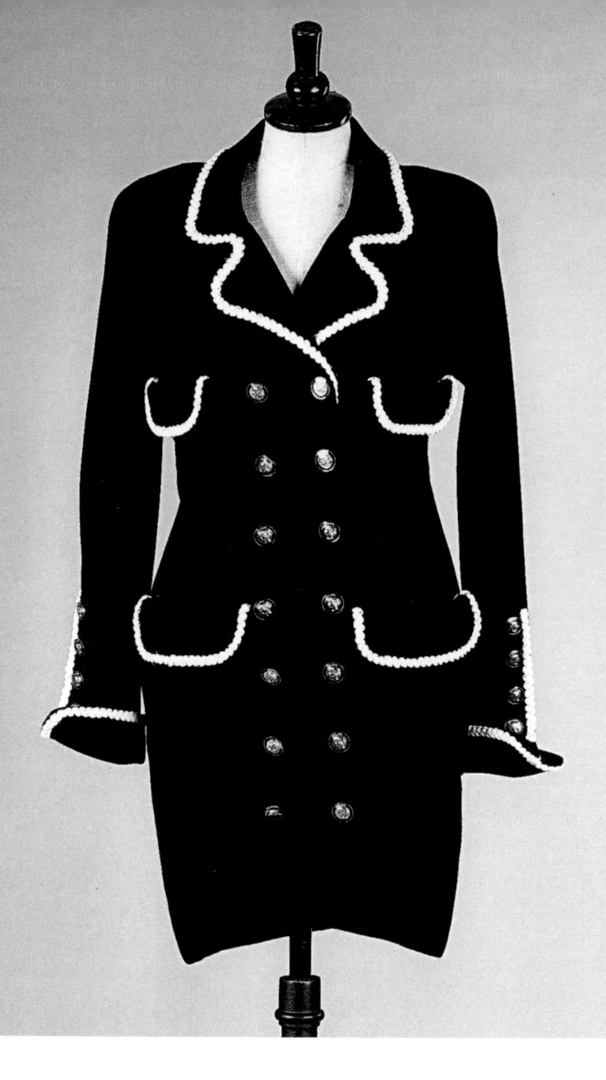

Above Black crepe coat-dress, edged in white rickrack braiding on the collar, cuffs and pockets and with Chanel cameo buttons, is an example of absolute elegance in monochrome, circa 1990.

Opposite Lagerfeld often combined wit with creativity to come up with his most surprising ideas, like this sporty sequinned surfer jacket with a zip-up fastening from the spring/summer 1991 collection.

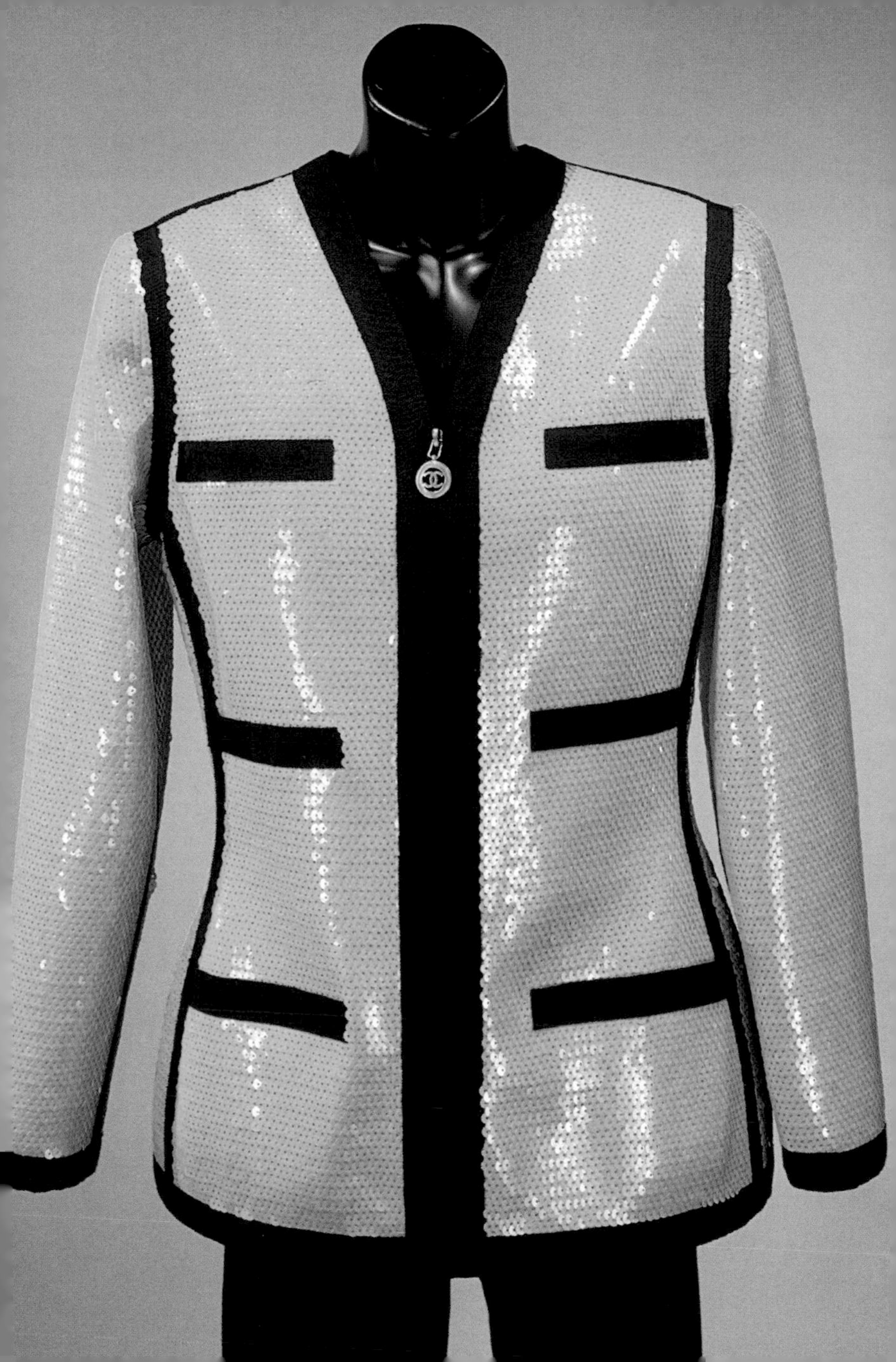

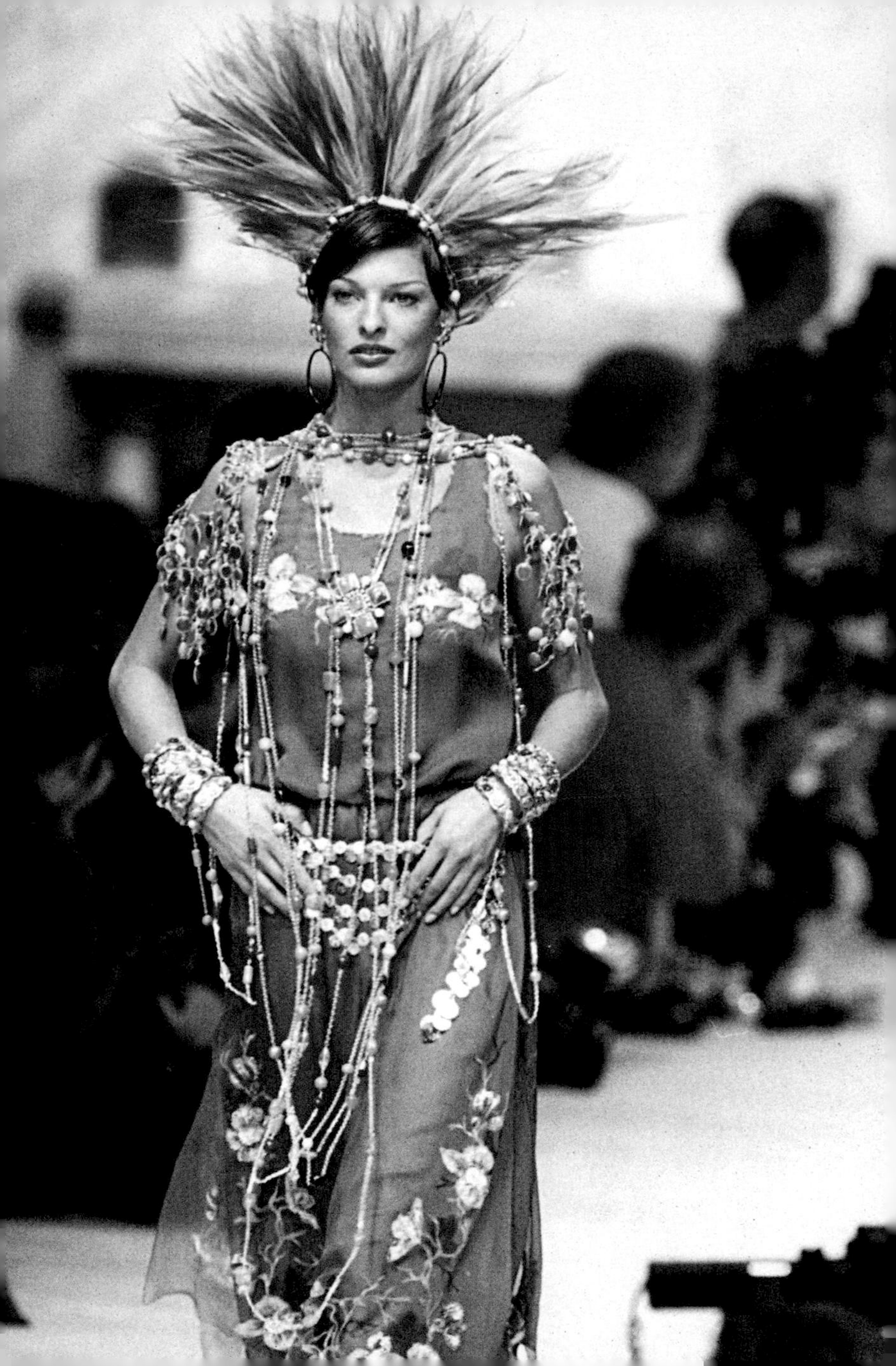

Opposite Linda Evangelista on the catwalk for spring/summer 1993. The abundance of jewellery and feather headdress create the spectacle, but the skills of couture are evident in the detailed flower embroidery decorating the simple grey tunic dress.

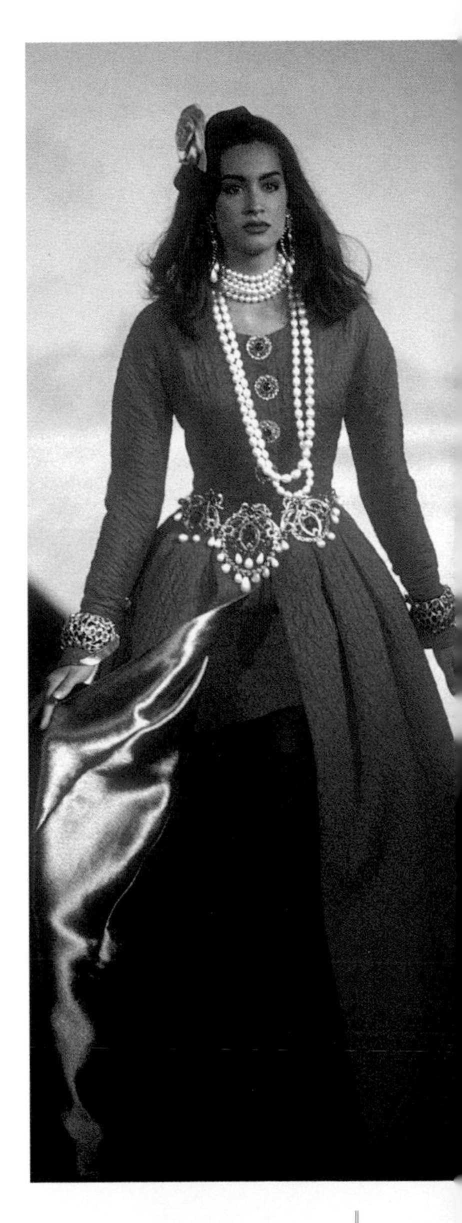

Right Suit proportions taken to extreme lengths for autumn/winter 1990–1. Model Yasmeen Ghauri wears a floor-length fitted coat with elaborate buttons and jewelled belt, with a gold lamé lining, over a short dark pink wool dress. On her wrists are the updated versions of the "mosaique" gold and jewelled bangles that Chanel used to wear.

Overleaf left A 2005 double-breasted trench coat in soft cotton becomes instantly recognizable as a Chanel trench when Lagerfeld adds contrasting braid to the front opening, shoulder seams, pockets, collar, belt and cuff edges.

Overleaf right Traditional tropes of the tweed suit, in a black and white colour palette, complete with braided trim and practical pockets, gets a high-tech update, accessorized with Stormtrooper helmet, plastic VR headsets and fembot-style gloves and Wellington boots in 2016.

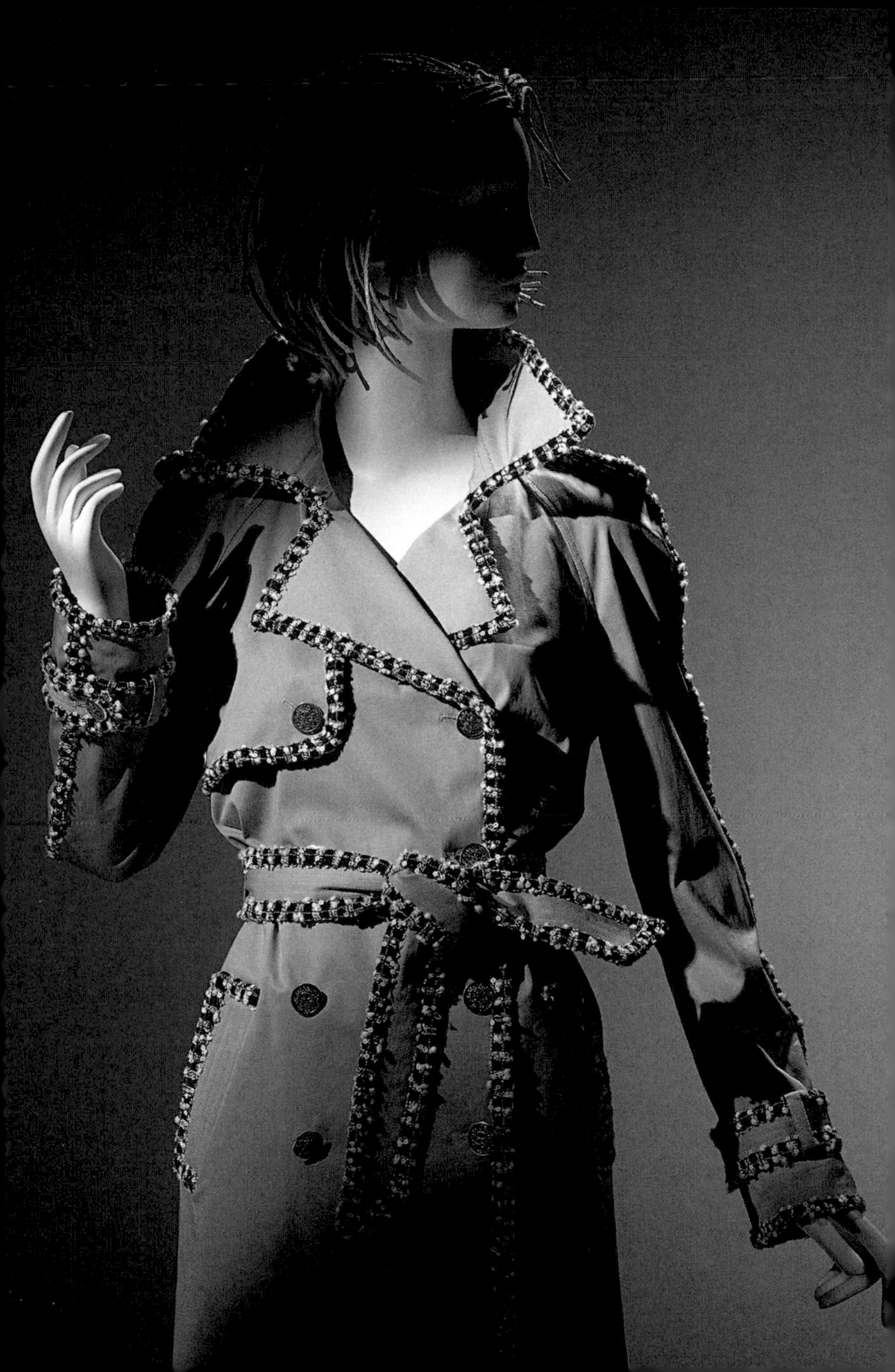

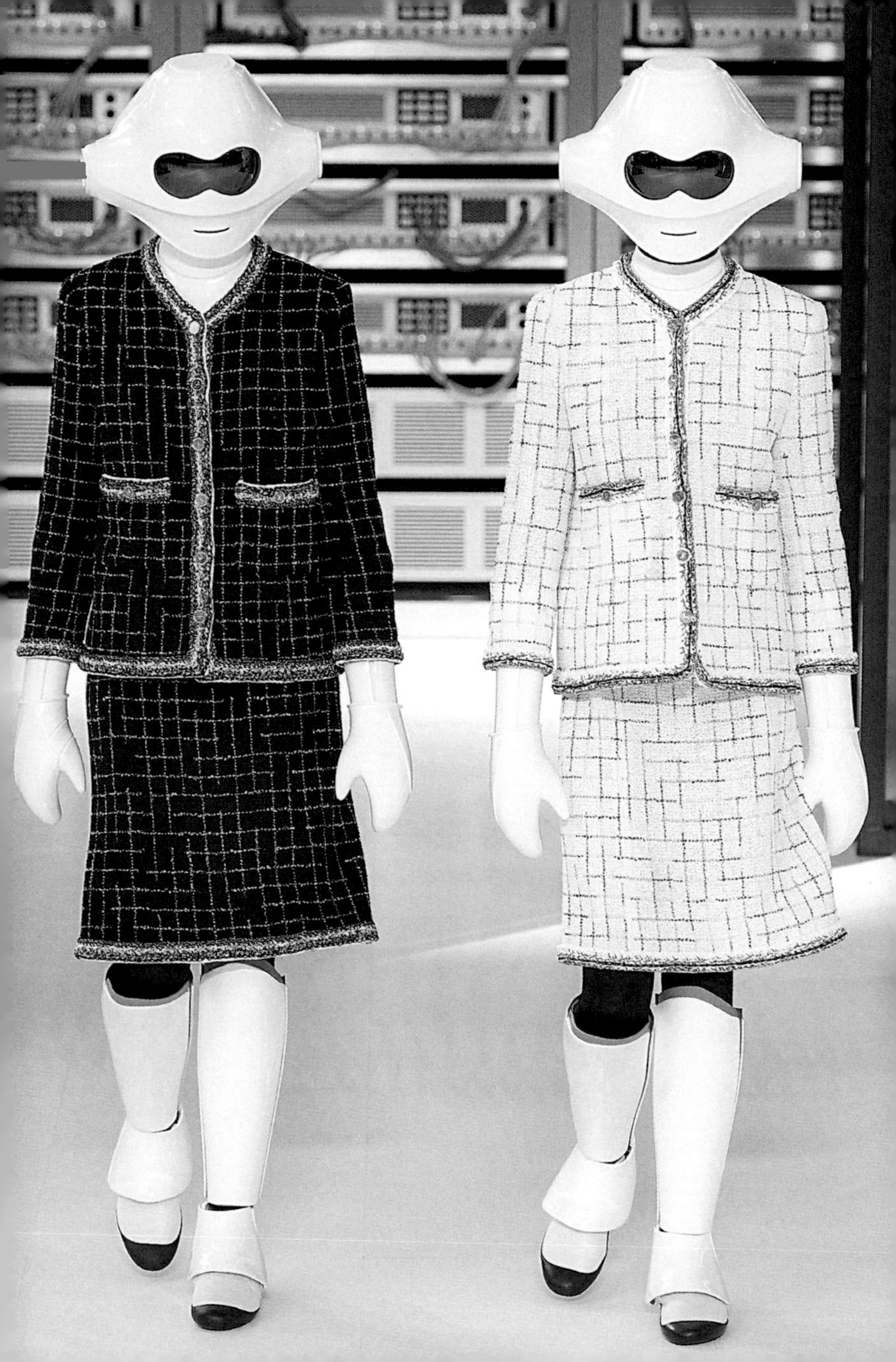

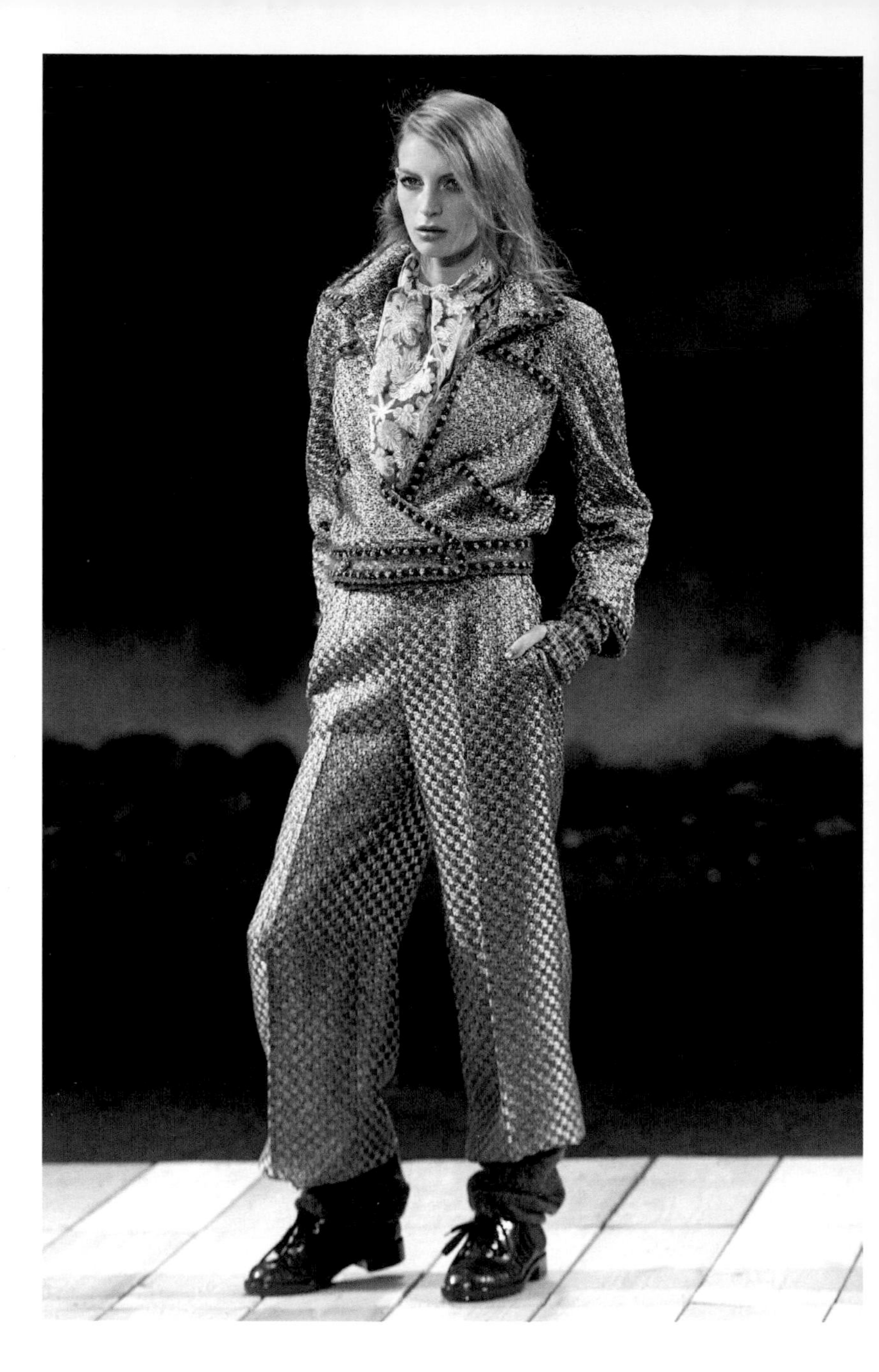

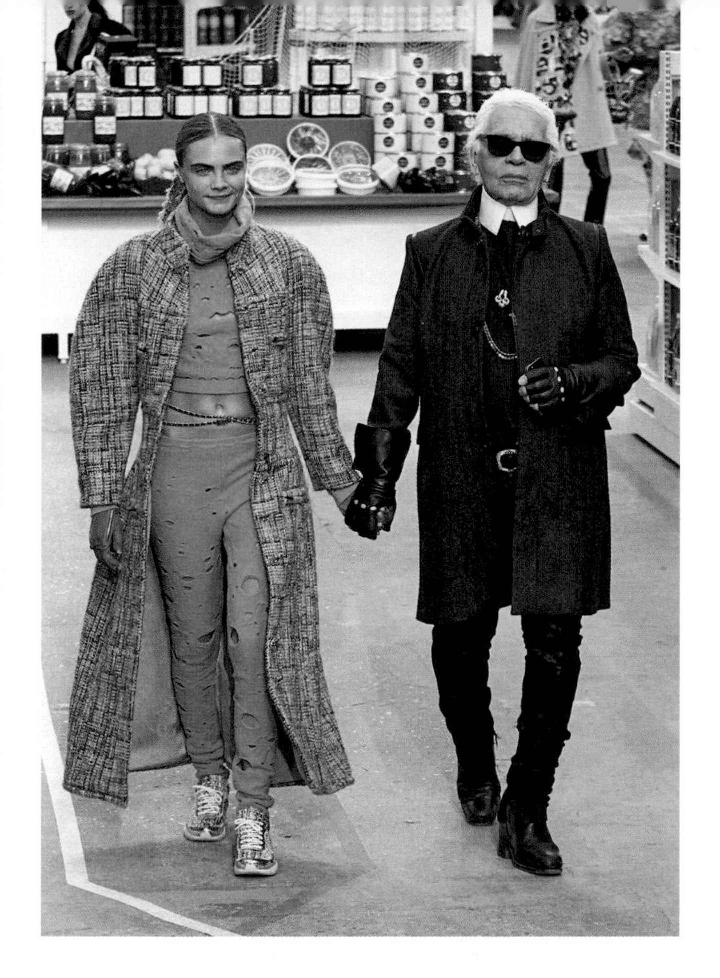

Opposite Chanel's signature jacket and staple use of tweed are reinterpreted in 2011. Lagerfeld was a master of reinvention with fabrics beautifully deconstructed, jackets resized to new proportions, and multiple layering. Masculine trousers were a mainstay of this collection worn with clumpy workman's boots.

Above At the autumn/winter 2014 catwalk show, models strolled the supermarket aisles as a nod to consumer society. Wearing sweetie necklaces and beautifully tailored tweed tracksuits, psychedelic iridescent trainers, with a classic Chanel handbag reinvented as a supermarket shopping basket.

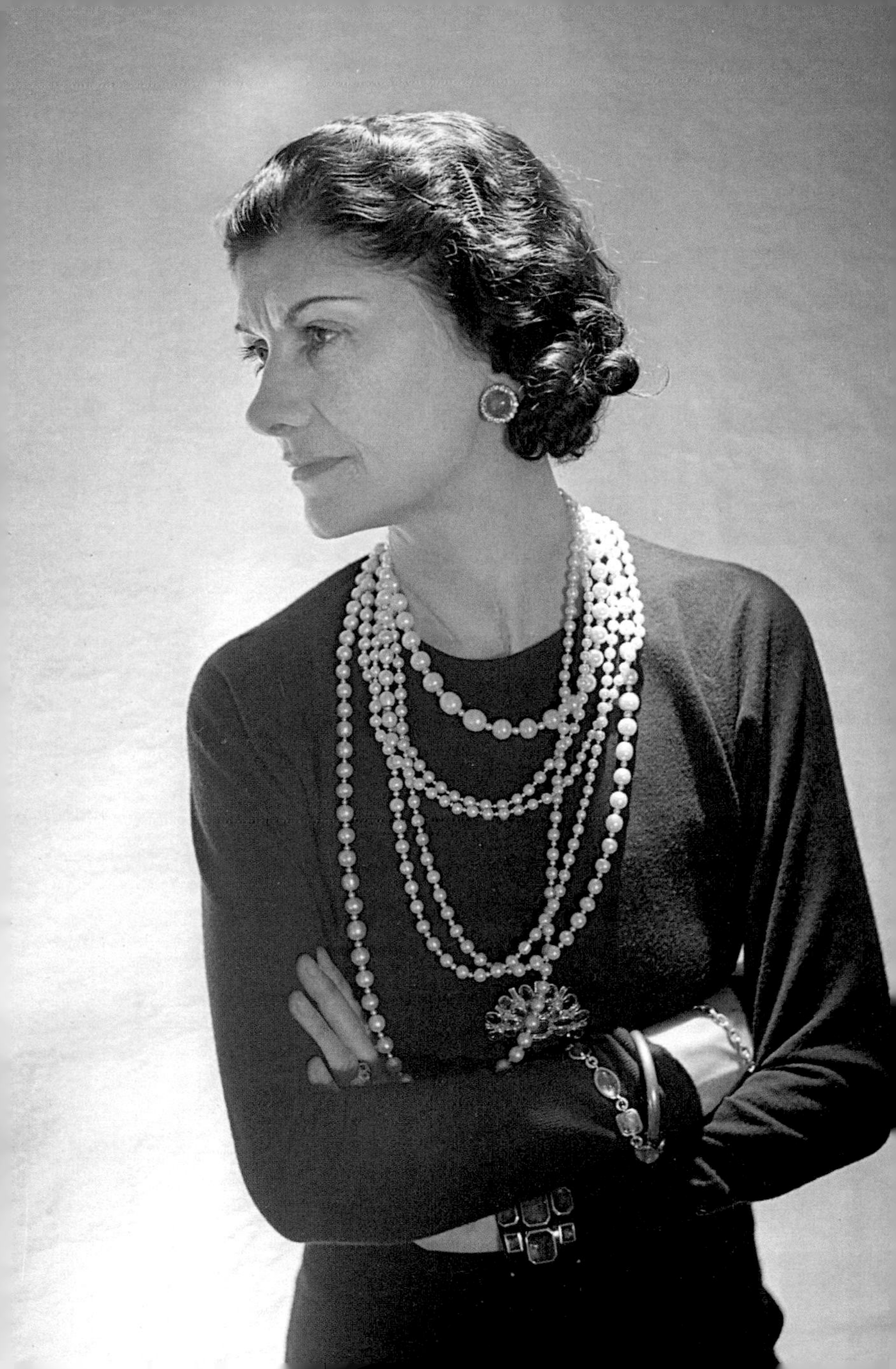

Accessories

Coco's unique style was always to champion what was of her own making: comfortable clothes devoid of decoration, short hair because it was easier to deal with, and costume jewellery because she found real gems ostentatious. In truth, the foundations of so many of her groundbreaking and original ideas can be traced back to her own desire to enhance women's lives in a practical and simplistic way that erred on classicism, never exaggeration.

From the beginning, Coco excelled in putting together a complete look. Later on, her repetitive use of the same accessories (bag, shoes, gold chains, pearls, camellia) visually provided a Chanel trademark that came to define the house style. The famous quilted handbag, made to be worn rather than carried, was born out of frustration – Chanel herself was always losing the bag she carried. The elegant shoes with a tiny heel and a black toe-cap were invented to trick the eye into seeing the foot as smaller than it really was; her love of pearls was entirely based on a belief that they could enhance the beauty of any woman by highlighting sun-tanned skin and capturing the light of sparkling eyes.

Today, women who cannot afford to buy a Chanel suit, choose Chanel's covetable accessories instead. These provide a more affordable and realistic way for a larger audience to buy into a brand that speaks volumes in the world of fashion.

Opposite The timeless vision of Gabrielle Chanel, as she will always be remembered, in a simple black dress adorned with jewellery. The pearl necklaces, which she was rarely photographed without, became as identifiable with her style as the Little Black Dress.

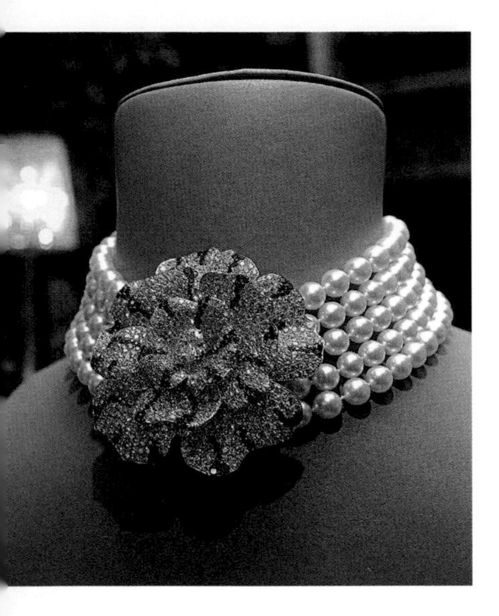

Left A black and white diamond Camellia brooch, attached to a five-strand pearl choker necklace, was shown at the Chanel Madison Avenue Boutique, New York, in September 2010.

Opposite A vision in white, catwalk model Natalia Vodianova wears strings of pearl and white bead necklaces, with feather flowers in her hair, for the spring/summer 2003 collection.

Jewellery

Chanel was, of course, a woman of impossible contradictions, and while she advocated the trend for extravagant paste, she herself was always loaded with the real thing, usually bestowed on her by an abundance of wealthy boyfriends. Her lover, the Grand Duke Dmitri Pavlovich, escaped the Russian Revolution with a string of Romanov pearls that he gave to Coco, and which she then copied for her customers, thus starting the trend for fake pearls. The Duke of Westminster also gave her fabulous jewels, initially to woo her, and then later to make amends for his regular infidelities.

Coco was rarely seen without her jewellery; she usually combined pieces from her own collection with the presents she received from the men in her life, and her ropes of pearls became something of a trademark. The luminosity of pearls captured the light, she felt, and gave a flattering glow to the skin and eyes. Like much that she did to democratize fashion, jewellery was not to be saved for impressive occasions. She made it contemporary and wore it casually and without grandeur, at the beach or slung over her tweeds to go hunting.

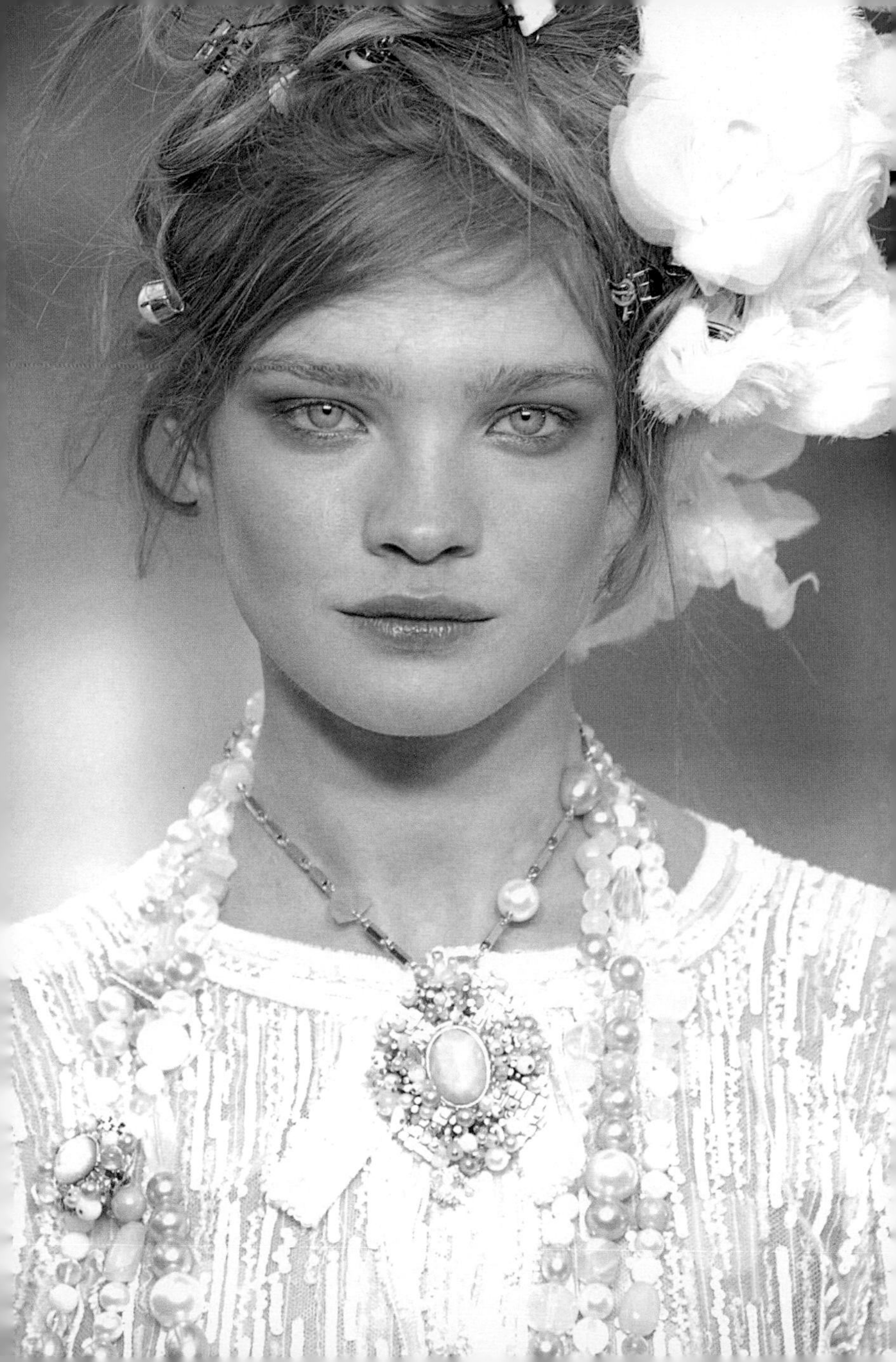

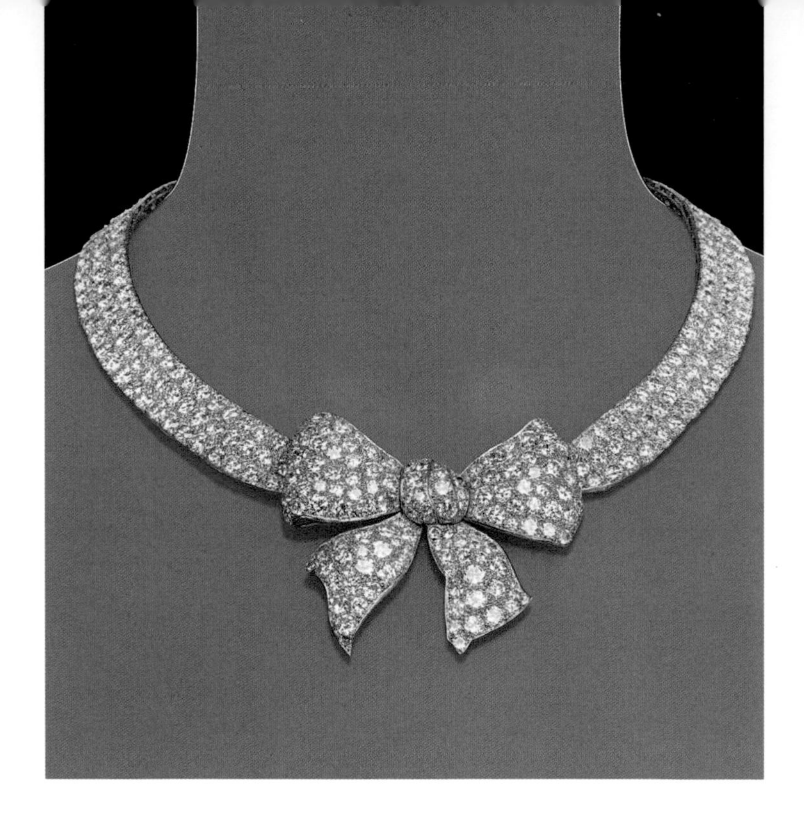

In November 1932 she surprised everyone with an invitation to view an exhibition of exquisite diamond jewellery that she had designed. At a time of financial depression, it was a controversial decision to work with priceless diamonds, taken by a woman who had previously shunned precious stones. But thousands came to her private rooms at Rue du Faubourg Saint-Honoré to look at Chanel's "Bijoux de Diamants", trailing past the glass cases that were guarded by policemen and which contained stunning pieces based on three main themes: knots, stars and feathers. The spectacular diamonds were estimated at the time to be worth 93 million francs! Lack of clasps and discreet mounts made the elaborate pieces cleverly interchangeable – a brooch could be worn as a hair ornament while a sunburst tiara could double up as a necklace. Two of the most memorable pieces from 1932 have recently been reissued: in 2007 the "Comète" necklace, made from

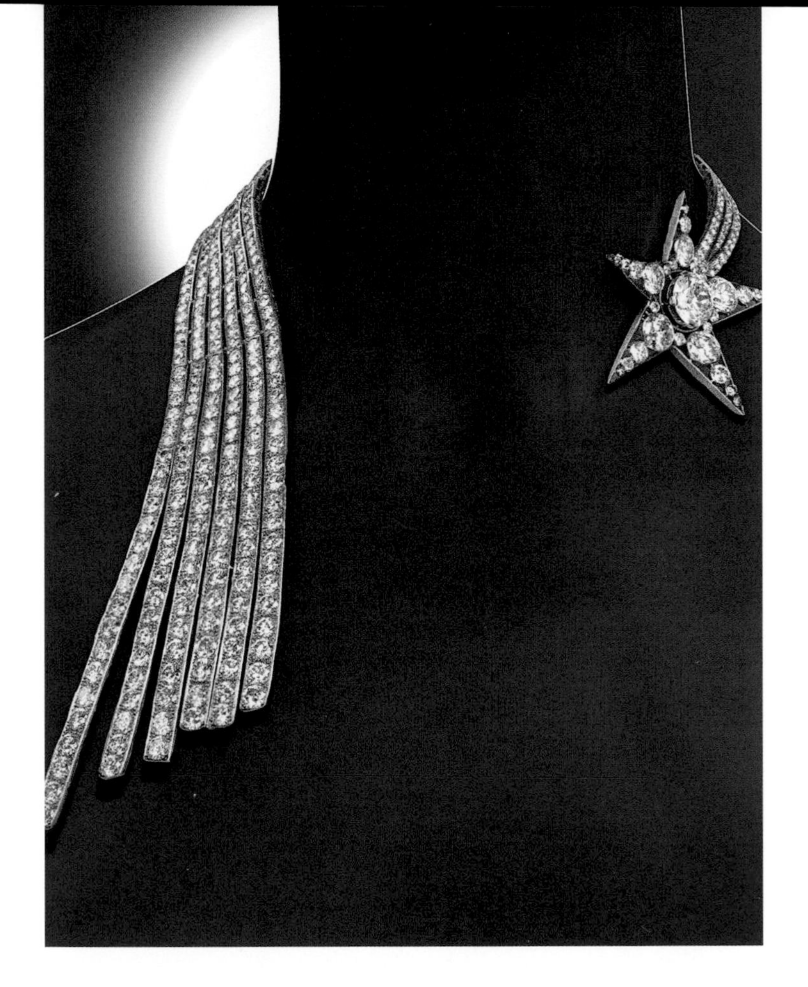

Opposite Chanel surprised everyone with her "Bijoux de Diamants" collection, which went on show from her own apartment in Paris in November 1932. This diamond necklace with ribbon bow mirrored Chanel's continual use of the motif throughout her long career.

Above The famous "Comète" diamond necklace, originally designed in 1932, was reissued in 2007 as a classic piece of jewellery. The necklace has no clasps or clips and is simply placed at the nape of the neck, with the diamond trail sitting on the opposite shoulder.

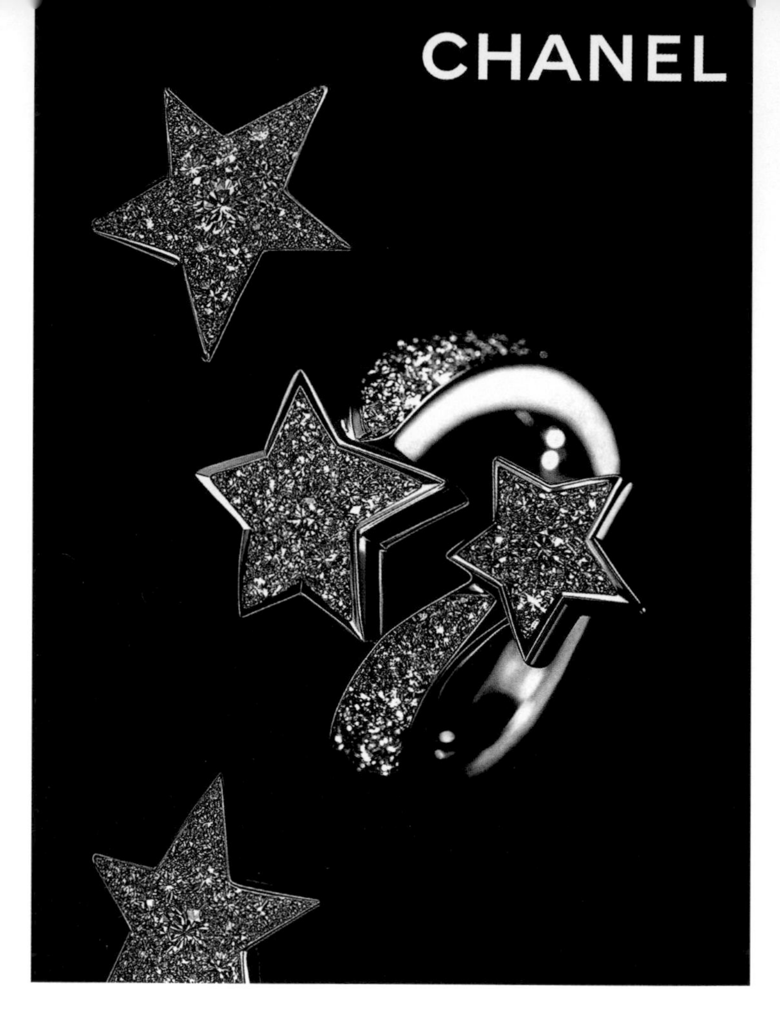

Above Based on the success of the original "Comète" collection (see previous page), new pieces have been designed using similar themes. This double-star ring and ear-studs, made from white gold and diamonds, is here shown in an advertising still for Chanel in 2001.

Opposite The Italian Duke, Fulco di Verdura, seen here with Chanel in Paris in 1937, designed some of her most memorable pieces of jewellery, including the baked enamel cuff, decorated with coloured stones in the form of the eight-point Maltese cross.

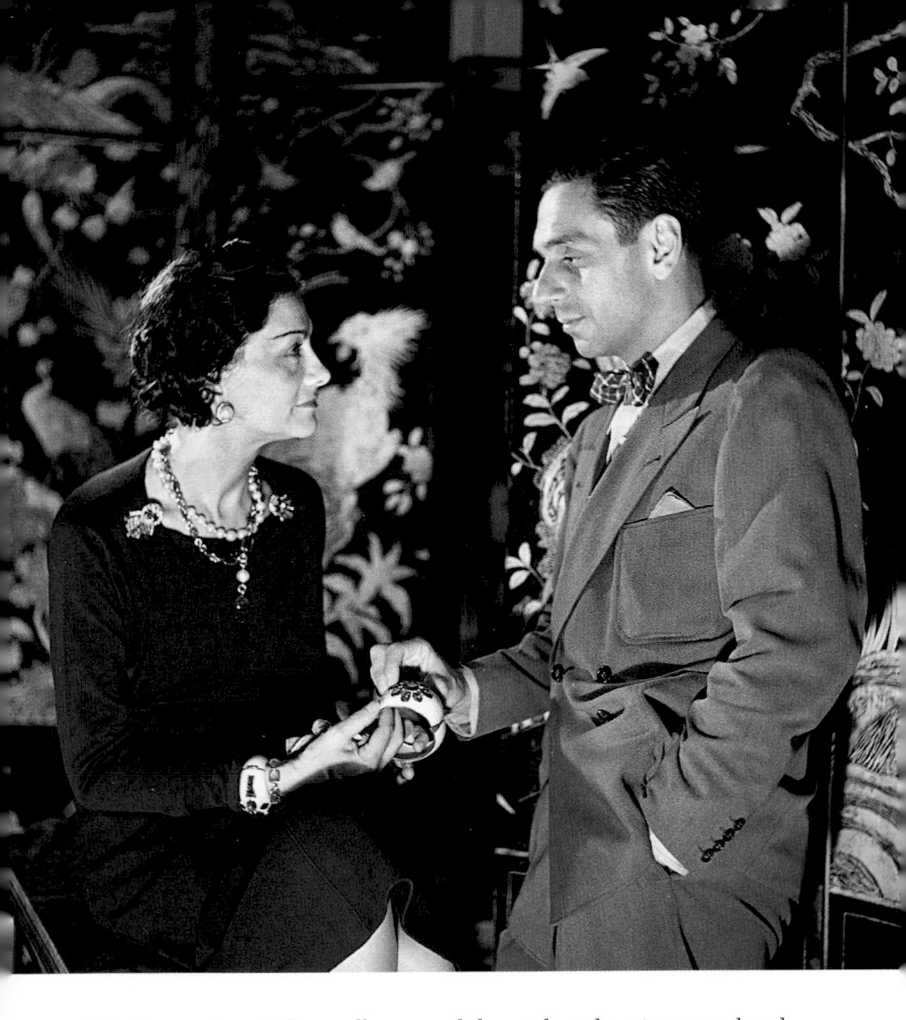

649 diamonds, sat like a collar around the neck, a shooting star placed on the collarbone with a cascading vapour trail designed to sit over the other shoulder; and the "Franges" bracelet, likewise inspired by the heavens, which had long diamond threads that fell over the hand.

These pieces she designed with Paul Iribe, an ambitious illustrator who was friends with Poiret and Cocteau, and with whom Coco had a serious romantic liaison, but he was not the only man to collaborate on her jewellery collections. For a short time she employed Count Étienne de Beaumont, and then another aristocrat, a Sicilian called Fulco Santo Stefano della Cerda, Duke of Verdura. The artistic Duke had originally wanted to become a painter, and had already worked with Coco as a textile designer before moving on to jewellery. Much of Chanel's most memorable work came from her collaboration with Verdura; they both shunned the boring "solitaire" rings that were popular at the time and instead took inspiration from the past. Verdura pioneered the revival of baked enamel, and taking motifs from medieval history he designed chunky bracelets that were studded with huge coloured stones in the form of the eight-pointed Maltese cross. The distinctive black-and-white cuffs became one of the most popular designs for Chanel; they were produced in many variations and Coco regularly wore one on each wrist. From 1924 onwards Chanel called on the expertise of an atelier called Maison Grippoix to execute her jewellery designs, using their skill with poured glass to create the boldly coloured baroque stones she loved. When Chanel relaunched in 1954 a young goldsmith called Robert Goosens developed the fashion for large pieces of artificial costume jewellery, which combined glass stones and pearls in a faux Renaissance gilt setting. Today the Goosens atelier has been bought out by the House of Chanel and continues to create exclusive handmade jewellery for them.

Opposite Chanel's signature use of pearls is taken to extremes in the early 1990s with this oversized choker, ropes of bracelets and large clip-on flower earrings made from pearls. Hanging from the neck is an outsize gilt cross, decorated with coloured glass and drop pearls. Yasmeen Ghauri was the face of Chanel, and the photograph was shot by Karl Lagerfeld.

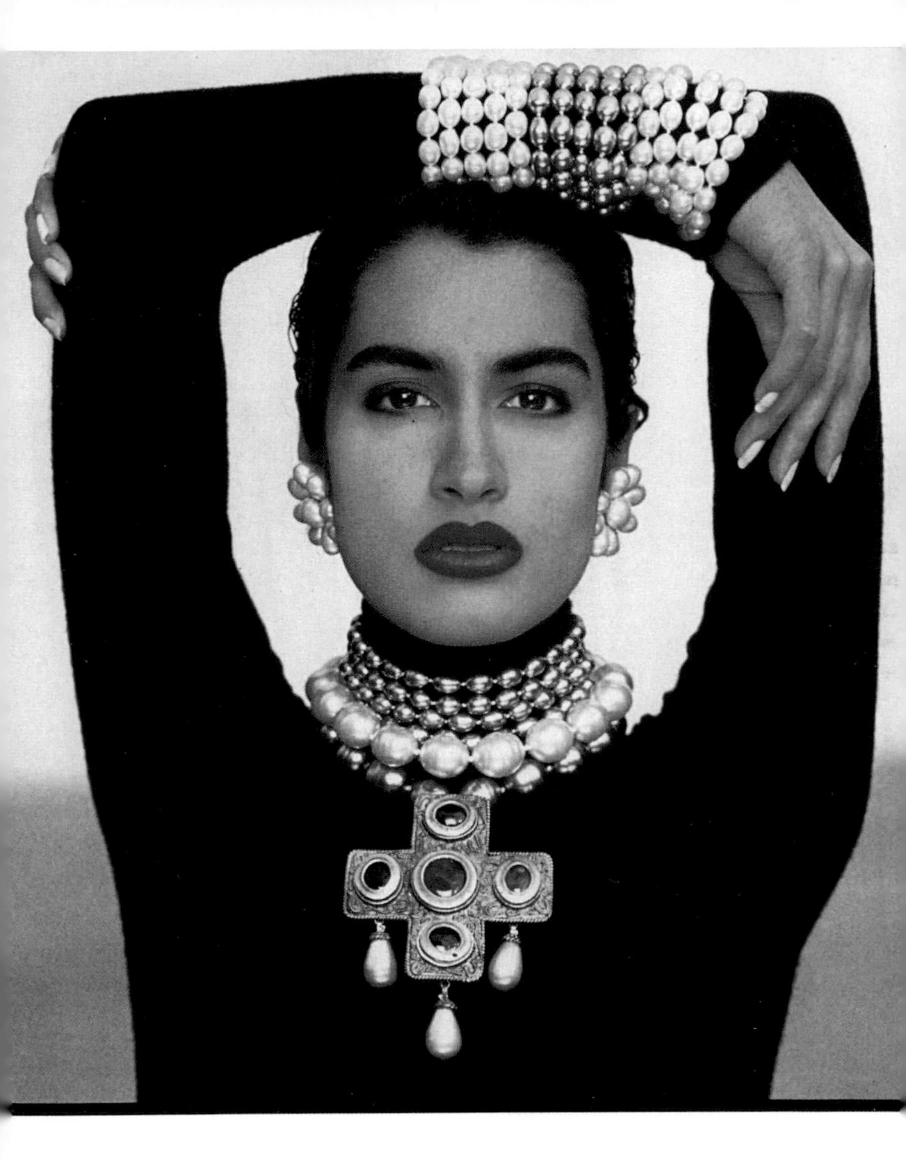

CHANEL

BOUTIQUE

26 OLD BOND STREET · LONDON W1

31 SLOANE STREET · LONDON SW1

The Chanel 2.55

In an era where a designer handbag has become the status symbol of a couture house, flaunted as a statement of wealth rather than taste, it is gratifying to find the original designer handbag still solidly aligned with the principles of its creator.

The Chanel handbag, like so much of Coco's fashion legacy, has become an instantly recognizable component of her iconography. The classic "2.55" was not the first bag Chanel produced – those came earlier in the 1930s – but it is the bag that has come to signify so much of Chanel's design philosophy within a single product. In much the same way that Coco used a number for her famous perfume, this bag was given a numerical name, which was derived from the month and year in which it was launched, February 1955. At a time when bags were usually held like a clutch, this was a new invention: designed to be worn over the shoulder rather than simply carried in the hands. The connection between Coco and her endlessly inventive design process can always be traced back to her own desire for simplicity and practicality. For her personal use she needed a bag that she wouldn't keep losing, so she added a shoulder strap, which left her hands free; she also wanted something that contained different compartments to hold her keys and cigarettes, so she conceived the idea of an inside pocket, a back flap, as well as a specific pocket for her lipstick so she would always have it to hand.

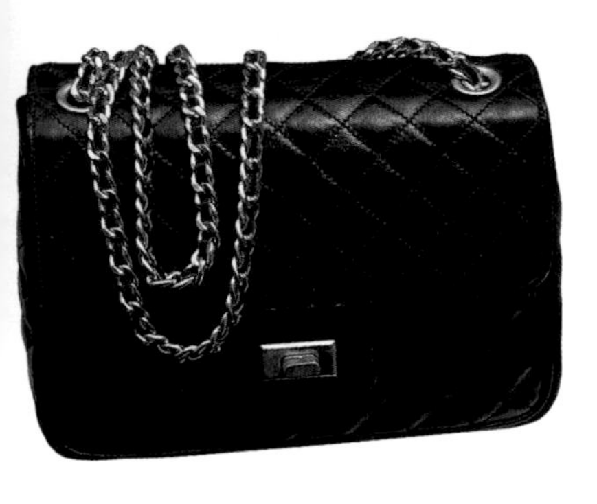

Left Designed by Chanel in 1955 for practical reasons – she was "weary of carrying my bags in my hand and losing them", this 1960s version of the famous 2.55 handbag remains true to the original design.

Opposite The overstitched quilted leather, chain shoulder strap and twist "Mademoiselle" lock are identifiable design details of the 2.55. This version is from 2005.

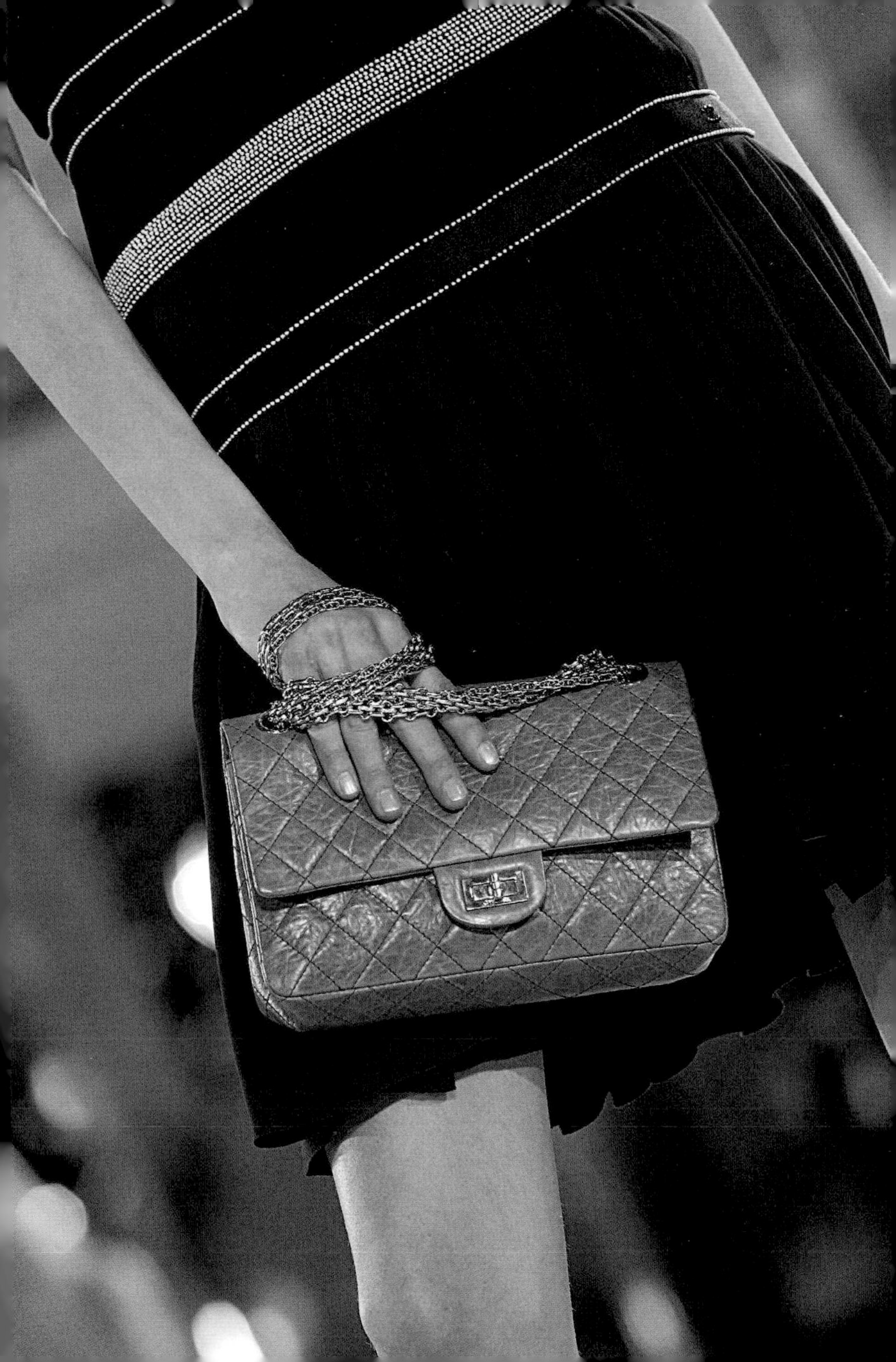

For the autumn/winter 1955 collection Chanel made two versions of her 2.55 bag, one intended for daywear, constructed from soft lambskin leather, which was strong but supple, and an evening version made from silk jersey. The distinctive Chanel quilting, or *matelassé*, was created by diamond-shaped top-stitching, meticulously sewn on top of the fabric and thought to have originated from the quilted fabric worn by the young stable lads that Coco met when she learnt to ride at Étienne Balsan's estate. The final component part was the metal chain woven through with leather, which may also have come from her memories of early days in the stables, as the juxtaposition of leather and metal is closely reminiscent of bridles and harnesses. There was an alternative metal strap made from flattened oval links (similar to the chains she used on the hems of her jackets to ensure they hung correctly). Both had visual and practical merits, and were strong enough to turn a handbag into an item that was wearable and useful. The front clasp was not adorned with the double-C insignia; instead it was a twist lock called the "Mademoiselle Lock".

Karl Lagerfeld reissued the bag in February 2005, as a commemorative product to celebrate the fiftieth anniversary of its debut, and has since continued to reinvent the 2.55 for each collection. Fabrics may be more inventive, colours more exotic, and dimensions deliberately extreme, but attention to detail never wavers. The Chanel signature turnlock closure and ID card with a unique number placed inside an interior pocket both guarantee the authenticity of each individual handbag.

Right Czech model Karolina Kurkova, in a British advertising campaign from 2004, carries a bright pink quilted leather tote bag. Lagerfeld often parodies the Chanel insignia, subverting and reinventing, as here where the discreet double-C logo is blown up to exaggerated proportions.

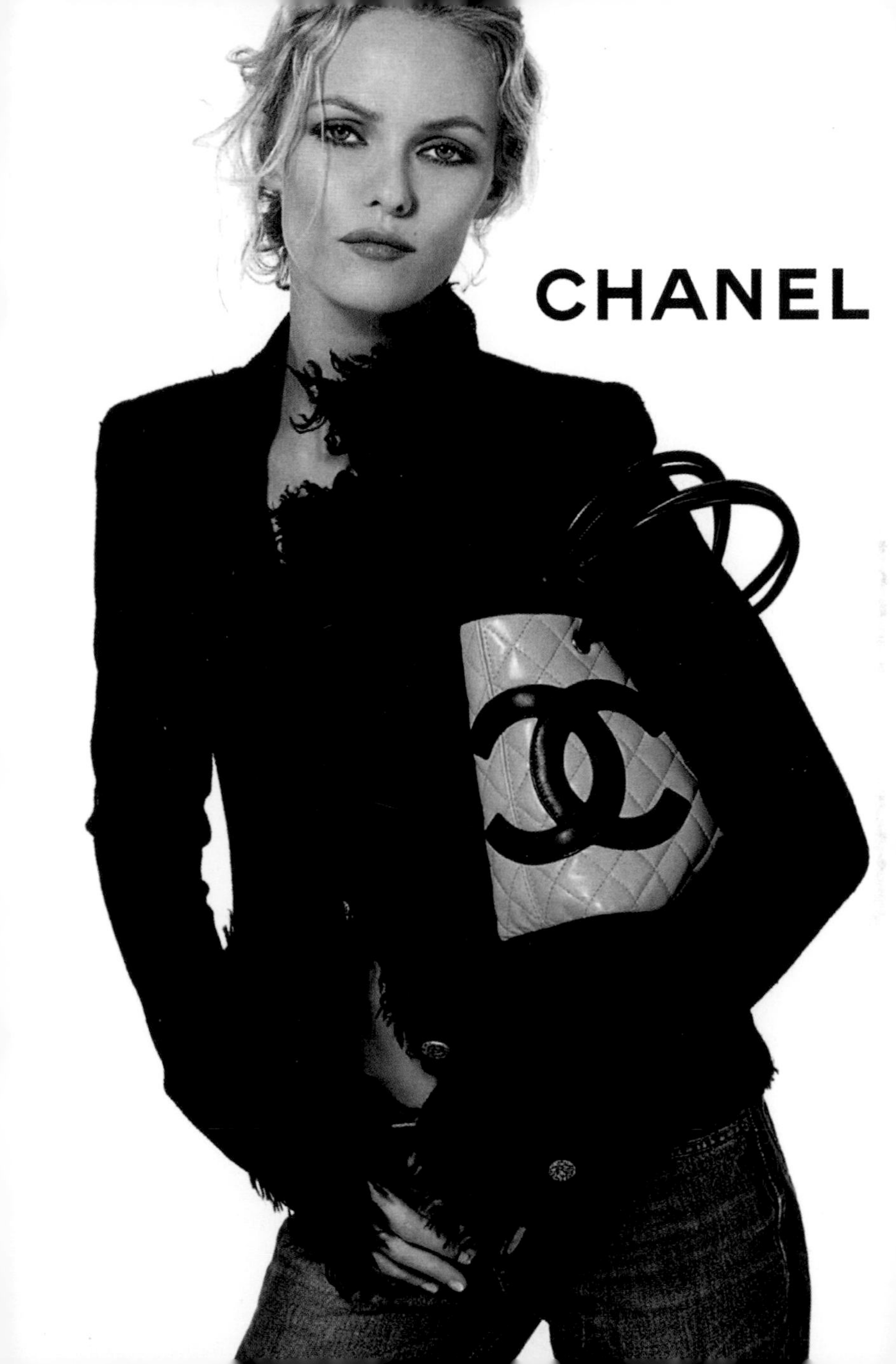
CHANEL

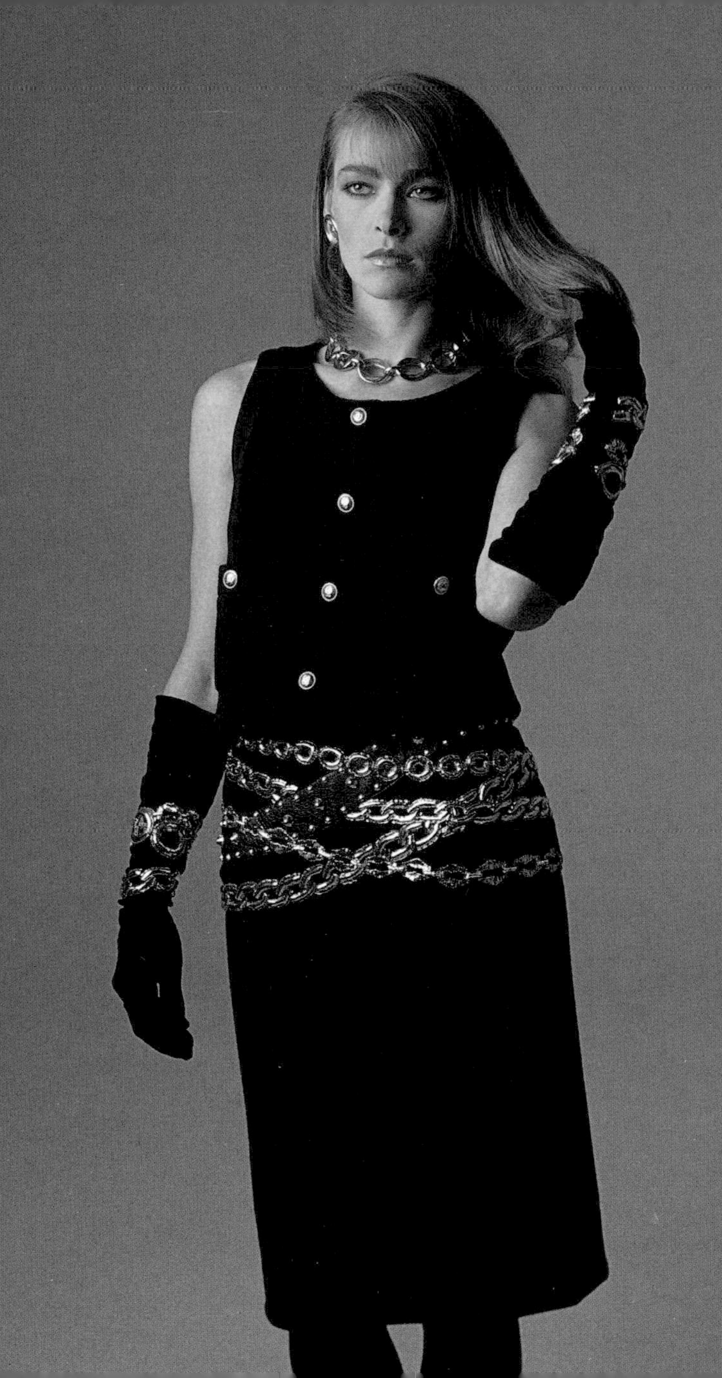

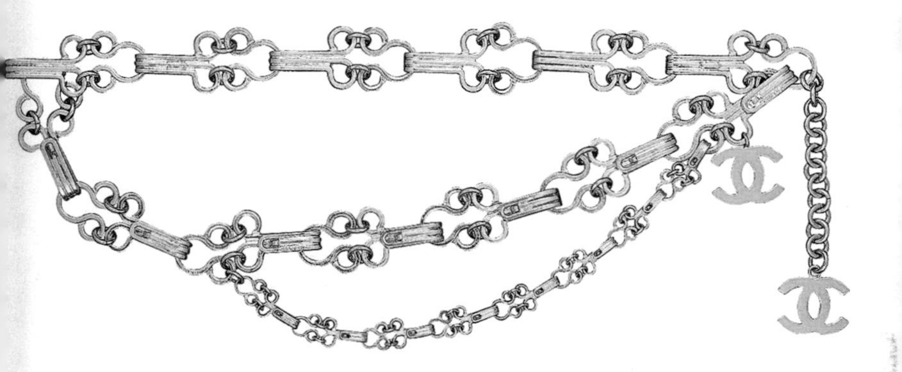

Opposite A witty reinvention of the iconic chains used for belts and handbag straps by Chanel, Lagerfeld here embroiders multiple chunky chains in a trompe-l'oeil style onto black suede evening gloves and a black jersey dress. Worn with gold earrings, a large gold chain necklace and gilt buttons on the dress front, the excessive theme from 1985 is indicative of the era.

Above A fine gold chain belt comprised of different sizes and types of decorative chain features the double-C insignia on the fastening.

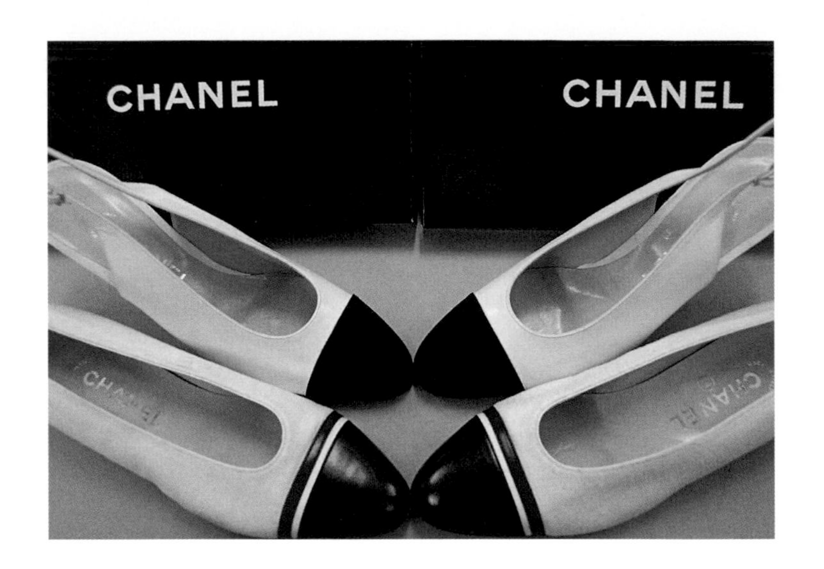
CHANEL
CHANEL

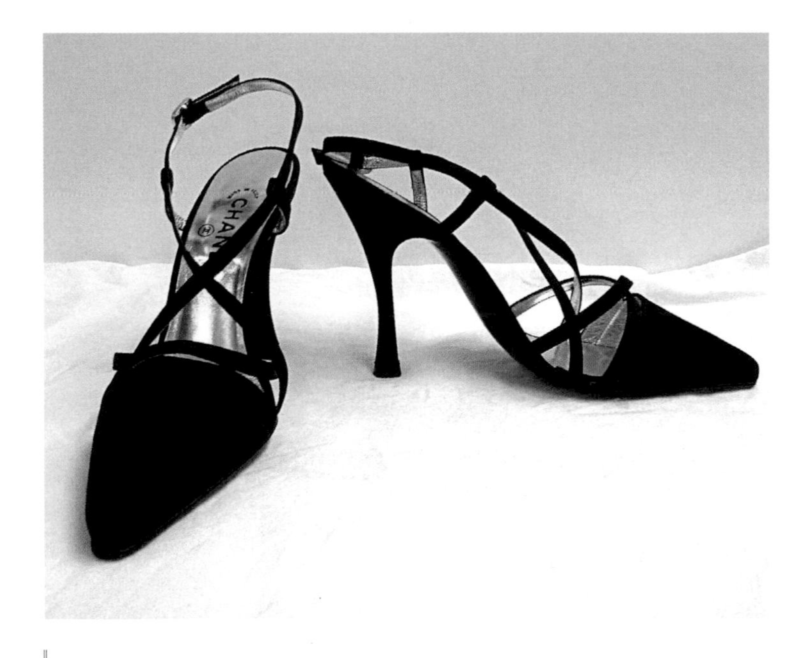

Shoes

There are pictures of Coco from as early as 1929 wearing flat shoes with a dark band across the toe and a neat little strap across the foot. Although she is unlikely to have designed this particular shoe herself, she went on to make the two-tone shoe her own. The first and now classic of these, which appeared in 1957, was very simple, elegant and comfortable to wear. Made by the house shoemaker, Monsieur Massaro, in nude leather to complement skin tone and visually elongate the length of the leg, the slingback slipper had very fine straps and a rounded black toe-cap that cleverly foreshortened the length of the foot. On a practical note, Coco was also aware that a shoe made entirely from pale leather would show every mark, and the invention of the dark toe would help to hide the odd dirty scuff!

Opposite top The classic two-tone cap-toe slingback style, with a small kitten heel, was the prototype for endless variations, like these flat ballet pumps with a thin red leather stripe.

Opposite bottom Lagerfeld has extended the Chanel shoe range to include every type of footwear, from jelly flip-flops to après-ski moon boots. These elegant slingbacks, made in soft black suede with crossover straps, date from the 1995 collection.

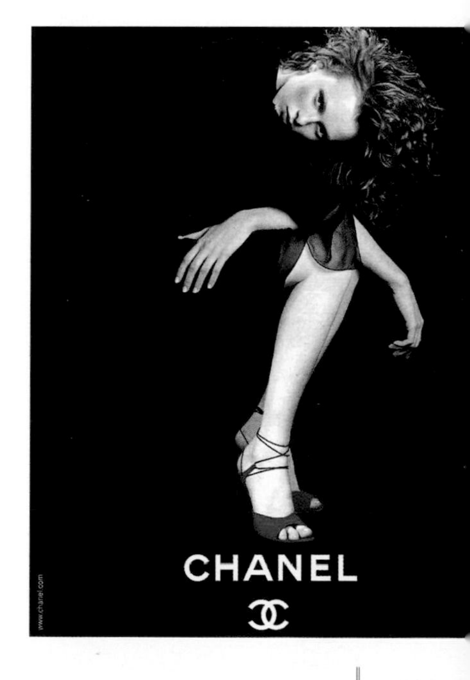

Right British model Karen Elson advertising Chanel shoes in a magazine campaign in 2006.

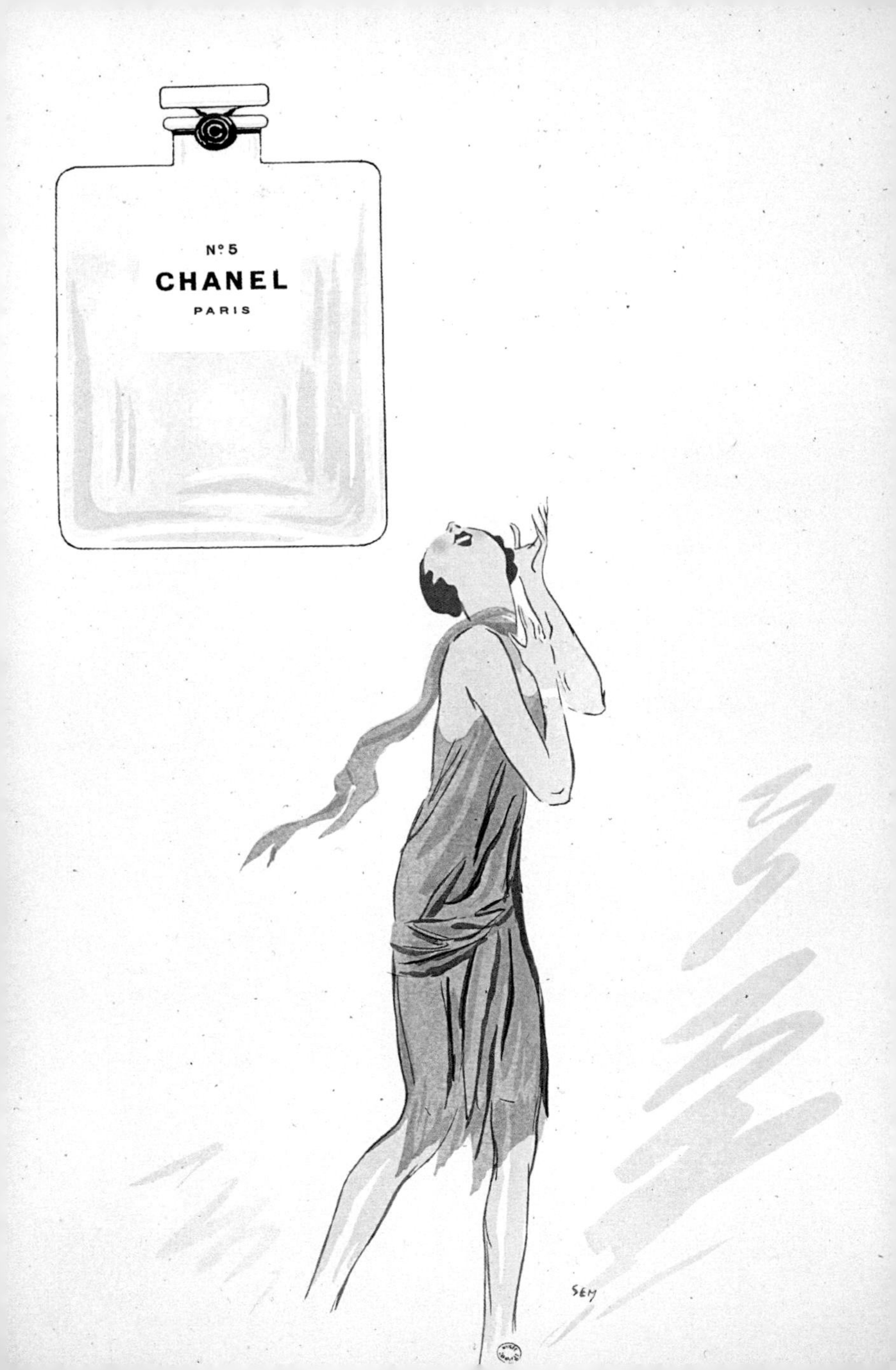

N°5
CHANEL
PARIS
SEM

Beauty & Fragrance

"...that is what I was waiting for. A perfume like nothing else. A woman's perfume, with the scent of a woman"

Coco Chanel, on *Chanel No.5*

Chanel No. 5 is the most famous perfume in the world, and it remains the greatest success in the ongoing story of a woman determined to leave her mark on the twentieth century. Coco loved perfume and had an exceptional sense of smell – she often quoted the poet Paul Valéry: "A woman who doesn't wear perfume has no future"– and so it's surprising she waited until she was nearly 40 to launch her own fragrance in 1921.

Chanel was not the first couturier to diversify into the market, but unlike the others, who relied on romantic flower potions, she was the first to create a secret cocktail of more than 80 natural and synthetic ingredients, and then present it in a minimalist pharmaceutical-type bottle labelled only with her name and lucky number. The original formula was created by Ernest Beaux, an eminent French perfumier. He had a factory in Grasse where Coco spent many days suggesting different combinations of ingredients until she was finally presented with a series of miniature vials to test, labelled Nos. 1–24; Coco settled on bottle No. 5. There has always been speculation about the significance of the name (some say it came from her astrological sign, Leo, the fifth in the zodiac), but it is most likely she chose this clinical name to set herself apart from her competitors, who were marketing floral scents with evocative names. Beaux expressed his fear that with so many ingredients, jasmine being the most prominent but also neroli, ylang-ylang, sandalwood and May

Left The first advertisement for *Chanel No. 5,* circa 1924, featured the image of the designer herself. Typical of the Chanel ethos and the machine-age ideals of modernism, the name itself was abstract, the bottle square-cut and masculine, and the design and advertisements lacked the usual flourishes and flowers associated with perfume.

rose, the perfume would be very expensive. Without hesitation Coco declared: "I want to make the most expensive perfume in the world."

She took the samples back to Paris, atomised the shop and fitting rooms with the scent, gave tester vials to her best customers, and almost immediately found she had hit upon a winning formula. The perfume sold from the shops in Rue Cambon, Deauville, Biarritz and Cannes, but Coco, always adept at grabbing the opportune moment, wanted more. She approached Théophile Bader, the owner of Galeries Lafayette, with the idea that he should sell her perfume in his department store. Knowing that he would require greater quantities of stock than Ernest Beaux could produce, Bader introduced Coco to Pierre and Paul Wertheimer, a meeting that was to result in a lifelong business association that changed all their lives. The brothers, who owned one of France's largest cosmetic and fragrance companies, Les Parfumeries Bourjois, agreed to fully finance production, distribution and marketing for all her beauty products, and in 1924 they set up a company called Les Parfums Chanel, giving Coco just ten per cent of the company. It was a decision she came to regret, as the profits from the business that bore her name escalated into millions, but despite many legal wrangles over the years, the Wertheimers (who to this day have kept Chanel in private ownership) were reliable business partners, and ultimately responsible for the vast wealth that allowed Coco to be financially secure and to live independently.

Ernest Beaux invented new fragrances for Chanel – *Cuir de Russie* (1924), *Bois des Îles* (1926) and *Gardenia* (1927) – but they were never to equal the success of *No. 5*, which came to be associated with the most beautiful women in the world. Other fragrances included the first men's cologne *Pour Monsieur*, in 1955, and in 1970, just before Chanel's death, *No.19*, which was aimed at a younger audience. The "nose" behind the House of Chanel today is Jacques Polge, who has continued to expand the line with many new fragrances including *Allure* (1996), *Coco Mademoiselle* (2001) and *Chance Eau Tendre* (2010).

Right By 2001, *Chanel No. 5* was seen as a symbol of idealized womanhood and advertised by visuals that linger on the glamour and beauty of Hollywood. In most of the ads, the bottle is transparent, in line with the original concept of the "invisible" bottle.

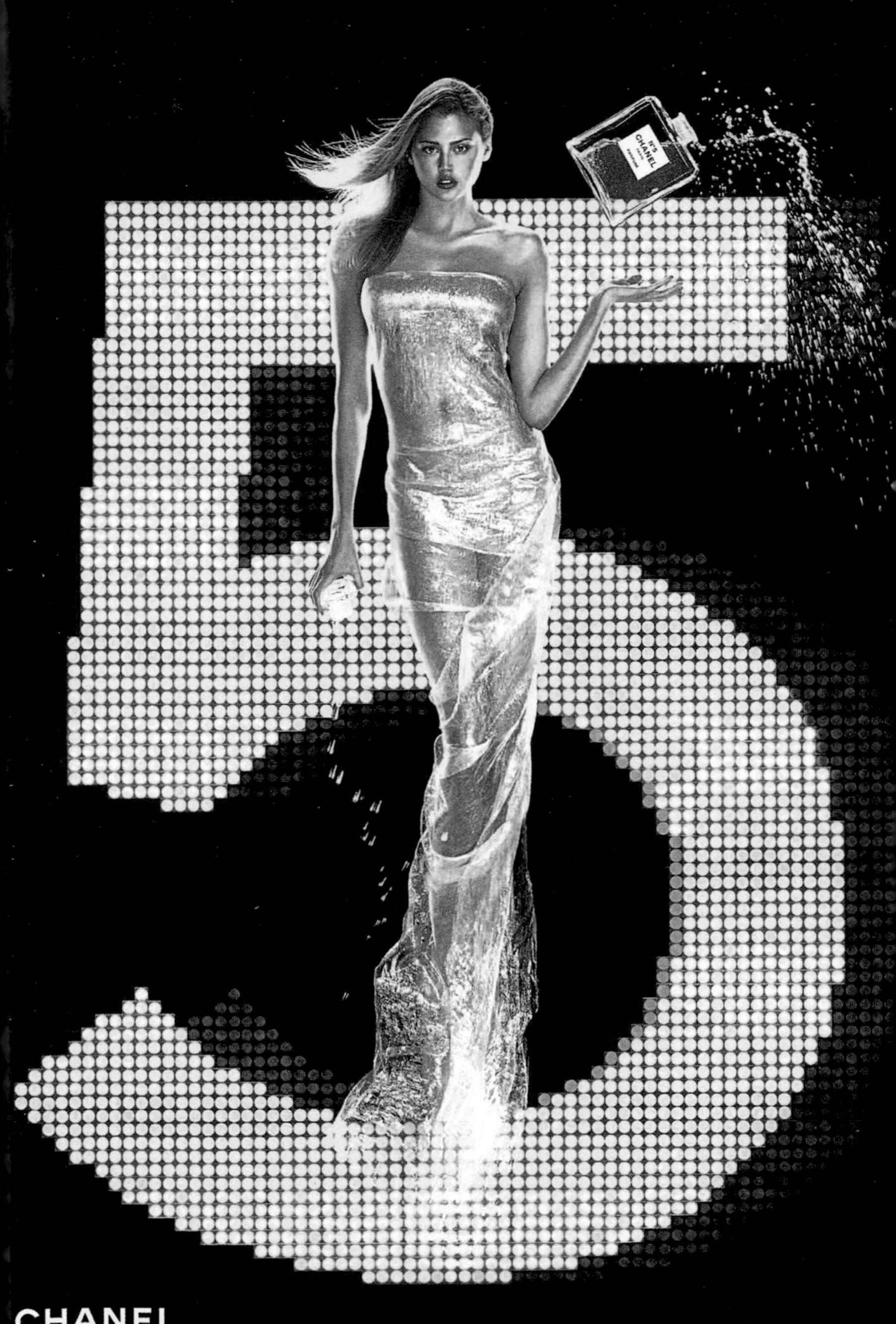
N°5
CHANEL
CHANEL

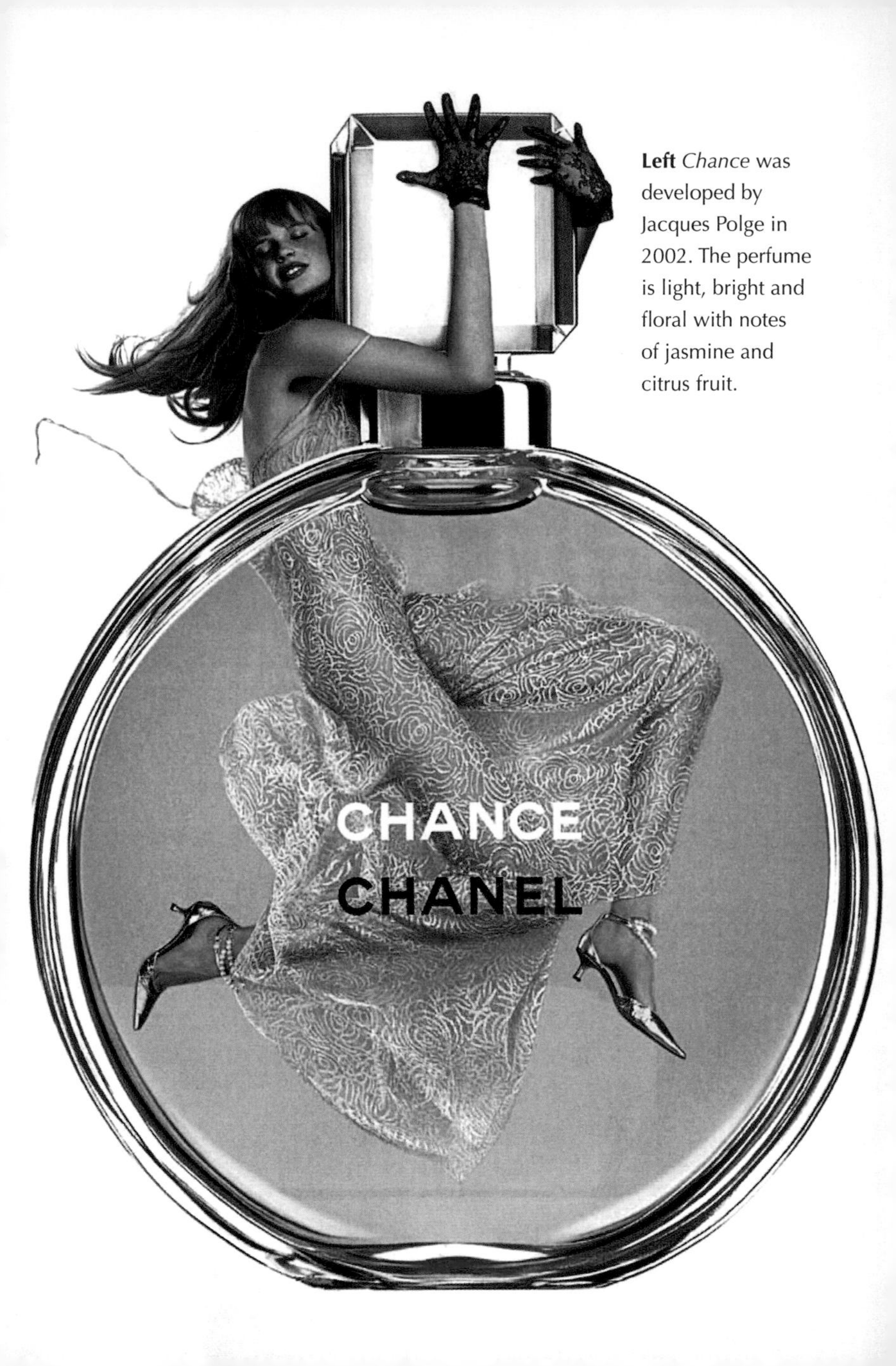

Left *Chance* was developed by Jacques Polge in 2002. The perfume is light, bright and floral with notes of jasmine and citrus fruit.

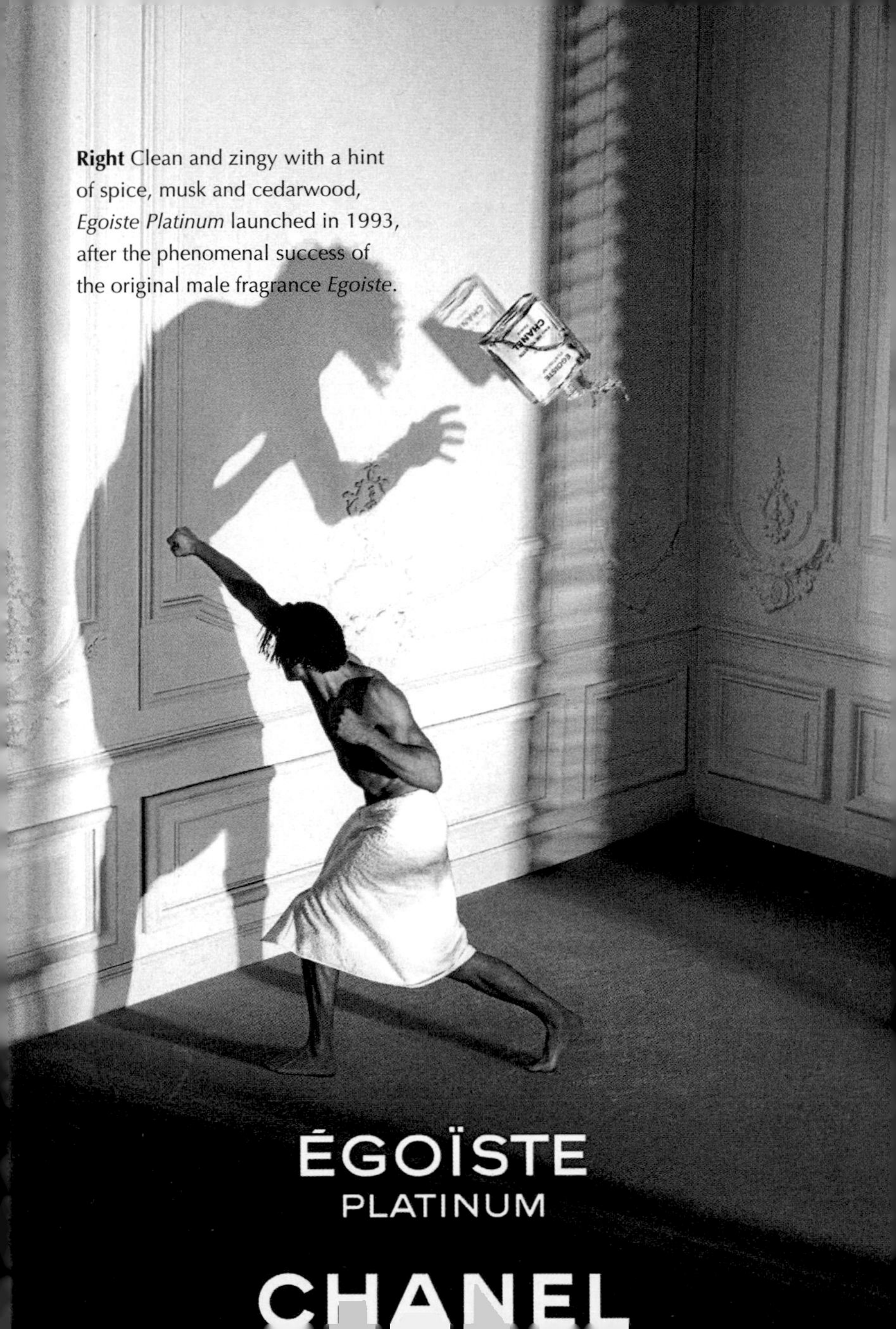

Right Clean and zingy with a hint of spice, musk and cedarwood, *Egoiste Platinum* launched in 1993, after the phenomenal success of the original male fragrance *Egoiste*.

ÉGOÏSTE
PLATINUM

CHANEL

Cosmetics & Skincare

Coco adored make-up: she thought it pretentious to leave the house barefaced, and was rarely seen without charcoal eyes and a slash of vermilion across the mouth. In 1924 she made an early blood-red lipstick for herself. Encased in a mother-of-pearl tube, this went on to become the prototype for countless shades of Chanel red lipstick. As with her instinctive requirements for functional clothes, her own beauty needs influenced her commercial products. From 1930 onwards, Coco produced an expanding range of beauty products including face powders, moisturizing oils, perfumed talcum powder and oil for sunbathing. All these products were marketed in ultra-modern black cases, with chic black-and-white packaging stamped with the double-C logo. Today the black packaging of the brand is instantly recognizable around the world as the creative team at Chanel combine scientific innovation with cutting-edge technology to produce a flawless range of beauty products. The house legacy remains intact: to provide women with products that enhance natural beauty and also cultivate individual differences, with the ultimate aim of being as unique as Coco.

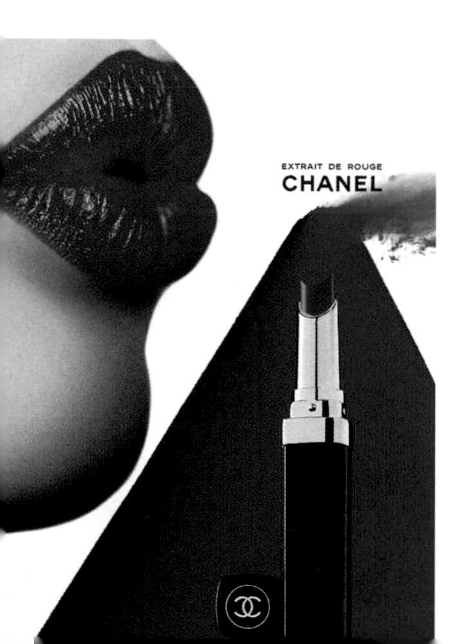

Left A magazine advert for classic red lipstick Rouge Extreme, 1997. Coco Chanel was never seen without her trademark vermilion red lips, and the legacy remains today with endless shades of rouge created for each new collection.

Opposite Chanel began the bodycare range with the launch of perfumed soap for the "toilet and the bath", infused with the fragrance of *Chanel No. 5*, the most famous perfume in the world, seen here in a 1940s advertisement.

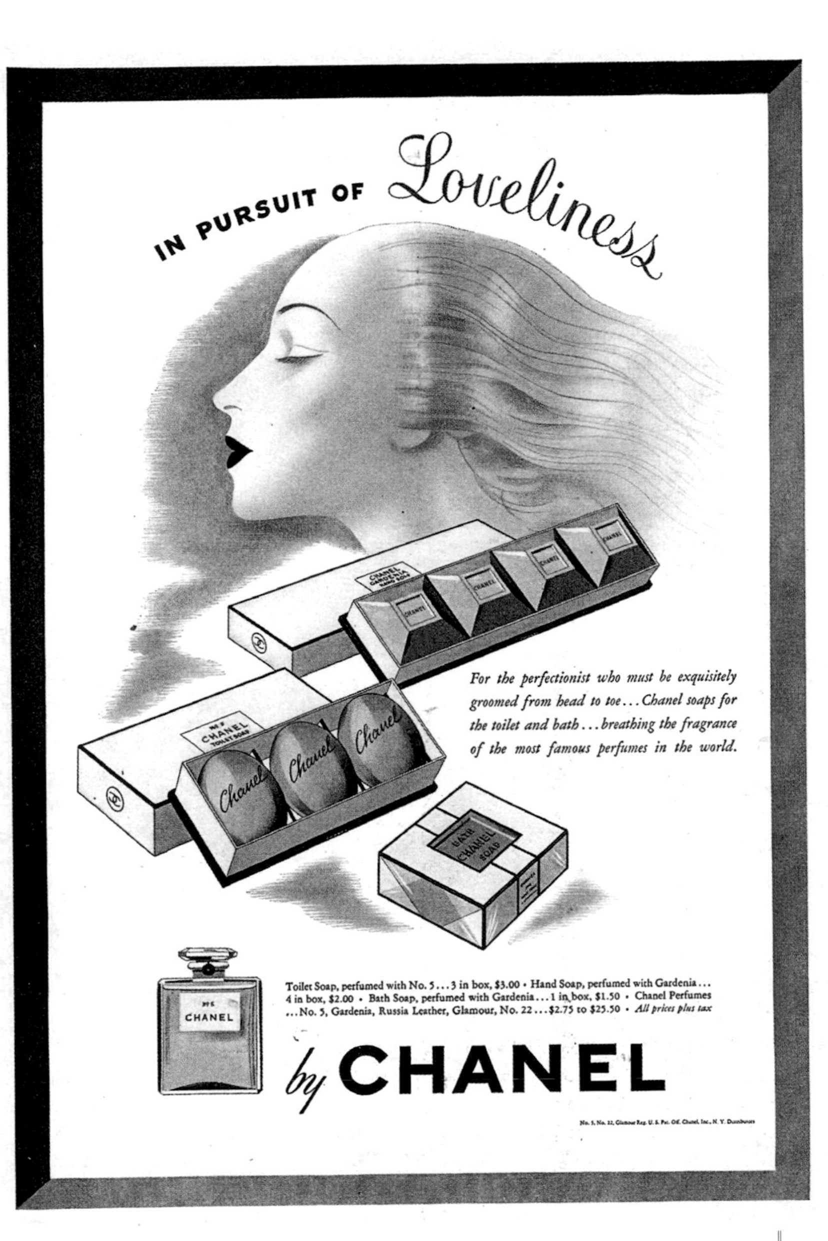
IN PURSUIT OF Loveliness
CHANEL GARDENIA HAND SOAP
CHANEL
No 5 CHANEL TOILET SOAP
Chanel
BATH CHANEL SOAP
For the perfectionist who must be exquisitely groomed from head to toe... Chanel soaps for the toilet and bath... breathing the fragrance of the most famous perfumes in the world.
Nº 5 CHANEL
Toilet Soap, perfumed with No. 5... 3 in box, $3.00 • Hand Soap, perfumed with Gardenia... 4 in box, $2.00 • Bath Soap, perfumed with Gardenia... 1 in box, $1.50 • Chanel Perfumes ...No. 5, Gardenia, Russia Leather, Glamour, No. 22... $2.75 to $25.50 • All prices plus tax
by CHANEL
No. 5, No. 22, Glamour Reg. U. S. Pat. Off. Chanel, Inc., N. Y. Distributors

Resources

Baudot, Francois, *Chanel: Fashion Memoir*, Thames and Hudson, 1996.

Bott, Daniele, *Chanel: Collections and Creations*, Thames and Hudson, 2007.

Charles-Roux, Edmonde, *Chanel and Her World*, Weidenfeld and Nicolson, 1982.

De La Haye, Amy, Tobin, Shelley, *Chanel: The Couturière at Work*, V&A Publications, 1994.

Madsen, Axel, *Coco Chanel: A Biography*, Bloomsbury, 1990.

Morand, Paul, *The Allure of Chanel*, Pushkin Press, 2008.

Picardie, Justine, *Coco Chanel: The Legend and the Life*, Harper Collins, 2011.

Wallach, Janet, *Chanel: Her Style and Her Life*, Mitchell Beazley, 1999.

Index

Page numbers in *italic* indicate images.

Acknowledgments

Author's Acknowledgements

Thanks go to the superb collections from the Victoria & Albert Museum, the Arizona Costume Institute at the Phoenix Art Museum, Kerry Taylor Auctions, and to Clare Hutton for her invaluable research. Special thanks to my fabulous editor Lisa Dyer and all the team at Carlton Books.

Picture Credits

The publishers would like to thank the following sources for their kind permission to reproduce the pictures in this book.

Key: t=Top, b=Bottom, c=Centre, l=Left and r=Right

Akg-Images: 8, 20, /Paul Almasy: 37–38, /Hervé Champollion: 10, /Ullstein bild: 22
Image Courtesy of The Advertising Archives: 47, 49, 134, 137, 141, 145, 149,150, 151, 152, 153
Bridgeman Images: /Archives Chamet: 50, /Bibliotheque des Arts Decoratifs, Paris, France/Archives Charmet: 13, 14
Camera Press: /John Launois: 87, /Petra: 143, /Mitchell Sams: 131, /J.L.Sieff /Queen: 86
Getty Images: 130, /AFP: 70, /Bettmann: 54, 69r, 96, 104-105, /Stephane Cardinale/People Avenue: 2, 110-11, /Stephane Cardinale/Sygma: 109, 139, /Condé Nast Archive: 35, 41, 53, 77, 92-93, 142, /Julio Donoso/ Sygma: 123, /Gamma-Rapho: 90, 94, /Hulton Archive: 12, 26, 44, 45, 58, /Massimo Listri: 80, 113, /Christopher Morries/VII: 4-5, /Thierry Orban: 108, /Time & Life Pictures: 57, 88, /Pierre Vaulthey/Sygma: 106, /Roger Viollet: 18–19, 128 /WWD/Condé Nast Archive: 126
Kerry Taylor Auctions: 30, 40, 78, 82r, 114, 116, 120, 144t
Mary Evans Picture Library: 21, /Interfoto: 119, 122, /National Magazine Company: 59, 66, 67, 71, 72, 73, 160, /Rue des Archives: 15, 56
Collection of Phoenix Art Museum: /Gift of Mrs Kelly Ellman, Photo by Ken

Howie: 124, /Gift of Mrs. Wesson Seyburn, Photo by Ken Howie: 32
Photo 12: /Wolf Tracer Archive: 63
Réunion des Musées Nationaux: /©BnF, Dist. RMN /Séeberger Collection: 17, /
Ministère de la Culture-Médiathèque du Patrimoine, Dist. RMN: 64
Shuterstock: 126, 127 /The Art Archive: /Collection Dagli Orti: 138, /
The Kobal Collection: /Goldwyn /United Artists: 61
Sharok Hatami: 85, 91, 95, 97, 99, 100, 101, /Marco Madeira/
Moviestore Collection: 62, /Geoff Wilkinson: 112
Topfoto.co.uk: 3, 74, 102, /The Granger Collection: 1, 6, 16, 46, /
Roger Viollet: 11, 24, 52, 82l, 84, 115, 135, /Roger Viollet /R.Briant
et L.Degrâces / Galliera: 42, 43, /Roger Viollet /R.Briant et P. Ladet/
Galliera: 27, /Roger Viollet / L.Degrâces et P.Ladet / Galliera: 38, /
Roger Viollet /Phillipe Ladet et Claire Pignol /Galliera: 29, /Roger
Viollet /Musée Carnavalet: 146, /Ullsteinbild: 98, 132, 133
Victoria & Albert Museum/V&A Images – All rights Reserved: 23, 31,
69l, 79, 81, 118, 121, 125, 144b

Every effort has been made to acknowledge correctly and contact the source and/or copyright holder of each picture and Welbeck Publishing apologizes for any unintentional errors or omissions, which will be, corrected in future editions of this book.

Page 1 *Portrait of Mademoiselle Chanel,* 1923, by Marie Laurencin. Chanel commissioned the portrait when the pair met working for the Ballets Russes, but then turned down the finished portrait as she did not think it a fair representation.

Page 2 Detail from Chanel spring/summer 2007 ready-to-wear collection by Karl Lagerfeld, with diamond Coco brooch and camellia cuff bracelet.

Overleaf Illustration of a Chanel dress by Jean Cocteau 1939, with red, white and blue cornflowers and poppies on the bodice.

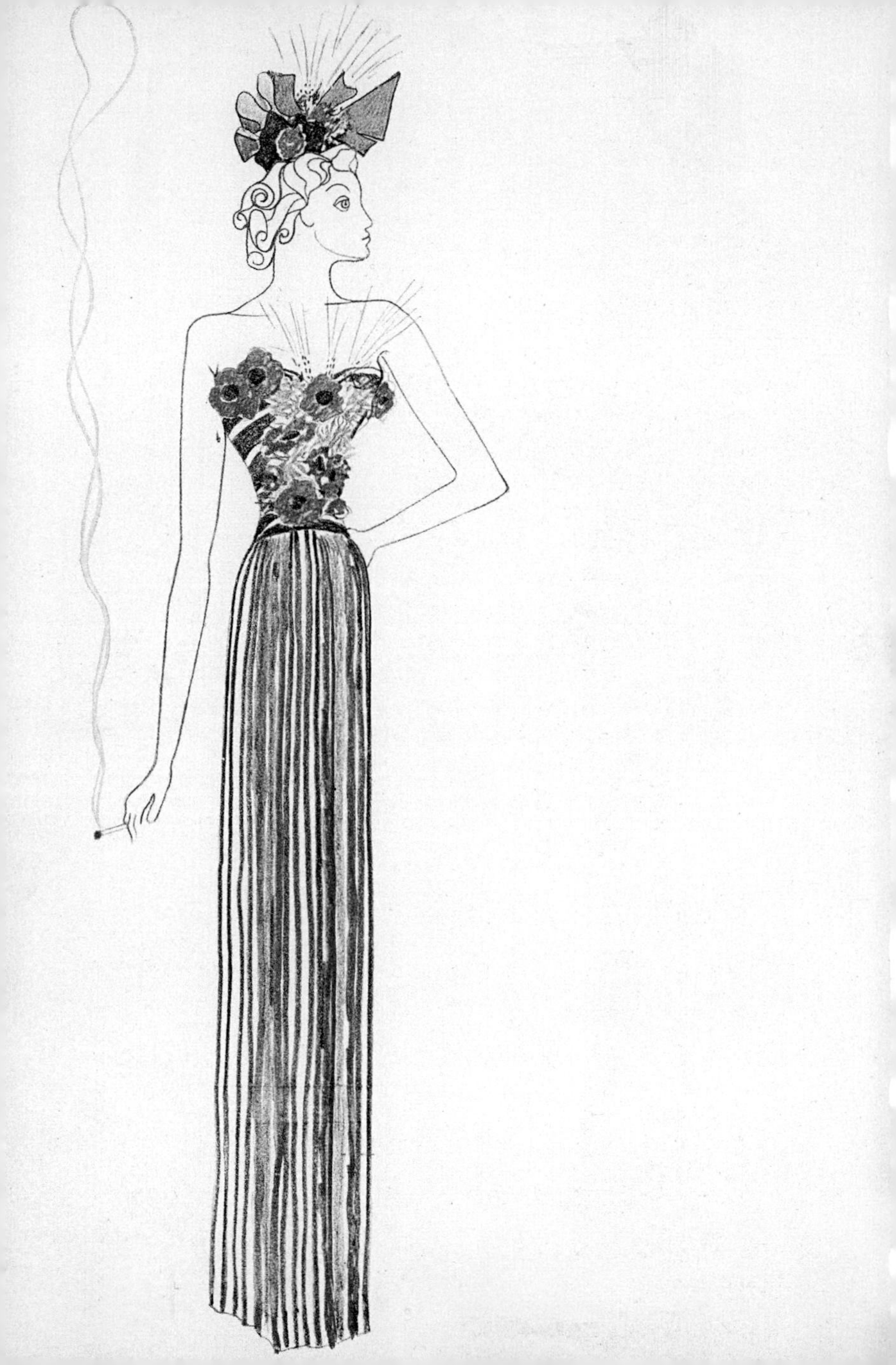